WITH A SONG IN MY *heart*

WITH A SONG IN MY *heart*

Margaret Dwyer

BALBOA
PRESS

A DIVISION OF HAY HOUSE

Balboa Press books may be ordered through booksellers or by contacting:

Balboa Press
A Division of Hay House
1663 Liberty Drive
Bloomington, IN 47403
www.balboapress.com.au
1-(877) 407-4847

ISBN: 978-1-4525-0475-9 (sc)
ISBN: 978-1-4525-0476-6 (e)

Printed in the United States of America

Balboa Press rev. date: 04/17/2012

DEDICATION

To my dear husband, who encouraged me in everything I tried to do.
I laughed with him,
Learned from him,
Leaned on him,
And loved him.

ACKNOWLEDGEMENTS

Firstly, a big thank-you to my young editor, Louise Bourke, whose enthusiasm, encouragement and expertise has smoothed the path to having this book published.

With a Song in My Heart may never have been written without the urging of my very dear friend and mentor, Sister Marie Therese Slattery R.S.J. OAM, who taught me at St Joseph's College, Perthville, and asked me several times over the years, 'Have you written that novel, yet?' I would reply that I had written a few chapters, which were 'gathering dust somewhere'. Finally, in 2009, I visited her in Oberon Hospital where, aged ninety-six, she was battling cancer, and though extremely unwell, she asked me again. Marie Therese died a month later, and as I attended her funeral, the first stirrings of wanting to attempt what I had considered was impossible for this eighty-year-old, surfaced.

As if on cue, and knowing nothing of this, my twenty-five-year-old grandson, Simon O'Donnell, wrote on a card: 'Mardie, write your story, for yourself, for your family and for our families to come!' I am exceedingly grateful to them both for motivating me, but it seemed a daunting task when I first sat staring at my computer. With no training in either journalism or creative writing, and no degrees of any kind academically, I still felt I had a story to tell, so I simply began to write it.

My husband was often my source when I needed information about the early days, and I would wake him in the middle of the night, knowing he would go straight back to sleep, and ask him something. He would tell me, and then say, 'Good God woman, don't you ever go to bed?!' Sadly, his health deteriorated and as I completed each chapter, I would take it to him as he sat on the veranda, and he would read it and verify its accuracy, especially things about his early life.

I am grateful also to family and friends who acted as guinea pigs, reading the first draft and giving me feedback. This included Sister Annette Tinkler, Sister Mary Galvin, Sue Ranger, Philippa O'Donnell, Poss Kelly, Virginia Dwyer and Sue Crowley, all of whom said encouraging things like, 'I couldn't put it down', or even, 'It's a good read, Mardie'.

Our dear family friend, Joanne Ford, used her artistic ability to produce the picture on the back of the book showing a young rider, presumably me, riding around the hills of Mt. Pleasant on my horse, Midget. Not for nothing do I think of you as another daughter, Jo!

The story is set in the Central West of NSW, the area referred to in the weather reports as 'the Central Western Slopes and Plains'. It traces the lives of two ordinary families, my birth family of Stella and W.B. Edwards and their six children, and the family of 'seven little Australians' that my husband and I reared together.

I think many people will relate to aspects of my story, and may have even experienced similar situations and struggles, especially in the years of high interest rates and escalating mortgages, through drought, fire, hail and deadly frosts, the last three necessitating crippling insurance cover. However, I hope I also showed the upside of life on the land, the freedom, the joy of working with the soil, through beautiful sunrises and sunsets, and the great feeling each night of a day well spent.

I have enjoyed writing my story. I hope you enjoy reading it.

CHAPTER INDEX

CHAPTER 1

TOTS, TEENS AND GRANNIES

It was 16ᵗʰ October 1932, in the village of Euchareena in central New South Wales, Australia. It was a small community, the village itself consisting of a couple of stores, two churches, a hall, post office, hotel, school, railway station and a few houses.

Like many early settlements in rural Australia, Euchareena had sprung up to answer the needs of the settlers in the district, mostly land owners and the seekers after gold, many of whom camped along the Macquarie river and worked their claims.

On this particular day, a small girl made her way purposefully through the orchard that separated her weatherboard home from the local school. Her name was Margaret Edwards and she was three-and-a-half years old. She scrambled through the hole in the fence and made her way to the school and knocked on the door. The startled schoolmaster surveyed his tiny caller, who announced, 'I've come to sing for you.'

Rising to the occasion, Mr. Shaw led the tiny prima donna into the classroom and said gravely, 'Children, Margaret has come to sing for us.' I was that slightly precocious child who loved to sing.

There were snickers of amusement and startled glances from Gwen, June and Harry who hoped their little sister wasn't going to embarrass them. All of this was lost on me as I stood on a stool and sang with all my heart, and in a very true voice, one of the songs of the day, 'I don't know why I'm happy, so happy, so happy. I don't know why I'm happy, but I only know I am.'

I followed this with a couple of other popular choruses and my brother and sisters relaxed when they sensed that their peers were more amused than anything, a little impressed as well, and that like themselves, they thought I was cute.

'She *is* cute,' thought Gwen, who was nearly thirteen and fiercely maternal towards me with my big blue eyes, rosy face framed by dark hair cut into a bob with a fringe just sweeping my eyebrows. 'Dad will have to cut it soon,' thought Gwen, 'It's nearly in her eyes.'

She and June avoided this monthly ritual with Dad by growing their hair long, but Harry and I had to sit on a high stool while Nana tied a towel around us and Dad snipped away and tidied his brood to his heart's content. 'Neat hair and clean shoes' was our father's eleventh commandment. 'Always polish the heels' he would say, 'It's easy to forget the heels.'

The impromptu concert over, Mr. Shaw kept up the charade and thanked me. 'Come again soon, Margaret,' he told me and then dismissed the school. The Edwards children raced the short distance home. Harry was first in the door, as the girls had slowed their pace to their little sister's.

'Mum, guess what!'

Estella Edwards turned from stirring something on the big fuel stove. She was a handsome woman in her early forties with a figure that was still good, despite bearing six children, and although she could be sometimes strict, she was mostly good-humoured and downright merry at times.

Now, as the other children clattered in behind Harry, she sensed they had something exciting to report, so she looked from one to the other enquiringly. Between them, they described how 'Margaret had come over all on her own and sung to them and how Mr. Shaw had been real nice.' While they were imparting this between giggles and fond looks at me, the cause of it all, a small, brown-looking woman bustled in and poured them all a glass of milk. Nana (pronounced Narna) was no more than 5ft. 2 inches tall and now stood on a step to reach up for the biscuits on the top shelf.

'Come on now children,' she scolded in a surprisingly deep voice, 'eat your lunch. You can talk later.' Stella explained to her mother-in-law, 'Nana, Margaret went over to the school and sang for them.'

Nana tossed her head and laughed, her brown eyes indulgent as she gazed at the moppet who now had her nose in a glass of milk, 'I think Margaret was born with a song in her heart,' she said. 'She's always singing.'

As they sat around enjoying their afternoon lunch, Stella studied her children. Gwen, at thirteen, was the second eldest as Jack, who was at an agricultural school in Sydney, had just turned fifteen. She had light brown hair, hazel eyes and a fair complexion, which had a tendency to freckle.

June, two years younger, was extremely olive-skinned, with the same flashing brown eyes as Nana and her father. Her black hair fell like Gwen's, nearly to her waist. Harry, like me, had Mum's brown hair and very blue eyes while the baby, Dick, at this moment sitting in his high chair, showed signs of being smaller in build than his older brother, but at two years old that day was brown-eyed and sturdy.

'Where's Dad?' asked Harry.

'Oh, he took Mr. Cousins to look at Mt. Pleasant, he might buy it, 'replied Stella. Then she added, 'if he doesn't, we might.'

While the children were digesting this, there was the sound of a car pulling into the driveway.

'Here's Dad now,' said Harry, pulling the lace curtain back to make sure.

Nana emptied the teapot. 'He'll want a cup of tea I suppose.'

The tall, well-built man who entered stopped in mock surprise when he saw his family gathered around the table.

'What! A party?'

'Shhh!' cautioned June, with a glance at the birthday boy, 'Later.'

Wilfred Boundy Edwards, commonly called W.B. by those who knew him, scooped his youngest son out of the highchair and held him high in the air. Brown eyes looked into brown, W.B.'s steady and sure as those of a man who, though not conceited, knew his own worth and was happy with his life. Dick's cheeks were rosy from his afternoon nap, whereas his father's were ruddy from his outdoor life and his naturally olive complexion.

With his curly black hair, noble features and strong physique, he was an attractive man physically, but it was his personality that endeared him to all whom he met. He combined a sweetness of nature with strong principles and would not tolerate anything shady, and his family was left in no doubt as to what was unacceptable behaviour. He had been given Boundy as a second name because his father was Edwin Boundy, but always called 'Boundy,' and his mother was a girl from Cornwell whose surname was Boundy.

Now as he drank his tea and ate a piece of cake, he said, 'Stell, I don't think Clarrie will buy Mt. Pleasant, he can't raise the money.'

Stella was startled. 'Does that mean you . . .'

W.B. cut her off. 'We'll talk about it later.'

His wife accepted this. She knew her husband's rule of not discussing business in front of the children.

Nana washed up the cups and mugs in the big tin dish and Stella handed tea towels to the two girls. When they grumbled a bit, she said in her jocular way, 'Hurry and get it done and when you have all had your baths we will have Dick's birthday tea.' This was incentive enough, especially when she added: 'Before tea you can take Margaret and Dick over to see Grandma and Uncle Alan. They will want to see Dick on his special day.'

Gwen and June loved taking us for walks, and Grandma only lived over the road. They usually sat us both in the big pram, one each end, and took turns pushing. Today I declared, 'I tan walk, I'm a big girl now.'

Gwen was ready first. June, of the long black hair and brown eyes, was the acknowledged beauty of the family and when she emerged from the bathroom, she had tied a bright red ribbon around her hair, giving her a gypsy appearance. W.B. was heard to ponder aloud to Stella one day that perhaps they had accidentally switched June at the hospital.

Gwen was more prosaic about her looks, she liked to look nice but there was always so much to do before and after school with two little ones in the family. She had assumed the role of mother's helper quite early and it brought a smile to her grandmother's face now as she saw her struggling with the latch on the gate with me on her hip. June followed Gwen up the path pushing Dick in the pram.

'Well, if it's not my two cleaning ladies,' cried Grandma, looking up from weeding the garden. 'Alan said you did a great job this week. He said he could nearly see his face in the linoleum, it was so shiny.' The girls flushed at the praise. One of their chores was to clean their grandmother's floors occasionally, especially when her rheumatism was playing up.

Like Nana, Lillian Sloane was widowed and in her mid-seventies, but where Nana was slight and wiry, Grandma was tall and large-boned, majestic in her long black dresses with a scarf and cameo brooch at her throat. She was fair complexioned and blue-eyed and always wore a hat to guard against the sun when she was outdoors, as she was now.

'And my little pets too?' she said, smiling at Dick and me. 'Come inside, I've got a birthday present for you Dick and something for you too, Margaret.'

They followed the old lady inside where she rummaged around in a drawer and brought out two gifts, one wrapped in tissue paper and a little tractor not wrapped. June helped me unwrap a white crocheted coat hanger.

'For your new dress,' explained Grandma.

'Oh it's pretty Grandma,' chorused the girls. 'Say thank-you, Margaret.'

I approached the old lady shyly and lifted my face for a kiss. Everyone laughed. 'That will do nicely for thank-you,' said Grandma.

Dick held out his hand for the tractor. 'What do you say, Dick?' asked June. The baby hesitated and then said, 'Ta.'

'We'd better go home now,' said Gwen, 'Mum will have tea ready.' She hoisted me on to her hip.

'She can walk, Gwen,' scolded the older woman. 'She's too heavy now for you to carry her. You'll do yourself an injury.'

They said their good-byes and crossed the road, waving to their grandmother who stood watching them from the door. Dick waved a chubby arm. 'Bye Bye' he said, as if to himself. June was disappointed. 'He could have said that before we left,' she remarked to Gwen.

Gwen was more philosophical. 'He's only a baby, June. Grandma understands, she did have eleven children you know!'

By this time we were at The Ranch and Dick and I ran in to show our presents to Mum and Nana while the girls finished setting the table. It was growing dark so Dad lit the gas light in the dining room. It cast a soft glow over everything and made the linoleum on the floor shine. It shone down on our family who sat around the table sharing Dick's birthday tea, which consisted of shepherd's pie, carrots and beans, followed by apple pie and custard. In the centre of the table was a sponge cake with white icing and two blue candles.

'I wish Jack was here,' said Harry who, at seven, hero-worshiped his older brother.

'We all do, Harry,' said Mum, 'but he'll be home for the long holidays soon.'

It was a happy meal, with Gwen, June and Harry recounting the morning events at the school for their Dad's benefit. He asked for a repeat performance so I hopped straight up and launched into 'South of the Border.' Our amused father hummed along with me until Mum broke up the party by carrying her two younger children off to bed. After the table was cleared and the dishes washed once again, Nana took Harry to the room he shared with Jack when he was home and the girls settled in the office to do their homework.

When they were alone, W.B. placed a writing pad on the table and said to his wife, 'Stell, I think I'll do it. I think I'll buy Mt. Pleasant.'

Stella was doubtful. 'But where would we get the money, Wilf? How much are they asking for it?' she questioned.

W.B. began writing on the pad, assets on one side, living expenses and the approximate cost per acre of Mt. Pleasant, the saving on a couple of leases he had if he relinquished them—all the calculations people make when they are seeking a loan. He would have included any stock he owned, a couple of paddocks he had bought over the years, the sale of our home, The Ranch, which was also on a few acres. He told me years after that he and Mum used up a writing pad working out how to buy Mt. Pleasant—a slight exaggeration, but it stuck in my memory. All of these, with the addition of his Stock and Station Agency, helped him to bring his sizable family safely through the Great Depression.

With mounting excitement he and my mother realised that they might be able to scrape up enough finance to convince the ANZ bank they were suitable candidates for a loan.

Mum found it hard to get to sleep that night. The prospect of the larger home in which to rear her family was enticing, but the hard days of the depression were still fresh in her memory and vague thoughts of droughts, poor seasons and failure to meet loan repayments plagued her for hours.

Finally, W.B. put his arm around her. 'What's the matter, Stell?'

'I'm not sure,' she whispered. 'I don't know if we should take such a big step.'

'It's a great chance for us,' he urged. 'George has practically gone broke there, but it's mostly due to bad management. It's over-run with rabbits and when we clean them up we can run two sheep to the acre and some cattle. I'll work the agency from home like I do here and Jack will be leaving school next year and he'll be a great help.'

Comforted, she snuggled into the crook of his arm. 'How lovely,' she thought drowsily, 'Jack will be working with his Dad.' She slept at last.

CHAPTER 2

MT. PLEASANT

The day our family made the six-mile journey to our new home was fine and sunny, but windy. As our mother, Stella, stepped out of the car, the wind blew her prematurely grey hair into her eyes.

'Ooh' she laughed, 'this place should be called Mt. Windy.' She was heard to repeat this often, though over the years the first comment people made when they arrived at Mt. Pleasant was mostly, 'Well this is certainly well-named!'

We entered the house, which was stripped of carpets, drapes and furniture, and, as I was led through the large, empty rooms by Gwen and June, I sensed their excitement, and loved the echoes that reverberated as we walked on the bare boards. Throughout my life, I've had a dream many times, and in it I'm always walking through the many rooms of a big house. I wonder . . . was that the beginning of the love affair with the house and the hills which cradled it, for us, the girls, which was to last all our lives?

W.B. took charge. 'Mother,' he said to Nana, 'you and Harry take this kerosene tin and get some chips. We'll light the stove and the dining room fire, and Stell, you tell the men where you want the beds, table and chairs. We'll sort out the rest of the furniture tomorrow.' Stella bustled away, followed by Gwen and June, who began to squabble about which room each one wanted.

By nightfall, when Dad lit the gaslight, the fire cast a soft glow over the meagre furniture, and soup bubbled gently on the stove. The big move to Mt. Pleasant had been made.

The house had a wide hall running north-south, off which there were four large bedrooms, two on each side. Stella and W.B. chose the top one for themselves and Dick's very large cot was put in there. June and Gwen had to share a room at this stage, and my bed was put in Nana's room. This meant the remaining bedroom became Jack's and Harry's, but later Dad gauzed in the long front veranda which ran the full width of the house, and built a sleep-out at each end, one for the two older boys and the other for Dick and me, because Grandma came to live with the family.

It didn't take long for Mum and Dad to transform the house into a comfortable home. Carpets brought from The Ranch were laid, and Dad had an inside toilet and shower built, and with open fires in the lounge and dining rooms, and grates with marble mantel-pieces in three of the bedrooms, it was indeed cosy. As time went by they didn't worry about lighting fires in the bedrooms, it used too much wood, and the house was warm enough.

About this time, Mum put me to bed one night and, after she had left the room, I started to play idly with my fingers on the wall. I realised I was following with my fingers the song that was playing in my head, 'I don't know why I'm happy,' the song I had sung to the school children at Euchareena.

Next morning, I climbed up on the piano stool and played the notes of the song with one hand, over and over. Eventually it registered with my mother and Nana that I was playing and singing 'I don't know why I'm happy, so happy, so happy. I don't know why I'm happy, but I only know I am.'

Each day this would happen but I would play different popular songs: 'A Beautiful Lady in Blue', 'The Isle of Capri,' and 'Harbour Lights'. The adults were astounded at this as I was just four, and then I surprised them even further by playing with two hands and putting a bass to the music. There may have been many children doing exactly this elsewhere, but these country people hadn't heard of any, so they thought this was very special.

Admittedly, it wasn't much of a base; I played correctly with the melody. The base was 'hit and miss,' but always in time. If it was a waltz,

I played it in 3-4 time, and if it was 4-4 time, that was what I played. My Dad was especially proud of this achievement of his youngest daughter, and, when friends visited, he would ask me to play for them.

Obediently, (Dad was strong on obedience), I would climb up on the piano stool and give it all I had. Of course, behind my back everyone would start laughing, and apparently I would swing around to catch them and Dad would say, 'That's lovely, Margaret, keep playing,' and off I would go again, and when I heard the smothered giggles next time, I would swing around once more and think to myself, 'Grown ups are strange, what's funny about playing the piano?'

As June said when telling a friend about it later, 'You couldn't help laughing, she was as funny as a circus, thumping away at any old base with the left hand, and her feet only a few inches below the stool, and playing like a veteran.'

When we two youngest children were about five and six-and-a-half, Mum's sister came to visit. To us she was Aunty Marion, and the only one of eleven in Mum's family to have had a thorough Catholic grounding while boarding at St Joseph's College, Perthville, for two years. As a result she developed a vocation to the religious life, and despite her father making her wait until she was twenty-one, she entered the convent at Perthville, and became Sister Mary Kostka. Another sister, Aunty Ol, had died so she and another nun were given permission to stay with us for a few days.

While she was with us, there was a rare dance on at the small local hall, which doubled as a church on Sunday. The older members of the family were going and we two 'little ones' asked could we go.

Dad was adamant. 'Definitely not, you can stay with Nana.'

I was desperate to go and Aunty Marion heard us talking about it in the girls' bedroom, so being of an inquisitive nature, she peeped in the door. As she told the others later in the kitchen, 'There was Margaret, in front of the mirror, liberally applying Gwen's powder and lipstick, Dick leaning up against the dressing table watching her, and he was saying, "It's no use Mard, he won't let us go," and Margaret, busy with the powder puff, saying confidently, "Leave him to me, boy!"'

They were hysterical about it in the kitchen, and of course we didn't go.

At the end of the year, preparations were made for Gwen and June to go to boarding school, as there were no high schools to which they could travel daily. Our parents contacted the Sisters of St Joseph at Perthville, near Bathurst, and the nuns were kind enough to let the two girls come for the price of one. W.B. appreciated this very much and later when he could afford it, he paid the deficit. Harry was riding his horse over to the small school at Store Creek where Mr. Frost was the teacher; Jack was still at Hurlstone Ag. College, and Gwen and June, of course, had started at Perthville.

Dick and I missed them, but Nana filled the gap quite nicely, finding things for us to do which were not totally 'boring,' as kids are wont to say nowadays. She taught us to play hopscotch and a game called Sticks, which involved running and jumping. With Mum's help, she would turn the skipping rope for us to jump over. Dad also built us a seesaw on which we spent many enjoyable moments, and Dick and I were great explorers, our main target being the large old shearing shed with its numerous yards inside the shed under cover. Looking back, Mt. Pleasant was a magical place in which to be a child.

Jack came home for the holidays and was enthusiastic about working with his Dad to rid Mt. Pleasant of rabbits, and the other curse, Bathurst burrs. With these under control, Dad brought the sheep and cattle home from the places he had been leasing, and gradually Mt. Pleasant took on a new look.

When he had first bought the property, and the news had leaked out into the Euchareena district, some men at the hotel decided over their beers that, 'W.B. has jumped from the frying-pan into the fire!' Sixteen-year-old Jack said 'man to man' to his Dad, 'They'll be eating their words soon.'

So the years passed and I was seven before I started school, as I had to ride my pony. Dick followed suit the next year and so there were three to get ready in the mornings. The good thing was that Gwen had left school and was a great help with us younger children, and just as well, too, because Grandma came to live with us when her youngest son, Alan, got married.

Harry and Jack would saddle the horses each morning and there was a small paddock at the school where the horses could graze all day until it was time to ride home, and then Harry would saddle them again. Three times a week we had to call at the Store Creek railway station to pick up the bread, and Harry had a wheat bag with a slit in the middle of it and this would go across the horse so he could carry two big 'tin' loaves on each side.

Fairly soon Harry went to boarding school at Wolaroi Methodist College in Orange, and then I graduated to riding the big grey horse called Bluey, and it was my job to carry the bread. One day, I was leaning over to tie one of the gates on the way home, and noticed Dick trotting off on his pony, Molly.

I called out to him: 'Don't canter down the hill,' and he could not have heard me, because when I caught up with him, I saw with horror, Molly was turning off to the dam for a drink and she tripped on a big stone and fell, and Dick was lying there unconscious.

I ran to him, and somehow knew that pouring water on people sometimes brought them around, but not having any water, I spat on his forehead and rubbed it in, at the same time babbling all the prayers I knew.

This didn't change anything so I ran up the hill to the homestead, into the kitchen, grabbed a metal jug, half-filled it with water, and was heading out the front door to go back to Dick when Mum and Gwen appeared, wondering what was happening. I had it all under control [as I thought!] and said, 'Don't worry Mum, Dick came off Molly and he's unconscious, but I spat on his head and prayed for him!' This story was to be repeated many times over the years much to everyone's amusement.

Dad rang the doctor, who was forty miles away in Orange, and his advice was to check for any breaks (of course, W.B. had already done that), to keep him quiet, (no difficulty there as he was unconscious!) and to keep in touch.

On the third day, a neighbour, Alan Stanford, came up to see how the boy was and when he walked into the bedroom, Dick opened his eyes and Dad said, 'Dick, do you know who this is?' Dick said, 'Yes, it's Mr. Stanford.' The relief within the family was enormous.

Shearing was always a busy time at Mt. Pleasant. There was a cottage that provided accommodation for the shearers but they had all their meals at the house. This meant an early breakfast as they would begin shearing at 7.30am then Stella would carry morning tea of scones or sandwiches and cakes over to the shed by 9.30am, then hurry back to the house to continue cooking the hot midday meal, which was served on the dot at 12.00 noon.

Afternoon tea was at 3.00pm, and knock off time was 5.30pm, followed later by the evening meal, which, like lunch, was served in the homestead. As to be expected, this, as well as getting the children off to school and with the two old ladies now in residence, was taking its toll on Mum, so Dad hired a middle-aged lady, Mrs. Dawson, as a cook for the shearing season. This helped greatly, and as well balanced things a bit because she favoured Dick over me, whereas Nana was inclined to do just the opposite and favour me during the occasional disagreements we had. Mrs. Dawson said to someone in Orange and it was repeated to Mum, 'Dick's a nice little boy, but that Margaret's a fair little minx!'

Life at the small Store Creek School included assembly each Monday morning at which we chanted, 'I honour my God, I serve my King and I salute my flag.' We could also join the League of Nations, the Junior Red Cross and the Birdlover's Gould, and we learned Maypole Dancing with ribbons streaming down from the maypole into our hands as we danced around it, always on the 1st of May, or the closest school day to it.

These are just vague memories but they made life at school more interesting than just having reading, writing and arithmetic. At recess we played cricket or vigaro, sometimes rounders or marbles, then when school was over for the day we saddled the horses again and, contrary to Jack's wishes, cantered and even galloped some of the way home!

One thing worthy of mention is that shearing was always in October, and Dick's birthday was the 16th of that month, so there was always a special cake which he shared with the shearers, and they would make a fuss of him. We children always went to the shed after school, sweeping the board and throwing the belly wool into the right bin, and of course acting as tar boy if a shearer nicked a sheep and called out 'Tar.' I always sang for them if they requested it and they 'got a kick out of it,' Dad would tell Mum that night.

The usual noises of shearing, the whirring of the machines, the click-clack of the wool press, the bleating of the sheep, plus the smell of the wool and the busy atmosphere in the shed, is something I still remember vividly.

CHAPTER 3

NANA AND GRANDMA

Nana had been with our family as long as Dick and I could remember, and she was 'Nana' (as in banana) to all who knew her. She was tiny and olive-skinned with brown eyes and grey hair pulled back into a bun. She wore her dresses shorter than women of her age were wont to do, and had an outlook which was modern compared to her contemporaries.

She enjoyed excellent health, marred only by increasing deafness, and kept herself occupied, mostly by raking up leaves in the back garden at Mt. Pleasant and then burning them, or taking the wheelbarrow over to the wood-heap and wheeling it back full of wood which she would stack in the wood box. She loved to take a kerosene tin, with a homemade handle, over to the woodheap with her and bring it back full of chips and pine for starting the fires, and these jobs as well as wiping the dishes when Gwen washed up after meals and setting the table kept her busy.

Nana always donned an old black felt hat when she was raking, or bringing the wood in, and in the years to come, my husband would say to me, 'Nana will never be dead while you're alive!' as I was inclined to do the same thing.

Nana loved to crochet, nearly always bed socks, and most people had a pair of Nana's bed socks in mainly blue or pink. I maintained in later life that the older members of the family got a better deal than Dick and I did because the older Nana grew, the longer and more pointed the socks became!

Grandma, on the other hand, could crochet exquisite doilies and table centres, and this art filled a lot of time for her, as she wasn't as active as Nana. Physically, she was much taller, and it was difficult to know how big she actually was because of the clothes she wore. She certainly wasn't fat, but she wore quite a few petticoats, flannel in winter, silk in summer, and over these she wore a black silk dress to her ankles, and finished her ensemble off with a scarf, held in place at the neck with a cameo brooch, and this was everyday attire! Her white hair was long, but always plaited and coiled on top of her head, and this gave her a regal appearance.

Grandma's skin was as fair as Nana's was dark, and she had blue eyes. She spoke quietly and gave every appearance of gentility, and it seemed to us that Grandma worked hard at being no trouble to our mother, and Nana worked hard to be helpful. Sometimes Grandma would peel the vegetables and then chop all the peelings up for the chooks, but she felt in such a busy household she was better out of the way.

This was possibly true, because Mum said to her, 'Mother, it is better if you stay in bed until I've got the shearers fed, and the children off to school, and I'll bring you a tray.' So she did stay in her room, and one day Nana passed by Grandma's door just as Mum was taking her tray in. Nana simply tossed her head and said, 'Oh, the Duchess!' and kept walking.

Despite these small jealousies, the two old ladies got on very well, and if either of them was going away for a short break, they would embrace each other saying good-bye, there would be a few tears, and one would say, 'we've lived beside each other all our lives and never had a cross word.'

Grandma's bedroom was in sharp contrast to Nana's. Each had a grate in her room with a marble mantelpiece above it, and Grandma's was lined with medicine bottles. Because of her rheumatism she had liniments to rub herself with, including red chillies in a bottle and various other remedies, and for her bowels there was paraffin oil, Epsom Salts and quite a line up of remedies.

On Nana's mantelpiece, on the other hand, there was only a jar of Corn cure and Ford pills! Jack was heard to say once that he thought Nana ran on natural gas; she was certainly very frugal, and the only thing she was ever heard to complain of were her chilblains. Dick and I were fascinated with the array of medications on Grandma's mantelpiece and would sometimes creep in to look at them. One night she mistook the liniment bottle for the paraffin oil and I vaguely remember she had burnt lips from taking a swig of it.

When Grandma was going away for a couple of weeks the preparations were mighty. I watched her pack many times and have never forgotten it. One thing she always packed was her porcelain chamber pot. (This vessel, one each, was a necessity for the three senior ladies of the household, the toilet being at the opposite end of the house from the bedrooms.)

Grandma called hers her 'piano,' and would wrap it lovingly in a big white towel so it wouldn't get broken, and then put it in one of her numerous suitcases. When they were loading the car, W.B. would look at the number of suitcases lining the path to the car and expostulate, 'Good Lord, Mother, what have you got in all these?' Nana's departure was just the opposite, generally one modest suitcase and her handbag, and she'd hop in the car and away they'd go.

Grandma had a favourite spot on the front veranda and she would sit there and either write letters, or crochet. If she wasn't writing, I would seek her out and she would tell me about her life and its sad beginning. When she was born at Beechworth in Victoria, in 1858, her mother died and her father contracted pneumonia 'from shock', to use Grandma's words, and died three weeks later.

Grandma was told there were three older children, Eliza, Kate and Richard, who were fostered by a sister or friend of their mother. The baby, Lillian Harriet, was fostered by her mother's sister whose surname was Snow, but when she was four, the family brought her by bullock wagon to NSW where she later became a teacher and eventually married Henry Sloane, my mother's father. This account of her birth, and subsequent foster care, was according to Grandma's memory, and records from authentic sources may vary slightly, but this is what Grandma told me.

She and Henry had eleven children: six girls first, followed by five boys, my mother Stella being the second youngest girl. What I found very poignant was that my grandmother, Lillian, never saw her siblings, but she did correspond with them by letter, and knew that her brother, Richard, died when he was twenty-two. Everyone who we knew had a car, and the fact that seventy or so years earlier the only mode of transport was by wagon, sulky or dray and no one could travel vast distances, was a concept I found hard to understand as a child.

Suddenly, Grandma changed the conversation. 'Margaret, see that big hill up there with only one tree on it? I call that One Tree Hill,' and then I pointed out several of the hilly paddocks around Mt. Pleasant and named them.

'That's Lanky-One, that's Lanky-Two, and over there is Flagstaff and Oakey-One and Oakey-Two.' All the paddocks were named, and when I married and went to a farming property, I was surprised to hear paddocks called 'the 100 acres', or 'the 250 acres' and so I gave them names that they still bear today.

When I thought later about Grandma's brother, Richard, dying so young, I wondered if that was why Mum called her youngest son 'Richard Gerard', known to one and all as Dick, but I didn't think to ask her.

The Hubbard family from Mt. Top, Euchareena, were very good friends of our family. Mr. and Mrs. Hubbard, or Frank and Beryl, as Mum and Dad called them, visited each other, not often, but on a regular basis.

Mrs. Hubbard drove a car and was always going to teach her friend Stella to drive, but it never happened. In those days it was uncommon for a woman to learn to drive, and, looking back, the family think perhaps we should have encouraged our Mum to accept her offer. In Dad's many absences on business trips when all of us had left home, she was often lonely and it would have been good if she could have been independent and visited someone for a cup of tea and a chat.

The Hubbard and Edwards children all got on well as Gwen and Claude, June and Ted, Harry and Margot, and Robert and I were of similar age, but Jack as our eldest, and Dick as our youngest, didn't have a match in the Hubbard clan.

One day, Harry, Robert, Dick and I were playing near the dip at Mt. Pleasant where the sheep had recently been dipped. Without thinking there was any danger, we walked along the sides of the concrete dip, hanging on to the fence posts as we went. It was a lot of fun until I lost my grip on a post and fell in the water, which the sheep had recently been swimming through during the dipping session and it was fetid with the evil smelling Dip powder.

Of course the boys pulled me out and sent Dick off to alert the adults who all came running in great alarm. Nana ran a deep bath with antiseptic and sweet smelling bath soap in it and wrapped me in a fluffy white towelling gown. All was well again, but we were warned not to play near the dip.

One day when my younger brother and I were playing in the shearing shed, we found, to our great surprise, two really old bikes in a state of disrepair. Excitedly we wheeled them out and tried to ride them. Neither of us had ever been on a bike before and we had great difficulty because of the very bad condition of the bikes.

The girl's bike was just the right size for me, but the handle bars were in a bad way as the horizontal part slipped in and out all the time, the seat tipped up and down, and there were no tyres on the wheels, only the rims. Dick's was not quite as bad, but very difficult to ride.

We persevered each day, however, and Nana was kept busy bathing gravel rash and applying iodine! We actually learnt to ride them in a sort of a way, and on Mt. Pleasant hill that was no mean feat. Then suddenly they disappeared, and when questioned about them, Dad told us they were too dangerous, so he got rid of them.

A good month went by, and one night when W.B. arrived home from his weekly trip to the Orange saleyards, he called us to help him unload the groceries from the car, and there were two brand new bikes! Or so we thought, but they were the old bikes done up and they really did look brand new. Dick's even had SPEEDWELL in big letters on it. Such excitement! Dad must have bought the two dilapidated bikes at a clearing sale with the intention of having them repaired, but we two young 'explorers' beat the gun, as they say.

The next day being Saturday, we persuaded Mum to let us ride our bikes over to Store Creek as practice for riding them to school on Monday. This eventuated without incident, so on Monday morning two very excited youngsters set off for school, schoolbags on our backs.

On the way to Store Creek, there is a long climb up quite a big hill. Having accomplished that, we proceeded to ride down the other side of it, which is even longer and it curves a bit. At the very bottom was a gate, now a ramp. I was nagging Dick all the way down: 'Don't go too fast, be careful', and then as the gate came into view at the last little hill: 'Get ready to stop, get your freeway ready'. (Freeway was the term for the only way to stop the bikes, you had to reverse pedal until the bike stopped.)

Dick pulled up like a little champion, but I hit the gate with such force that my bike broke, the handlebar section came off, and I had to carry the two sections to the local post office where I left them, and then walked the remaining distance to school, minus my pride and joy.

Later that morning our parents drove through the gate on their way to town, and when Mum was opening the broken gate, she called out to Dad, 'Oh Wilf, there are ball bearings everywhere here!' They called at the post office to get the mail, picked up the bike, and took it with them to Orange to get it repaired. And that story was repeated over the years as well.

One could not finish this chapter on Nana without telling of her toffee making. This was a small trial to our Mum, who hated the stickiness of the saucepan, the trail of syrup, and then cleaning the remains of the hard toffee off the enamel pie dishes, as well as the ants that seemed to be drawn to it all like a magnet.

However, on the day when she drove to Orange with Dad to do the shopping, or for an appointment, she would leave us in Nana's care. We would wave them off, watch them go down the hill, past the dam, then over the ramp.

As soon as this happened, Nana would say, 'Well, they're over the ramp!' and this would be the signal for the honey, butter and whatever else went into toffee-making to come out and she was in her glory.

She would carry the two pie dishes out into the gauzed-in meat house and leave them there to cool and harden enough for her two charges to enjoy later. No wonder we loved Nana, in some ways she was a real Mary Poppins, but with her feet on the ground!

Mum and Dad would arrive home after she had fed us with bread and milk for our tea (yes, you might well look blank and wonder what sort of a meal that was, well to be honest we didn't like it much as it was white bread with sugar sprinkled on it and then hot milk poured over) and Mum would pull a face when she saw the pie dishes soaking in the sink and with that merry laugh of hers she'd say, 'Oh Wilf, she's been at it again!'

Another small irritation Nana caused her daughter-in-law was if Mum had baked a cake and it was in the oven, especially a sensitive one like a sponge, the energetic and well-meaning lady would come in with a big stick of wood and put it in the fire box of the stove. Mum would rush into the kitchen, take it out if she could, all the time saying, while nearly wringing her hands, 'Oh, I'm to be pitied!' And you know, sometimes she was—to be pitied, that is.

While this was happening, Grandma would be sitting quietly darning or something, and wisely keeping her own counsel. Another thing was that if Mum was mopping the kitchen floor, or had just mopped it, Nana would march straight across it, whereas Grandma would come to the door, notice the wet floor, then put her hands up in front of her and say, 'Oh Stella, the floor's wet, I'll come back later,' and she'd retire to her room. As I said, chalk and cheese.

I like to finish on a positive note, and there were more positives than negatives in this household of growing children, busy adults and ageing grannies. Dad liked music in the home, and he loved it when the girls, or his wife, and even Nana sometimes, played the piano. He especially liked it when I played and the two old ladies sang.

I still see it in my mind's eye; me, small and dark, sitting on the piano stool with a grey-haired lady each side, and they would sing, 'Abide with me, fast falls the eventide,' or 'Nearer my God to Thee, nearer to Thee'. Another one they knew was 'Silver Threads among the gold.' The first line of this one began: 'Darling, I am growing old, silver threads among the gold.' It was very poignant, especially when they came to the last line, and they would harmonize: Grandma singing the melody and Nana dropping into alto.

It is one of my earliest and most treasured memories, me sitting on the piano stool with my pudding basin haircut, per favour of Dad, and the two dear old ladies singing in harmony.

CHAPTER 4

THE BOYS

The family thought Stella and W.B. arranged their children very tidily, three girls and three boys, and Jack, christened John Wilfred, was the eldest. He was a good-looking boy with blue eyes like his mother and his grandmother and was of sturdy build and had brown hair.

He attended Hurlstone Agricultural College, in Sydney, and on his return told his Mum and Dad of events that happened at school, the most scary to his younger brothers and sisters being the practice that was rampant in some boarding schools at the time, of initiation ceremonies carried out on new arrivals. One example was the holding of boys' heads down in the water trough. We heard later that these practices had been outlawed in all schools, which the family considered a good thing, as it was potentially dangerous.

Jack gave everyone a good laugh at times. He had a young girlfriend, Melva Whitehead from Boomi, near Molong, and the night he met her when she was sixteen, he told his friend Kevin, 'I'm going to marry her one day!' She later became his wife, but the courtship wasn't easy as there was only one car, so he would ride his horse twenty miles to see her at weekends.

Once, to prove he had become a man, Jack assured his mother and father that he would look after Mt. Pleasant while W.B. drove the family to Manly for a week's holiday in the summer, so after mighty preparations, Dad, Mum, Nana, Gwen, June, Harry, Dick and I set off. Cars were bigger then and there were no restrictive seatbelts so everyone fitted in, and luggage was on top. Dad was the 'packer' for the family. Mum would get it all ready and Dad took pride in packing each suitcase, something he did methodically and well.

A great week of sun and surf, lots of fish and chips, sliced devon and tomato sauce and lots of milkshakes ensued, all of which was a great treat for this family from the bush, who mainly only ate the mutton from the sheep that were killed on the property.

On arriving home after our holiday, we could see no sign of Jack, and W.B. was dismayed at first, but found a note inside telling him he had ridden Bluey out to see Melva and he would be home at six o'clock. We heard Stella's merry laughter from her bedroom and all rushed in, and she pointed at her bed. Jack had put the valuable canteen of silver cutlery in the middle of his parents' bed and then covered it with the lace bedspread! It stood out like an elephant in the room, when Jack's intention was to hide it from potential thieves!

Another incident caused some amusement too, but this was at W.B.'s expense. Jack asked his father if he could borrow the car to go to a dance at the local hall, and, as these dances were very few and far between, Dad agreed with the proviso that he was to be home by midnight. Jack assured him that he would be and off he went. Harry asserted in later life that Dad could be very strict, and this is an example of that.

At 12 o'clock Dad started to pace up and down, as there was no sign of Jack. He said to Mum, 'I'm going to teach this fellow a lesson, I said 12 o'clock and I meant 12 o'clock!'

So he caught and saddled a horse, (not easy in the middle of the night!) and rode over to the hall at Store Creek where the music was playing and the dance still in progress. He tied the horse to a tree for Jack to ride home and drove towards Mt. Pleasant in his car, but when he pulled up at the first gate, he heard a baby crying lustily and discovered a basket on the back seat with a baby in it.

He quickly turned back to the hall where there was great consternation awaiting him. Mena and Les Mills were outside with Jack, all wondering what had happened to the car, and more importantly, the baby! Apparently they had asked Jack if they could put Maureen's basket in the car, away from the loud music in the hall, and Jack's excuse was that the young couple were having such a good time that he didn't like to cut it short by taking the car.

I never heard who rode the horse home that night but I can make a good guess! The baby who W.B. Edwards nearly abducted that night is now Maureen Ostini of Parkes, and a very good friend of mine.

After a while, Dad and Jack started to have disagreements, which would develop into outright rows and this caused great distress to Mum, Mel and me while they lasted. The worst one ended in Jack declaring he was leaving home and his father said, 'All right then, off you go but let your mother know where you are.' Jack rode off on his horse, to Mel's home, twenty miles away as Mum heard later.

A few days later Dad was working up in Oakey-One paddock and he thought he saw something moving way off in the distance. He kept his eye on it, as he told Stella that night, and sure enough it was a horse and rider, and the wanderer had returned by a very circuitous route! Jack rode up, W.B. extended his hand for a handshake and that was that.

This tension erupted from time to time, and wasn't pleasant, but no one could doubt the affection each had for the other. The funny thing was that when after a few years in the army Jack returned, there was never a recurrence of this problem, and, when Jack, Mel and the kids came to Mt. Pleasant, Jack would spend most of the visit in the office sitting on the floor with his back to the wall, talking to his father who would be seated sideways at his roll-top desk, giving his eldest son his full attention.

When the Second World War started, Jack and his best mate, Kevin Peters, joined the Light Horse Regiment. They had to take their own horses, so Jack took his father's horse, Byng, which was a big chestnut and a very stylish sort of horse, and Kevin took old Charley. The aim of the Light Horse Division was to train the boys and their horses for active service in the Middle East, and there were 1800 horses in the camp near Parramatta.

However, when Japan entered the war, the emphasis changed to prepare them for combat in the islands and the boys joined the A.I.F. (Australian Infantry Forces) and were posted to Geraldton, Western Australia, on the edge of the desert. Kevin told me recently that Jack made sure they all made their beds and even planted a palm tree outside their tent. He was always very tidy, and displayed this later when he owned his own home.

Jack and Mel were married in Holy Trinity Anglican Church in Orange. As it was wartime, and the coupons issued for clothing were in short supply, Mel didn't dress as a bride but wore a lovely beaded suit and a snappy little hat, and Jack wore his army uniform.

For twelve months after this Mel followed her new husband around the various camps where he was stationed, found accommodation and a job, sometimes in ammunition factories where she was in a division of labour set up for making ammunition for the war effort. Jack visited her as often as he could, legitimately or otherwise, and according to Kevin, who was with him, went AWOL a few times in order to be with her.

One night their division went on an overnight march—I think it was called a bivouac—and once clear of the camp Jack slipped out of his line and spent the night with his wife. When the division returned in the early morning, tired and weary, he slipped back in and remarked to the soldier in front of him, 'It's been a tough march this time.' The poor soldier readily agreed, saying 'My oath it has!'

They were then sent to Geraldton on the edge of the desert where they remained until the end of the war. When speaking to Kevin prior to writing this, I asked him, 'Did you ever get into Geraldton while you were in camp?' Kevin's reply amused me: 'As often as possible,' he said with a chuckle and the old familiar twinkle in his eye.

Kevin also told me that one day Jack said to him, 'A lot of these fellows are just loafing about and wasting time. You and I are going to get stuck in and get as much done as we can,' and then Kevin said, 'So that's why he was made Sergeant, and I was only a corporal.' Then he added in the interest of truth, 'I was on my way to getting my stripes when the war ended.' I always detect a note of hero worship when Kevin speaks of Jack, and I wouldn't want to be the one to denigrate Jack in front of Kevin. Mild as he is, he would defend his mate strenuously, and after all those years with him under difficult and primitive conditions one has to wonder, 'Who would know him better?'

One day Jack said to Kevin, 'I've just seen Hubbard,' (meaning Claude, who had just arrived) 'and he's as pissed as a parrot!' Kevin also told me of an incident that happened when he was packing his gear in his tent to come home. Some of the young soldiers were training to use hand grenades up the hill from where Kevin's tent was, and apparently after the pin is pulled one only has a few seconds to throw it. A grenade came rolling down straight for the tent and went under it . . . Kevin woke up in hospital and has no memory of any of it.

I thought of June's friend who had his hand blown off in the camp near Singleton. He probably hung on to it a fraction too long. It's dangerous being a soldier even when one is not at the front, and I can't imagine how Manny and Alice Peters would have handled it if their youngest son hadn't survived packing to come home after all he had been through.

When Jack returned from the war, Mel became pregnant and they designed their new home, which was built just outside Euchareena. Robyn Narelle Edwards, who arrived on 6th March 1944, was a very beautiful baby and their home, Woodlands, was finished so they moved the few miles away to set up on their own. Five years later, Stephen John arrived to complete their family, and Mum and I were the babysitters whenever the young couple went to a function.

Mel was a pretty girl, always immaculate, and as different in temperament from her Edwards' sisters-in-law as was possible. Phlegmatic by nature, she took life very calmly, which was in total contrast to Jack's gregarious nature, possibly causing tension between them sometimes.

One day Mum and I called in on our way home from shopping in Orange to give Mel the things she had asked us to get for her. She put the kettle on as it was a long drive from Orange on a bad road, made the tea and as usual, put out some bought biscuits. Stella, as I said before, sometimes didn't weigh her words before she spoke, and she said: 'Mel, why don't you make some little cakes occasionally?' Most girls would have bridled at this, but not Mel. She just answered her mother-in-law calmly, 'But Ma, they would only eat them!' Mum and I chuckled about it on the way home, but not maliciously as we really loved Mel.

One night when Kevin, Harry, Dick and I had been to a ball, Kevin said to me, 'I might as well sleep at your place tonight and then I can drive you and your mother to Mass tomorrow.' So we lifted Robyn, who was sleeping over, out of her bed and put her in with me, and Kevin crawled into Robyn's bed.

Towards morning Robyn gave a cry, so Mum, who didn't know Kevin had stayed the night, bent over him in her night attire saying 'Come on pet, come and do wee-wee!' Kevin ducked his head out from the covers and Mum realised her mistake. There was a good laugh about it over breakfast.

Jack was very aware of his responsibilities as far as we children were concerned. If he was in charge and Mum and Dad were out, we were not allowed to read in bed with the kerosene lights on in case of a fire, no lollies in bed in case we choked (it wouldn't have been good for our teeth either, but he was only concerned for our safety on his watch) and after he saddled the horses for the ride to school, he would lecture us on the danger of cantering downhill and instruct us not to do so. I wonder what he would think of the cover of this book, as I am most definitely cantering downhill!

One day after heavy rain, he issued this directive: 'And no cantering downhill, you kids. Walk your horses down all the hills.' Dick and I rode off and of course once over the crest of the big hill, and out of sight of the house, we broke into a canter. When we arrived home that afternoon, Mum said to us: 'You'd better keep out of Jack's sight, he knows you cantered down the hill!'

That was enough for us so we raced out to the huge leafy tree in the garden and climbed right up into it, hiding from our big brother and growing increasingly hungry all the time. In fact, it was our hunger that finally brought us out of hiding when Nana called us for dinner and we had to face Jack's wrath. Dick said sullenly, 'Anyway, how did you know we cantered down hill?' I thought, 'Good question!' but Jack would rival Hercule Poirot as a good detective. He told us that he had ridden that way himself after we had gone, and he could tell by the way the horses' hooves dug into the road after the rain that we hadn't been walking them, but definitely cantering!

I sometimes find myself being defensive about Jack, when some family members denigrate him a bit, though affectionately, and refer to his drinking and generally cast him as the scallywag of the family. I may be blinkered where he's concerned, but in all the years I knew him, I never saw him the worse for wear with alcohol, although I knew he liked to drink. Where W.B. would walk into a pub and say to the men in the bar, 'My shout boys' and then to the barman, 'and I'll have a squash, Les' Jack would do the same thing but there would be no squash for him. Like Dad, Jack was a Stock and Station Agent, and business was often carried out in a pub, with many sheep or cattle deals being instigated there.

I only saw the good side of Jack I guess, and I know he was a well-loved man in the district as many people have told me what a good man he was, and generous to them as well. When my third child, Philippa, was born, Mum and Dad were in Oslo in Norway. When I came out of hospital with three children under three to care for, Jack and Mel drove the eighty miles from their home just to make sure I was all right and had everything I needed.

This was a repeat of his responsible attitude to me as a child, and his way of doing what Dad would have done if he had been home. Yes, I am defensive, and I vowed not to write a fairy story but to write the truth as I saw it, and that is how I saw him, like all of us, flawed in some way, but caring, very funny and loving.

When I was told Jack had bowel cancer and had only a couple of months to live, Frank and I drove over to Woodlands to see him. I was unsure how to greet him and approached his bed hesitantly. As soon as I sat down on the bed, he said, 'Well Mardie, what do you think of me dying?!'

It was a typically Jack way of breaking the ice, and we had no trouble conversing. He was fifty-five when he died and Father McGuin visited him in Dudley Hospital a few days before. Father said to him: 'Well Jack, according to the records, you were baptised a Catholic. Do you want to do anything about it now?' Jack's reply was also typically Jack. 'No, Father,' he replied, 'I think I'll stay with the strength!'

That was Jack, and now we turn to Harry, a different kettle of fish, and very different from his older brother in temperament. Where Jack was the eldest of the six Edwards children, Harry was the fourth, and the second son. He was of average height for many years, but at puberty shot up to be 6 foot 2 inches tall. He joined the Air Force the week he turned 18, and soon developed broad shoulders, a slim waist and became a very attractive man. I always considered him to be a deep thinker, and he read a lot and was quieter than Jack, but he had a great sense of humour and could see the funny side of almost everything. He and I were the readers in the family and would often discuss the books we were reading. When Harry and I were reading, we sometimes didn't hear if someone spoke to us.

One day Harry rode his horse home from Store Creek and produced from inside his shirt this tiny black puppy. I don't remember who gave it to him but he named him Shaggles and grew very fond of him. Shaggles was not of royal birth but resembled a terrier of some sort and he fitted into the household immediately.

Every time the family rode out 'rabbitting' which is the term we used for the almost daily exercise of taking the dogs out to hunt and catch rabbits, all of the other dogs would follow Dick, except Shaggles, and there would be this lone horseman, Harry, with one little black dog following and jumping up on his hind legs every now and then to see over the high grass where Harry was. It looked very comical and Dick would have a menagerie of dogs following him, but Harry only had Shaggles.

On one excursion out in Lanky-One, which was hilly, a huge hare was tearing down this steep hill and Dick, and his large contingent of dogs, was nowhere in sight. No need to panic everyone, Shaggles is here! The little dog spotted the hare and ran as fast as he could to cut it off but the force of the collision rolled Shaggles over and over down the hill . . . and the hare just loped off along the creek.

This episode endeared the little dog to the family even more. Just to finish the story of Shaggles: years later, when Harry was preparing for his wedding, the tiny dog died suddenly a few days before. I don't think his master was joking when he said he was going to wear a black armband to the wedding!

Harry's days in the Air Force were spent as a fitter and turner working on the Catalina Aircraft as part of the ground staff, fitting nuts, bolts and rivets. His daughter Lesley told me recently that Stella didn't want him flying planes and that was something I had never known. When Mum and Dad were flying from Vancouver to Calgary in Canada, in 1956, there was a dreadful storm and they eventually had to turn back. At the height of the storm Stella looked out her porthole and saw the lightening flashing on the rivets on the wings of the big plane, and her thoughts flew to Harry.

During his Air Force training he started at Tocumwal, then was transferred to Sale in Victoria, and finally to Rathmines on Lake Macquarie where he stayed until the war ended. He must have liked the area because when he retired at the age of fifty—four, he bought a home at Toronto on Lake Macquarie where he had a jetty and a small boat in order to catch fish, and when my husband and I visited, he took us to Rathmines pub for a drink. In fact, from his veranda at Coal Point one could look across the lake to Rathmines.

After he came out of the Air Force, Harry joined the Rugby Union Club in Orange, as did his brother Dick, and friend Kevin Peters. Harry played Outside Centre and in a game against the Maoris in Orange, he scored the only try. The New Zealanders were very tall and very big, and very scary when doing their war cry, the Haka. He also represented Country against City a couple of times and played cricket with a local team. In a game against Yeoval he took all ten wickets as bowler, which was a local record. Harry also played a good game of tennis, and on a good day he was spectacular to watch.

Girls seemed to like him, too, and once or twice Harry and Kevin went for a holiday and met a couple of nice girls and Harry brought them home for a few days. After they had gone, he asked Mum what she thought of the girls and she said, 'Very nice girls Harry, but not suitable.' Then Harry had a serious romance with a lovely titian-haired girl who matched him in height and whom he had known when they were in primary school. They both went to different towns to boarding school and from there Harry went into the Armed Services and so they didn't meet for many years.

When they did eventually meet again, the attraction was mutual, but the lass was engaged to someone in another state. Nevertheless, the romance blossomed at dances and tennis days, so much so that they approached her mother, who seemed to rule the roost and her daughter told her she wanted to break her engagement. Her mother wouldn't hear of it and that being the late 1940s, the young couple had to accept the situation.

The day of the wedding, Harry saddled Byng and took off for the day and we didn't see him until early nightfall. He was a bit down for a while but the newly married couple went to live in the other state and slowly the old Harry returned. One of his friends, Ted Hubbard, married Gladys Dunlop from Ardlethan, and she had a beautiful sister, Olive.

At the wedding he renewed his acquaintance with her and his luck changed, and I would say he won the jackpot! When he asked his Mum what she thought of Olive, she told him, 'Very suitable Harry, but isn't she a little pony?' As I said, Mum sometimes spoke before she thought, but she was very happy with Harry's choice of a wife, and by 'pony' she meant she was petite. I was delighted as I now had two sisters-in-law and I got on very well with both of them, different as they were.

Harry and Olive were married in Temora where Olive had worked in a bank. I sang at the wedding, and Jack and Dick were the groomsmen while the bride's two sisters, Jessie and Amy Dunlop, were bridesmaids. And, Olive made her own and the bridesmaids' dresses! The newlyweds eventually built a home on their property, Avoca, between Stuart Town and Mumbil and it wasn't too long before Lesley Gaye and Pamela Joy arrived, two great little girls who shared their father's sense of humour.

Harry worked diligently to rid Avoca of rabbits with the assistance of myxamatosis and the help of his two small daughters, and of course Olive was a great support with her cooking, sewing and gardening. There were always homemade cakes, scones and biscuits, and from the fruits of her vegetable garden, she produced jams and chutneys. Often when she visited Mt. Pleasant, she would bring some of these as a surprise for her mother and father-in-law, and when she was leaving, Mum would always pack a box of goodies, including grapes which Olive really liked, but didn't grow. So life at Mt. Pleasant had changed, with Jack and Harry each managing his own property, and Dick working with his Dad at Mt. Pleasant.

Dick was the baby of the family, and in some ways that made him special, especially to W.B. From an early age he had his own horse and saddle, and Dad would send him off to shift sheep, telling him to count them as he drove them through the gate. Dick would scratch the number of sheep on a part of his saddle and then report to his Dad when he got back how many there were. I don't know how accurate he was in this but I never heard it queried.

He, like Harry and I did, rode to school at Store Creek for his primary schooling, then, like Harry, he attended Wolaroi Methodist College in Orange, where he attained his Intermediate Certificate. Wolaroi amalgamated later with PLC to become Kinross, the fine coeducational school it is today.

He came home after that as both the other boys were 'at the war' as we used to say, and workers were scarce. A fond memory comes to mind of Dad when Dick was younger, sitting in his armchair in front of the fire, nursing Dick who was quite a big boy by then. He would be reading the *Sydney Morning Herald*, which was a large paper and it would be spread out in front of them both. Grandma would be reading too, near the fire; I was mostly playing with the two cats, Fluffy and Pal, on the carpet; Nana would be sitting well away from the fire crocheting as the fire 'stirred up' her chilblains; and Stella would be trotting around in the kitchen, soaking the porridge and setting the fire in the stove for a quick start in the morning.

As children, Dick and I had quarreled at times and it would sometimes get physical, but boarding school ended that, and when we were both home on holidays we were the best of friends. The boys spoilt me a bit as they would always saddle my horse, I was exempt from milking cows and when I looked back in later years, I realised how good they were to me, never teasing me and seeming to respect me. They were like this with Gwen and June too, though Jack was a bit tough on June, maintaining she looked in the mirror too much when she was setting the table: 'preening', he called it. June would bridle at this and Mum would intervene and chastise Jack.

Harry had one irritating habit where I was concerned. As he passed through the kitchen where I would be carving the meat, or cooking, and my hands were occupied, he would deftly untie my apron strings and go on his way whistling! They were happy days though and I treasure the memory of them.

Like Harry, Dick played a good game of Rugby Union, playing hooker in the Wallaroos team with Harry and Kevin, and he also played in Fiji once. Both boys managed to get some skin off—Harry would have gravel rash down his side but it was Dick's nose that suffered, never broken, but often skinned. Nana and Gwen treated their injuries and would just have them healed and the following Saturday it would happen again. Dick played a good game of cricket and he also rode well and loved riding in gymkhanas.

This is as good a time as any to tell a story about Dick riding Byng, Dad's prize chestnut, in a race at Stuart Town. Unbeknown to their father, the boys had been training Byng for the race for some time, and somehow they loaded him and took him to Stuart Town without his knowledge. Dad arrived late at the race venue and was sitting with Stella when the big race started. Startled, he noticed Byng at once, but just then the gun went off. The horses sprang out, but it was a false start so they had to bring them back. Byng was a fairly highly-strung horse, and W.B.'s only comment was: 'No horse will beat him now!'

The boys and Kevin had bought an old Rugby Durante car to drive in to Orange each Saturday to play football and I used to go with them.

The trip in had its problems because Harry would drive and they would get to a certain spot near Spooner's Bridge and the old car would peter out. Kevin would fly out, give it a few good cranks with the crank handle and it would then make it to the oval. After the match, we would go to a cafe and have a cup of tea, and, of all things, scrambled eggs on toast before heading home. The two girls who ran the cafe were from Forbes, Ora and Marie Mahlo, and we thought they made the very best scrambled eggs.

Sometimes we would stop at the Royal Hotel, the boys would have a couple of drinks and I'd have a squash before setting out. The boys liked their beer but they would not drink to the extent some young people do these days. Boring, you say? Well it didn't seem like it then.

Dick met and married a lovely girl from Orange called Maree Stewart and W.B. built a small three-bedroom house for them a few hundred yards from the homestead at Mt. Pleasant. Their children arrived in due course and the first-born was another W.B. Edwards, only Warren Bruce, not Wilfred Boundy. A girl was next, Margot Elizabeth, and finally Stewart Richard.

Stella enjoyed these grandchildren very much as they were close at hand and she could see them every day. She would tell me on the phone about the cute things they were doing and saying, how Margot stood on a chair beside her while she was cooking. She loved the grandchildren and was never lonely when they were around, and they made their way most days up to Mt. Pleasant to Grandma and Grandfather.

So, as with the other two boys, we leave Dick working with his father and rearing his children. In time, he sent the boys, Warren and Stewart, to St Joseph's College, Hunter's Hill, and Margot to Loreto College at Normanhurst, thus ensuring they had a well-rounded education. Warren's career is outlined in a later chapter, but Stewart's heart was in the land as was his father's and his grandfather's and that is where he is today, on his own property near Wellington.

CHAPTER 5

THE GIRLS

By the time the Edwards family arrived at Mt. Pleasant, Gwen and June were ready for high school, so, as there was no chance of travel to a secondary school from Store Creek, they were sent to St. Joseph's College, Perthville, a boarding school for girls near Bathurst. They went together, but as time went by, their closeness in age and their natural rivalry caused trouble between them during the holidays when they came home.

The harmony of the home was upset by their quarrelling and, in fact on one occasion, one chased the other up the hall with a broom. This, as well as a little upset in Gwen's health, which necessitated regular visits to a doctor for a while, caused our parents to separate them, so Gwen was enrolled at St. Mary's College in Bathurst and June stayed at Perthville.

My eldest sister, Mary Gwenda Datson Edwards, was born on 5th December 1920, the second child in our family. At a very early age she was a responsible child, and as the other four siblings came along, she became 'mother's helper' to my Mum and was particularly motherly in her interaction with Dick and me, the two youngest of the brood.

One of my earliest memories is of the two of us being pushed along the dusty Euchareena road in an old pram by Gwen to the gate into the cemetery, which is quite a distance from the village. Near the gate was a sort of ladder spanning the fence, and here Gwen would unload us and allow us to climb up and down the ladder for a while before reloading us for the return trip. I would have been less than three years old, and Dick only about 12 months, but the memory, though vague, is still with me.

After Dad bought Mt. Pleasant several months later, and Gwen was sent to boarding school to St. Mary's College in Bathurst, she really blossomed, and not only in her character, but her weight ballooned too, and it is incredible how this slim girl we all came to know later could have put on so much weight at school. Nevertheless, she joined in all aspects of school life and there are photographs of Gwen building gymnastic pyramids with other navy-clad girls and looking attractive despite being a bit plumper.

She joined in physical culture lessons, and Dad and Mum managed to get to Bathurst for a concert in which Gwen was on stage as part of the act where several girls stood on each other's shoulders, making pyramid patterns. Dad was very amused when the girls were marching and Mum exclaimed, 'Oh Wilf, look! Gwen's the only one in step!' It may be a colloquialism to write it, but Dad 'made a meal' out of that remark for years at Mum's expense.

Whilst at college, Gwen learnt to play the piano, discovered she could sing well, became proficient at needlework and painting, and returned home to Mt. Pleasant. Jack gave June a break from teasing her about her so-called vanity, and turned his attention to Gwen, telling a few friends that when she came home, 'Gwen couldn't fit through the door.' A gross exaggeration of course, especially as Gwen soon slimmed down and was never more than a 12-14-dress size in her life, earning my envy, as I was the tallest, and one could say the 'largest' of the girls, and as well had very big feet!

Gwen showed at once that she was a natural homemaker, and while at home before her marriage, she showed her artistic flair in flower arrangement, though never having had a lesson. The homestead always had a graciousness and charm about it when Gwen was there as she would pick poppies, stocks and nandina from Mum's garden, and fill bowls and vases in the lounge and dining room, and Mum and Dad loved this.

At about this time, a young teacher arrived at the one-teacher school at Store Creek, which Harry, Dick and I attended. It was his first school, he was 22 years of age, and his name was Bill McCloughan. He was a presentable young man, of slim build, with grey intelligent eyes, and it wasn't too long before he noticed the young Edwards girl with her fair to light brown curly hair, a few freckles and a zest for life. Their romance blossomed, especially on the golf course at Stuart Town where they often played. They also played golf at Mt. Pleasant, using the long front paddock as their course and, instead of putting into holes, they putted to chosen trees. Not always welcome, but blissfully unaware of that, Dick and I would follow them around the entire course!

Then, after dinner after the washing up was done, and Mum, Dad, Dick and I, and the two old ladies, had gone to bed, the young couple would sit in the lounge and talk. Not for long though! W.B. was a nervous father of young girls, and very much of the old school, you know, avoid not only the sin, but 'the occasion of sin,' and he would soon start clearing his throat, then coughing, then more clearing of his throat, and then finally, 'It's getting late Gwennie, it's time for bed!' Poor Bill would depart, and Gwen was always a quick mover—she would be in bed before Bill was at the bottom of the first hill.

I felt I bore the brunt of this romance, as Gwen would make sure I was immaculate before riding off to school, my tie neatly tied, long white socks up to the knees, a hair ribbon tied in exactly the right spot to keep my dark hair out of my eyes all day, and, worst of all, *my nails cut*. This was the worst assault on my body as I hated the feel of my nails freshly cut, and would run out and rub them in the dirt to make them feel 'normal'. Poor Gwen!

On looking back I can't believe I did that, but I remember doing it at least once. In the afternoon the little sister she had sent off would arrive home with her hair ribbon and tie tied to her saddle, socks rolled down, ink smudges on her fingers and not bearing much resemblance to the pristine child Gwen had sent off in the morning. Then Gwen would have to do it all over again the next day.

Nevertheless, the couple was married on August 22nd 1942 in St. Mary's Cathedral, Sydney, and like Mel, she did not dress as a bride because of the war, but wore a beautiful, blue suit and had a fetching blue and navy hat perched on the side of her head. I've just read in June's diary that she was Gwen's bridesmaid and wore a dusty pink dress, knitted by one of her patients . . . something else I didn't know.

Dick and I went off to boarding school and Bill accepted a move to Gumly Gumly, near Wagga, where Gwen, like Meg in 'Little Women', became the perfect teacher's wife. So we leave them there furthering

Bill's career, Gwen eventually giving birth to two children in Wagga, Jayne Estelle and Robert William. Later in the story we will see her welcoming a third child, Gerard Edward, but in those days there was just the pigeon pair.

As Jack and Harry were like chalk and cheese, so were Gwen and June. June was as dark as Gwen was fair, with olive skin and brown eyes, always slender, and with a certain air about her of sophistication and elegance.

It was June who was selected in mannequin parades for charity in Orange, June who had flair when it came to wearing hats, so she was the first one the committee chose when it was hats that were to be modelled. She would turn her head this way and that, a dimple would come out in her cheek and it would make her look very fetching. No wonder Jack thought he should bring her down a peg or two by teasing her!

Her hair was long in her early years, as was Gwen's, but one day Mum asked Nana to take June to 'get a little bit off her hair,' but June persuaded the hairdresser to cut it short and when it was washed at home, it fell into natural curls and her hair always had a beautiful curl, another cause for envy for me as mine was straight.

When the family went to Manly for holidays, the fair-skinned siblings would burn despite tanning oil and cover-up shirts, but June and I would end up 'brown as a berry', to quote Nana.

June also had a very vivacious personality and a love of meeting people and this drew them to her like bees to honey. She left Perthville College aged seventeen, and after a short stay at home, went to Maitland Hospital to do her nursing training. She chose Maitland because a friend, Lorna Hansford, had an aunty who was Matron there, so the girls went together. There was another Nurse Edwards there training, so it was decided June would be Nurse Sloane-Edwards, as Mum's maiden name was Sloane, so that was what she was called throughout her nursing career.

After completing her four years training, she started at the Women's Hospital in Crown Street, Sydney for a year of training in Obstetrics and Gynaecology. This was during the war years and there were many soldiers in Sydney, and, as part of her training, June had to deliver babies on her own with a junior assistant who was called a scout. They were mostly called out at night but June said the nurses made sure they wore their uniforms and then felt relatively safe. On checking her certificate much later, June saw that she had delivered thirty-nine babies alone, and even more with an assistant.

I felt quite proud of my sister when I read this in June's diary, because those nocturnal trips by public transport, mostly in the slum area, must have been very scary with so many soldiers, many of them American and a lot of them Negroes, roaming the streets. Today, one does not look twice at a coloured person, but back in 1942 Negroes were unfamiliar in Australia, and in those unenlightened times presented an added risk. And as for feeling safe in a nurse's uniform, now in 2011, even a nun wouldn't be safe on some streets at night with drug use so widespread!

After finishing obstetrics, June had a short break at Mt. Pleasant, but she received an invitation from the Matron of the Royal Hospital for Women at Paddington, who had been Deputy Matron when June was at Crown Street, to 'pack your bags and come back.'

The job was great and just up June's alley, working with unmarried mothers who had fled their home town or district to come to the city, work at the hospital until their babies were born, then have them adopted and return home, having finished the 'course' they had been doing in the city, with no-one the wiser.

June was asked to set up a department for these unmarried girls and to be in charge of it. It was a great success as they were paid for the work they did in the kitchen and day room and with Matron's permission and signature, June set up accounts for them and would sit at her desk and call them over on their way from the office on pay day.

They would try to dodge June, but were really grateful when they left after their babies were adopted, and, thanks to Sister, had a tidy sum to help them to a fresh start.

Just after she turned 30, in June 1950, June and a couple of her nursing friends left on the liner Otranto for London, where they planned to finance their travels to Europe by working, as Aussie nurses were very much in demand then. Her diary reveals some short term jobs specialling patients, socialising with young Australian doctors in London furthering their studies, sometimes with their wives there as well, and one other job that lasted nine months, which she described as 'a great job'.

Mr. Cohen was a very elderly Jewish man who owned the factories that created the Marble Arch and the entrance gates to Buckingham Palace. He and his wife Maud were lovely people who were very good to June who, in turn, delighted them with her professionalism and happy disposition.

Mr. Cohen's health problem was bladder and he wore a colostomy bag strapped to his leg. June lived within walking distance of their home at Palace Gate, Kensington, and her first task each morning was to bath and dress him (he was 92) and then take him for a walk through Kensington Park. He used a walking stick, was very slow, and he would say, 'I think we should empty the bag.' June would reply 'No, wait until we find a big tree we can hide behind.' He would shake with laughter and say, 'You, Sister, are a very naughty Aussie girl.'

He had a chauffeur and they took June on many drives around London and Kent and she became very fond of Mr. and Mrs. Cohen. When she was returning by ship to Australia, a parcel was delivered to her when they had been three days at sea. It was a beautiful Royal Doulton figurine of a girl and it was accompanied by a note, 'Good-bye my special Aussie girl, my heart will break and I shall miss our walks!'

I feel I could write this whole story about June and her wonderful travels throughout her single life, but there is a younger sister, me, Margaret, waiting in the wings. June arrived home from England and spent time at home but finally married an old beau, Lester Moran, who at the time was the Advertising Manager of *The Brisbane Courier Mail* in Sydney.

They were married in St Canice's Church, Elizabeth Bay, and though a late starter, June gave birth to two children, Lynne Louise (Lindy) and Philip Lester. Just after Lindy's birth, Lester was moved to Brisbane with the *Courier Mail*, so that is where we leave her at this stage of the story, and turn to a short, and less interesting profile, of me.

I, Margaret Philippa Edwards, was born in Orange on 15th April 1929, the second youngest of Stella and W.B.'s six children. Like Dick, I don't remember a time when Nana didn't live with us, but of all the children, I have the sharpest memory of incidents that happened, or were told to me. (Ask me what I did each day last week though and I would have difficulty!).

I was four when the big move to Mt. Pleasant, Store Creek, was made, and had dark, shiny hair cut into a bob by my father, with a fringe. Like Harry and Jack, my eyes were blue, and I always thought these were my best feature but that wasn't for many years, as my looks were the furthest things from my mind in those days. I was a tomboy and loved climbing trees, riding horses and playing cricket or marbles with my brothers, and reading.

Not too many demands were made on me as a child, so I roamed free, but I did have one task which children today would probably baulk at. Because the bedrooms at Mt. Pleasant were at the opposite end of the house to the bathroom and toilet, and because there were two elderly grandmas and Mum as well, sleeping a long way from the toilet, they used crockery chamber pots during the night.

Dad put a handle on a kerosene tin, (no plastic buckets in those days!) and each morning it was my job to empty each pot into this tin and empty it down the toilet, wash the pots, and return them to their respective rooms. This would be deemed 'gross' by today's children but I thought nothing of it, it was just my job.

Gwen was a hard taskmaster though, and she made me (not enlisted my help, not persuaded me to) but *made* me help with polishing the strip of linoleum each side of the long Axminster carpet runner in the hall. She would apply the polish and I would rub it off and polish it until it shone. I went well for the first half, but then I would start to whine, 'Oh Gwennie, I'm tired now, can I go?' The reply was instant, 'No way, we have to finish it, keep going.'

The next request would also be ignored, so desperate situations call for desperate measures and I would lie on my back pretending I had fainted, with my eyes closed and my arms flung out crosswise. I got some reaction then, but not what I expected, 'Get up, I know you're only faking. Keep polishing!' So I'd keep polishing, mumbling things like, 'You'd be sorry if I did die,' and then for the rest of the time, my fertile imagination would conjure up my sad family weeping and wailing because of my untimely demise! And Gwen would be saddest of all.

I was seven when I started school as I had to be a good enough rider to undertake the two mile, very hilly ride to the school, and I shared this journey with Dick, and for one year with Harry, when he did seventh grade at Store Creek before going to Wolaroi College in Orange.

Mr. Frost was my first teacher and I gave him a bad time with my questions. For example, when writing a composition about my cat: 'Please sir, how do you spell Ussey?' Mr. Frost made a stab at it, 'O-o-s-e-y' he spelt. I wasn't satisfied with that. 'No sir, that's Oosey.' Then another day I told him I was going to do something 'to-morning' and of course Mr. Frost told me there was no such word. 'Yes there is' I assured him, 'to-day, to-night, to-morrow and to-morning!'

Speaking about Ussey brings to mind an episode that was upsetting for me, as like most little girls, I loved my cat and hated suffering of any kind. One day the boys had been rabbitting, and arrived back with a pack of bloodthirsty dogs who were stirred up from chasing, and catching, rabbits. Ussey chose that time to streak from the tree she'd been climbing to the dairy, and of course the dogs spotted her, probably thought she was another rabbit, and surrounded her.

No one could do anything and the dogs were barking all around the terrified cat. My family became alarmed when I rushed in among them all and finally, with everyone screaming at me to 'Come out of there!' I picked her up and ran out. She was in a bad way and we laid her on a towel in the laundry, but she died. The family thought I would get torn to pieces as well as poor Ussey, but I didn't give that a thought.

I remember clearly the day my younger brother Dick swallowed a little pencil. It was only a pencil stub really, and a small child should not have had it, but another boy took Dick's long pencil and gave him the small one . . . and Dick swallowed it. There was great panic, and someone was sent to bring Mrs. Frost who held Dick by the feet and swung him around, or tried to.

Finally, Harry went across to Mrs. Quirk's and rang Dad and he came over and took him home where, in his good old bush doctor's style, he gave him a cotton wool sandwich and rang the doctor. The doctor approved of his action, and told him to watch for the pencil in Dick's motions. I'm here to tell you it was never seen again, but the next day Nana said 'Shhh!' and when we all looked up, she said: 'I thought I heard Dick's pencil writing!' Everyone laughed, and the pencil episode was over.

The school at Store Creek only had an enrolment of fifteen pupils and a priest used to come from Wellington once a month to teach

Scripture. There was only a handful of his flock at the school, so the priest would take us on the veranda. One day Father Foley, a nice young Irish priest, put a question to his young congregation, 'If you were on your way to Heaven and you lost your way, what would you do?'

No response, except I flung my hand up. 'Yes, Margaret?' asked Father Foley, surprised. My reply brought some mirth: 'I would follow the fence Father.' (Dad had always told us that if we got lost in any of the paddocks, to follow the fence!) Of course the correct answer was 'to go to confession and tell God you are sorry' but I knew nothing of that.

It must have been hearing about Jesus in these sessions once a month that caused me to be a bit religious because every time there was an emergency of any sort, I would be somewhere praying. One day Gwen and Harry had gone for sheep and when they got to the spot where the boys had, unbeknown to our father, been training Byng for the gymkhana, he bolted, with Gwen, terrified, on his back.

Pandemonium broke out in the house when someone shared the news, and Jack, Mum and Dad were running out to the tennis court where, if Gwen made it, the horse would stop. Dad was issuing instructions to Jack, where to go to stop the horse etc. and then he said to his wife: 'And Stella, get that child out from behind the door!' I was in my usual position babbling prayers non-stop.

During these years, Bill McCloughan had become the teacher of the three youngest Edwards children, and now he was going to marry Gwen, so we had to stop calling him 'Sir' except at school. It was really strange to call him 'Bill,' but it wasn't for long as Harry moved on to boarding school that year, and Dick and I the next, and the numbers were down so the school closed and Bill was transferred to the Wagga area.

Every few years Mum would invite our city cousins to Mt. Pleasant for a short holiday, boy cousins for the boys, and Ailsa and Judy Sloane from Artarmon, for me. They were Uncle Jack and Aunty Glad's daughters, and though Judy was a bit older, Ailsa and I were only six months apart and we got on very well. We loved riding the quieter horses, which Jack had picked out for safety reasons, and every day saw us cantering off somewhere.

They both had long hair, Judy's was black and with her very blue eyes she could have passed for an Irish colleen, but Ailsa's hair was brown and her eyes more hazel, and she was of slighter build than Judy. Like June, these two girls had an air of refinement about them, which is as natural and evident in Ailsa today as it was then, Judy having unfortunately died several years ago.

Ailsa had washed her hair one day and when we asked Mum if we could go for a ride, Mum said: 'No, not until Ailsa's hair dries, it is cold today and she might get a chill.' I can't remember who thought of it, (perhaps I can!) but we decided to hurry things up a bit, so we decided to put her hair through the clothes ringer. Everything went well for a while until I started to reverse the wringer, and then we had big trouble as the hair started to get caught, and tangled, and then . . . 'MUM! COME QUICKLY!'

Well I'll draw a veil over the next twenty minutes, maybe I've blocked it out but things are a bit vague in my memory. I know that scissors were involved, and I would assume Aunty Glad wasn't amused when she saw her daughter's hair, but she never upbraided me, and being the sweetie that she was, she wouldn't. In fact she had a wonderful sense of humour and I am sure she and Stella had a giggle over the phone about it.

Now you have met all the family and learnt a little about each one, so at this stage we leave Jack in the Army, Gwen just married, June pursuing her nursing career, Harry in the Air Force and we two younger ones on the verge of going to boarding school.

That meant Dad was on his own again except for casual labour and Mum and the two elderly ladies 'keeping the home fires burning' while knitting socks for the war effort and writing copious weekly letters to those who were away. Mum undertook this task to keep her children informed and each one always received a weekly letter. If either of us at boarding school wrote saying we 'needed' something, she would walk over to the post office if Dad was away, to send it as she knew we would not ask for it if we didn't need it. It was a hard two miles, being so hilly, but a valiant woman was Stella Edwards!

I consider myself very fortunate to have had such a happy childhood as I don't have even one bad memory. If only children everywhere could say the same! Drugs are so prolific in our modern society, babies are being born to mothers who are drug addicts and the babies have so much pain from withdrawal that their first days and weeks are spent being rocked and comforted by volunteers. Looking back I realise it was a gentler age I lived in, at least in Australia, but it seems to me we have been just ten years behind America in most things, especially in being inundated with drugs, and they have certainly caused a surge in crime here.

CHAPTER 6

THE FAMILY SPREADS ITS WINGS

The early forties saw many changes in the lives of the Edwards family. Dick and I went off to our respective boarding schools, Harry joined the Air Force and looked quite dashing in his navy blue uniform, Jack was already in the Army, June was furthering her nursing career and Gwen and Bill got married.

There was no television then so the progress of the war, or any disaster, wasn't present in our living rooms as it is today. The most graphic evidence we ever saw of the war was in films like 'Mrs. Minniver', when planes were bombing London, people were crowded into air raid shelters and Greer Garson was weeping and hugging her children.

There were many such films, but it was years after the diabolical reign of Adolf Hitler that we even heard of the Holocaust, when six million Jews were persecuted and put to death in the notorious gas chambers in concentration camps throughout Europe. We relied on our radios and documentaries from the ABC and the BBC for information, but I don't remember hearing about the Holocaust until much later.

When we children were home there was always music at Mt. Pleasant. I was often at the piano playing and singing, sometimes Gwen would play a piece she had learnt at school and June seemed to know only one piece of music, and that was 'My Rosary', and this she would play expertly and with all the elegance that was her signature!

Sometimes, Mum would accompany me on the piano but I mostly played for myself when I sang. W.B. played by ear and he would incline his head to the side so he could hear us singing, and he would tell us to keep singing so he could pick up the tune as he went along. Nana would sometimes sit at the piano and belt out some songs she knew, so there was quite a variety of music played.

The boys didn't play any instrument but they enjoyed it and would stand around the piano and sing while I played if their friends were there. Over the years we had many gatherings of friends and neighbours, and singing around the piano would always be part of the evening. Jack, Harry, Dick and Kevin particularly enjoyed these singalongs, and they would lift the roof singing when I played 'McNamara's Band'.

I had always been friendly with a girl from Store Creek who was three years older than me, but because she had rheumatic fever as a child, she had missed school and so we were in the same class. Her name was Dorothy Quirk and we spent a lot of time together at the Store Creek School, and then at weekends riding my bike. Because Dot was delicate, I would double her and we would ride quite far afield and just enjoy each other's company. I really loved my young friend.

When I was going to Perthville, Mr. Quirk decided to send Dorothy too, so Dad and Mum took both of us to the College at the beginning of the school year in 1941.We settled in fairly well for the first week, and did what we did at home, and that was explore, and a couple of times one of the nuns told these two bush kids gently that they were out of bounds and 'the boarders are not allowed up here dear, this is the nuns' domain.'

Suddenly I felt sick one day and was put to bed for a couple of days with a tummy ache, and I only heard from my mum later that the nuns were sure I was only homesick. However that passed and in no time we were home for Easter and regaled our families with tales of all the exciting things about boarding school. The boys offered me two shillings if I could speak for five minutes without using the phrases 'I nearly died' or 'I nearly fainted!' as my conversation was peppered with these words. No money exchanged hands in the end, so enough said.

A truly exciting thing happened shortly after my return to school after the Easter break. I had never had a birthday cake, only a little tea party with Nana, Dot Quirk and Dick, and when my 12th birthday came in April, a big parcel was delivered from Bathurst. Excitedly I opened it and it was a birthday cake beautifully iced in blue, and it took pride of place that night on the table I shared with seven other girls at dinner, and of course everyone in the dining room sang 'Happy Birthday'. As Eliza Doolittle sang in the movie 'My Fair Lady,' it was 'loverly, loverly, loverly!'

In August of that year Gwen and Bill were married in Sydney. Dick and I were looking forward to it but just before the wedding, we both landed home from school with the measles, so Nana looked after us at Mt. Pleasant. We were quite ill really with very high temperatures, and, in my case, severe nosebleeds, but Nana was equal to the task of nursing us.

If you had an earache, Nana would warm olive oil and pour a small amount in and give you an aspirin. If it was toothache, another aspirin and oil of cloves for your tooth, and if it was a stuffed-up nose due to a cold she would put eucalyptus on a hanky and some on your pillow and off you would go with the fairies. Dad kept a wary eye on Nana's ministrations in the sick room; he would say to Mum, 'I don't like Mother giving the children drugs.'

June had written a couple of times about going out with a young soldier named John from the Greta Army Camp which wasn't far from Maitland where she was training. They had become good friends so she was upset when she rang to tell the family that he had his hand blown off by an exploding detonator. After she married Lester, quite a few years later, she met him again as he was involved in advertising, as was Lester, and came to dinner in their home in Brisbane.

Then she had another boyfriend named Bill who was in the Scottish Regiment and he would always know which ward she was working in. They all wore kilts and used to march past the hospital and Bill would command, 'Eyes right, Salute!' and all the nurses would rush to the window. Sadly, Captain Bill Watson was shot down during war service and June received word while on night duty. Naturally she was devastated, so I think that explains why such an attractive girl didn't marry until she was thirty-five.

Gwen was very happily settled into marriage and Bill was teaching a few miles out of Wagga at a place named Gumly Gumly. She would ride her bike out each week to teach sewing, and eventually Bill was transferred to a bigger school in Wagga itself where Gwen continued with the sewing classes. They were a popular couple and made friends wherever they were sent during Bill's teaching career, and in Wagga Gwen continued with her singing, entering a couple of Eisteddfods. In one she sang 'One Fine Day' from 'Madam Butterfly', which suited her light soprano voice. While I was supposedly the acknowledged singer in the family and won all the accolades and the odd medal, Gwen's voice was delightful and more like Mum's whereas mine was more that of a dramatic soprano.

I really loved singing and always knew it was a gift from God to me, so I sang to give myself happiness as a child, but later I sang to give pleasure and sometimes comfort, to others, especially when I sang at many, many funerals. It wasn't long before the nuns put me in the choir at the College and I sang in that for the six years I was there. Then, when my voice was deemed mature enough, I began lessons with Sister Veronica who herself had a beautiful singing voice. Sometimes at night when we were supposed to be sleeping in our dormitories, we would hear the nuns at their recreation downstairs and Sister Veronica often sang. My voice and the songs in my heart were trained and nurtured by my years in the choir at Perthville and by the tuition of Sister Veronica, and later Sister Lucy, and for that I am indeed grateful.

When the Japanese crept into Sydney Harbour in 1941, Mr. Quirk became very nervous about Dorothy being away from home and, regrettably, brought her home, so I was on my own there. This didn't worry me as I had already made friends and I had so much to learn. For instance, I couldn't darn socks, so every Saturday morning I had to join a class having lessons. I was very proud at the end of the first term when I won a prize for my darning, a big, green piggie brooch; a ghastly thing and I never wore it. Then I was having music lessons a few days a week, and this involved daily practice.

Sister Marie Therese was the basketball coach and she tried the new girls out, and surprisingly, I made the A team and was in this team for the whole six years I was at the College. There is not room here to detail all that filled the days but with Mass first thing every morning, duties, classes all day, choir practice, sport, meals of course, piano practice daily, and supervised study every afternoon from 4.00pm until 5.00pm and in the evening from 7.00pm until 9.00pm, life at boarding school was very busy. All the girls had to help hang the washing on washday and collect her things from the clothesline (no mean feat when we got out of classes at 3.30pm and study began at 4.00pm, and when sometimes our clothes had scattered halfway up the hill if it was windy).

Another thing this young girl from Store Creek had to learn to do was to iron her clothes, my incompetence a result I guess of my free life at Mt. Pleasant when Nana or Gwen would do the ironing. Anyhow, at the end of my first year at Perthville, I had come a long way. My 'duty' each day right from the age of eleven-and-a-half, was to sweep the back veranda and I must have passed this test because I was promoted to the very long front cement veranda, and I retained this duty for the term of my life at the college.

There was a bonus to sweeping the front veranda as I could often share a conversation with the elderly chaplain, Father Howard, who was an uncle of the former Labor politician, Fred Daly, and he was very like him in looks. As to Father's politics, well, we didn't go into that, but he was a beautiful old man. I usually glanced in the door of the parlour where the portraits of the co-founders of the St. Joseph's Order, Father Julian Tennyson-Woods and Mother Mary MacKillop, now Saint Mary of the Cross, were hanging each side of the fireplace in big oval frames.

At the beginning of the next year, I was deemed too young and immature to proceed to second form, so I repeated first form, and that was the beginning of life-long friendships for me. Joan Morrissey came from Granville and was the most homesick young girl you could imagine, but she overcame this and, after the Intermediate, applied for entrance to the order as a postulant at the age of fifteen. Special permission from the Bishop had to be sought and was granted, and she is still, at the age of 82, giving devoted service to God and her religious order.

Margaret Baker came from Cessnock and became another of my closest friends and she also entered the convent, as did Carmel Sheridan from Coolah and Philomena Gearon from Oberon. These wonderful women all celebrated their 80th birthday at a luncheon with my husband and me in May 2009, in Bathurst, except for Phillo Gearon who sadly died from a brain tumour in April 1999.

The year that I met all these women as schoolgirls, 1942, two lovely auburn-headed girls from Alectown, near Parkes, came to Perthville and, becoming friends with these two had a huge impact on my later life.

The Dwyer girls, Molly and Kath, had sadly lost their father in early September, and they came to the college two weeks later, still grieving for this father of eight children who had died as a result of pneumonia. An elderly nun died a short time later and, knowing how upset the two girls would be, one of the nuns suggested to some of the senior girls that they might take Molly and Kath for a picnic in the bush above the college while the funeral was going on.

In the evenings, these two girls sometimes entertained us by singing, with very sweet voices, and in harmony, 'Whispering Hope'. Mother Elizabeth wasted no time in recruiting them for the choir and they remained in it for the duration of their time at Perthville.

Although I enjoyed college life and having so many new friends, let no one assume that life at boarding school was a bed of roses. On the contrary, the nuns took a holistic view of training the students in their care and some of this involved 'formation of character.'

At that time, as the youngest girl in a big family from the bush, I had only ever experienced unconditional love, and when this formation was apparently going on, it was hard for me to differentiate between character-building episodes and a plain clash of temperament between one nun and myself in particular. I was a prefect and later on, captain of the school, so not irresponsible, and found the unpleasant episodes with Sister, who, in the interests of charity, shall remain nameless, very upsetting.

One particular incident happened when I was just twelve-and-a-half, and it affected my self-esteem for many years, as our opinion of ourselves is either affirmed, or denied by those with whom we interact. We did not receive phone calls at school so my mother had phoned and the sisters had passed the message on to me that my Aunty Grace had died suddenly, but no details were known. As I was filing into the dining room for dinner, the mail was handed out and there was a letter for me from my mother.

As soon as I sat down and was waiting for the food to be brought to the tables, I eagerly opened the letter, mainly to find out what had happened to my aunt. Immediately the Sister, who was the source of my only area of discomfort at the college, pounced—that is the only word to describe her action—snatching the letter, crumpled it up and put it in her voluminous pocket, saying as she did so for the 100 girls and several nuns in the room to hear, 'Margaret Edwards, you with your airs and graces, how dare you read at the table!'

There was more of the same about my airs and graces, but I didn't wait to hear it. I bolted from the table in shock and ran up three flights of stairs to my dormitory where I shut myself in the bathroom and cried my heart out. After they had finished dinner, Molly and Kath Dwyer came upstairs and finally persuaded me to come out.

The next afternoon, dear little Sister Sabina came to me, and said, 'Margaret, the only way you will get your letter back is if you go and apologise to Sister X.'

I sought her out and apologised for reading my letter at the table and Sister X rather shamefacedly took the letter from her pocket and handed it over. There had been an attempt to iron it but somehow the joy of opening a fresh letter had gone, and I felt wounded. With the maturity of years now, I think I should have sought out the Mother Superior and reported it, as perhaps the punishment didn't fit the crime. Sister X was obviously feeling the strain of her job and needed a break from dealing with young girls.

I said nothing of this and many other incidents at home as I knew how disturbing it would be to my parents who had enough worries with the boys in camp and likely to be sent to the war zone. I also knew that Dad, if he knew, might even remove me to a Sydney school, and, to this day I have a deep and abiding love for the college, the Josephite spirit, and for the many wonderful nuns who influenced me in my growing up years there.

Many years later I was in a group and the priest lecturer was speaking on healing. He asked the group to look into their hearts and isolate one hurt that still bothered them, so I chose this incident with Sister X, which was not an isolated incident by any means, and asked, as he suggested, for healing in that area. Perhaps someone reading this may benefit from that as I did, as most of us have hurts that linger long after they perhaps should, and it is better for our health if we put them to bed.

While all this was happening to their younger sister, Gwen and June were forging ahead with their lives. Gwen was pregnant and gave birth to Jayne in 1944, June was delivering babies out of Crown Street Hospital, and Mum had to face a hysterectomy in a Sydney hospital. She and Dad had been married 'out of the Church' which was the usual way of saying a Catholic had married in a church other than Catholic. They had in fact been married at All Saints, Church, Woollahra.

I have no idea why as Dad was not bigoted about religion. Mum had been excommunicated as a result and wasn't allowed to receive the sacraments. She had something in common with Mother Mary MacKillop, our recently canonized saint, who had suffered the same fate at the hands of a bishop, but for wanting to keep the autonomy of her order and not have it controlled by the bishop in each diocese.

Stella was not instructed in the laws of the church as I was, because at school, these rules and regulations were taught as part of the religious lessons. In 1915, when Mum and Dad, who had grown up together, were considering marriage, the priest from Molong came once a month to say Mass and that was the extent of her instructions.

When, in 1944, she was to face what was then a very serious operation, Stella asked her husband to agree to another marriage, this time before a priest. Uncharacteristically, Dad refused, stating that they were already married, as of course in the eyes of the state, they were, but he didn't understand his wife's desire for the blessing of the Church on her 28-year-old marriage. It was a big worry to me who had only just learned these rules and the dire consequences if they were disobeyed, and I didn't think of asking Gwen for an explanation as to why they got married out of the church, and perhaps she didn't know either.

Dad would often say he woke many times in the night with Mum's rosary beads under his back and he always drove us to Mass so there didn't seem to be much bigotry there. Thankfully Mum came through the surgery and went to Gwen in Wagga to recuperate.

Dad took me with him when he went to Wagga to pick her up and we drove via Cowra so that he could show me the graves of the Japanese soldiers who had either been shot during the recent Cowra break-out or committed hari-kari soon after. I was amazed to find the soldiers were buried in a couple of long mass graves, which resembled the ensilage pits I had seen on farms. Later of course these men were remembered in rows of graves with white crosses on all of them and with a name as well, but to my knowledge, no bodies were removed from the mass grave.

Basketball, then similar to today's game of netball, was the main sport that the girls at Perthville played, although a few occasionally had a game of tennis and we all played baseball. There was no swimming pool in those days; that came later, much to the envy of us, the earlier students. I was in the basketball team and Sister Marie Therese was our coach and sports' mistress. She wore the full habit, a long black serge dress with a large leather belt around her slim waist and huge rosary beads and a crucifix. She also wore the starched white gamp which curved nearly to her waist and a black veil which she tied back, and yet she ran and jumped and sprang in the air, and blew that whistle and kept up with the game as well as if she had on a pair of shorts.

Sister Marie Therese taught me and most of my friends in 3rd year and was an inspirational teacher, in many ways ahead of her time. The college had an enviable record for winning matches against all other schools in the region, and the coach of the Bathurst High School team asked Sister Marie Therese's advice, as they had the Ashley Cup coming up and she thought they could benefit from her input. Of course she willingly helped in any way she could.

While June was doing obstetrics at Crown Street Hospital, and learning to deliver babies on her own except for a junior 'scout', she was on her way back one night after a delivery. The two girls were chatting on the train with two young doctors who were also doing the course. June wondered why they got off at a stop before the hospital and when she went to get off at the right stop, she discovered the bag with the placenta in it was missing. This had to be brought back after each birth, so June cried all the way to the hospital, and when she got there the two young doctors were sitting on the steps and they had the bag! They had taken it when they got off 'for a lark', but when June told the family about it we failed to see that it was funny.

When my friends, Joan, Bake, Carmel, Philomena, Molly and Kath and I were in 3rd year, an incident occurred which, when narrated at home, merited the remarks 'I nearly fainted' and 'I nearly died' that the boys had banned in my first year there. There was an apple tree in the back garden laden with apples and the whole of the Intermediate class had been keeping an eye on it. One afternoon someone declared the apples ready to eat, so most of the class gathered around the tree and a few started picking them, and then eating them.

Suddenly there was a loud clapping of hands and Sister Marie Agnes sang out in a loud voice, 'All the girls anywhere near the apple tree, come up here immediately!' We obeyed and then Sister sent us all up to bed without any dinner. Shortly after we could hear heavy footsteps and then Sister Marie Agnes appeared carrying a large bottle of the dreaded castor oil and a huge tablespoon, and approached each bed in turn. She was followed by little Sister Sabina, who bore a tray with orange quarters and small squares of bread. The dose was administered in that dormitory and then they went upstairs to treat the other offenders.

After they had gone, chatter broke out; Philomena took the remains of an apple out of her pocket, and said, 'Well, I've had the oil, I might as well finish the apple!' Joan said, 'I only had one bight,' and I said, just as Sister Marie Agnes was coming back down the stairs, 'I could hardly stop laughing when she was giving it to me!' Sister heard me but didn't know what I said, so demanded to know. I spluttered and stammered and finally admitted that I had said I could hardly stop laughing! Sister glanced at me balefully and said, 'I've a good mind to give you another dose! That would stop you laughing.'

Of course she didn't, and the girls thought she would entertain the other nuns at recreation with the story because sometimes she did have a sense of humour. And this must have happened, because when we went into our classroom next morning, Sister Marie Therese was writing on the board the parsing and analysis for the English lesson: 'I MUST NOT EAT GREEN APPLES BECAUSE THEY ARE BAD FOR ME'! Other than that not a word was said, and in fairness I have to say that we were aware that we had done wrong as regards the apples and accepted our punishment in the right spirit.

I can't leave these references to the Sister X I spoke of earlier without saying that she was very kind to me when I was sick once with a vomiting bug, and, if the truth be known, I as a twelve or thirteen year old secretly wanted her to like me . . . but it didn't seem to ever happen, and this left me thinking there was some flaw in me.

Holiday time again and we all caught our various trains home. Because of the war, petrol was rationed, so only parents who lived in Bathurst, or somewhere close to the college could collect their children by car, and the rest of us travelled by train. The trains were often crowded with servicemen but there was no strong drink allowed on the train so we were fairly safe.

As we topped the big hill and Mt. Pleasant came into view, I felt my spirits rise with the feelings my home always inspired in me. The words of Sir Walter Scott formed in my mind: 'Breathes there a man with soul so dead, who never to himself has said, this is my own, my native land', and here it was before me like a picture on a postcard; the homestead on the hill with its several chimneys silhouetted against the sky-line, the surrounding hills coated a soft green from recent rain, the creek running through, fringed by drooping willows, and to top it all off, Hereford cattle grazing under a huge gum tree and newly-shorn sheep dotting the hillside.

This was the Mt. Pleasant I loved. And inside, my family was waiting to greet me with their love, their acceptance of my shortcomings, ready to laugh when I expected them to, and not today anyway, a critical thought in their heads. It would be balm indeed for anyone's wounded heart, and I revelled in it.

CHAPTER 7

SUMMER HOLIDAYS

Up until I was nine months old, Stella and W.B. drove to Cronulla, or some other beach for a camping holiday in the summer, taking Nana and the five of us with them. I have no memory of these trips, but my sisters told me that on that last camping holiday in January 1930, when I was nine months old, I started to walk. They remembered me walking between them, with my hands in theirs.

Later, when I was older, Dad would rent a house or flat at Manly and we would stay a fortnight, though he himself would return to Mt. Pleasant in case of a fire from the steam trains, and then come back to bring us home. Our property was only two miles from the main western railway line, so in summer, fire was a very real danger because a spark from the coal fire had been known to ignite the grass along the railway line. I can remember Dad having the odd swim with us in the surf at Manly, though he couldn't stay long, but when Jack was old enough to look after Mt. Pleasant he would stay and enjoy a well-earned rest.

These holidays at Manly were memorable because they enabled our family to play together whereas at home it was mainly work, work, work, and I can remember our arrival at Manly each time, and with what joy we all dashed into the surf. Mum would ensure that we all had cover up shirts on as well as suntan oil, but Dick and I always stayed in the water too long and usually suffered sunburn on our shoulders. We loved it too much to come out when ordered to by the older members of the family, so suffered the consequences, and we were always blue around the lips and shivering when we finally did.

Dick and I always made friends with other country kids, either at the Manly pool or the surfing beach, and we'd bring them back to our flat, or we'd go to theirs. Dad and Mum would sometimes meet friends from our district, and one of them said to them one day, 'No matter where we go in Manly we see Margaret,' and that was true as I roamed freely over most of Manly with my new friends, from the main surfing beach, along the Corso to the little Manly pool where the ferries came in, and then to our flat.

Things had totally changed when Frank and I took our children there in 1965 and we didn't feel they were safe on their own at all, as drugs had caught on, and the atmosphere was different. In our day, we loved the roller skating rink and spent all our pocket money there skating happily to 'O Johnny, O Johnny, how you can love' and 'Nursie, come over here and hold my hand, I feel awful bad'. Harry had a brush with fame there when he was knocked over by Chips Rafferty when he was about twelve and we all rushed back to the flat to tell Mum and Dad about that!

Our whole family loved the open-air concerts along the promenade where we would sit in deck chairs and the artists would perform in a big shell, and one could hear the surf pounding in, and smell the sea and listen to the beautiful singing. Dad would buy us all an ice cream, and to kids who lived where the nearest shop was eight miles away, it was all-magical. Why didn't I have the maturity to put my arms around my Dad's neck and thank him for making it possible? You know, I never did.

Actually, we were not a demonstrative family, even though we cared for each other deeply, and still do. June was an exception and hugged me sometimes but Gwen, who was more motherly towards me than her, didn't as a rule. Sometimes, when beds were short and I had to sleep with one of them, it was June who loved to cuddle up, whereas Gwen would snap: 'Move over. Don't touch my feet! Keep on your own side!' Later, I wondered how Bill got on sleeping with this touchy sister, but obviously that was different!

I can remember holidays at Manly with Gwen, June and Harry there, but perhaps June was nursing in Sydney and came for a few days and Harry must have got leave from the Air Force because we were there for New Year's night. It was a repeat of the dance at Store Creek when Dick and I were judged too young to go, but the three older ones were allowed and we were so sad because it sounded so much fun.

The crowd would surge up the Corso at Manly and we could hear music, horns tooting and much frivolity, and we knew our sisters and brother were there . . . and sure enough just after midnight they would arrive with newly-made friends and put the kettle on and talk in loud whispers in the kitchen so as not to disturb their sleeping family. As if I was asleep! My ears were attuned to everything going on outside in the street and then in the kitchen. By the time Dick and I were old enough to join in the New Year celebrations at Manly, the war was on and soldiers were everywhere and we were still not allowed to go. Responsible parenting, it's called!

My cousin Ailsa, who I've mentioned before, came over from Artarmon to spend the day with us once or twice when we were at Manly. She, Judy and Aunty Glad would arrive on the ferry, and the grown-ups, as we called them, would have a lovely time together while Dick, Ailsa, Judy and I would have a *great* time. We would do our usual traversing of Manly on foot, from South Steyne to Circular Quay, to North Steyne and then back to the Quay. There one day Dad shouted us a ride on the big Ferris Wheel and, when Ailsa was a bit reluctant, Dad said, 'Go on Ai, from up there you'll see the whole of Sydney,' and we could see a lot of it, too.

During the school holidays I was often asked to sing at functions and one was when I was about thirteen and the Convent school at Stuart Town put on Snow White and the Seven Dwarfs. I played Snow White, and Joan Peters from the post office at Store Creek made me an exact replica of the dress worn by Snow White in the film. The dwarfs were fully grown young boys, not at all dwarf-like, and we had so much fun at rehearsals as we had a scene where we had to eat at a table, and we were given real food each time, apple pie actually.

One of the dwarfs was Leo Hannelly, who later lived in Parkes until his death a few years ago, and he and my husband worked together in the St Vincent de Paul society. Leo was very dedicated, and he worked tirelessly for the Society, and died far too early.

When I was about fifteen, Mum played for me to sing at a function at Euchareena, and I chose to sing 'The White Dove' from the show 'White Horse Inn'. It was the only time my mother accompanied me on the piano in public, and I remember she had trouble playing while wearing bi-focal glasses, as she had to tilt her head up and down to read the music.

She managed beautifully, and everyone was sitting around the hall listening, when an old coloured identity, named Charlie, wanted to leave. He couldn't find his hat, so he went around the entire hall asking everyone politely, and loudly, 'Excuse me, is my 'at under you?' It caused quite a disruption as each one would stand up and look under the seat, and it took the length of the song for him to locate his 'at! I battled on, and Mum kept playing, thankfully oblivious to Charlie's antics. Not one of my best performances, but we all had a good laugh about it afterwards.

During these holidays Nana's deafness seem to have worsened, so she went to Sydney to see about it. When she returned after a week away we were all stunned. Where was the Nana with the tight little bun at the nape of her neck? Where were the practical thick black stockings? And her skirt, which was usually mid-calf at least; what was different about her skirt? Well! The Nana who emerged from the train that Jack met at Store Creek station, wore a skirt to her knees, had on black silk stockings and her hair had been permed!

W.B.'s sense of decorum was outraged. 'What is Mother thinking of?' he spluttered to Stella, 'Permed hair and short skirts!' Nana went her merry way unperturbed. The perm eventually grew out, and Stella lengthened her skirt just a little, but Nana felt better for asserting her independence even if it was short-lived. Meanwhile, Grandma continued with her crochet, clad in her long silk dresses, watched the proceedings from over her glasses, and wisely kept her own counsel.

Gwen and Bill came for school holidays and, despite having two children, they always pulled their weight. Bill often did some painting in the house for Mum, while Gwen, who was always a quick worker, would organise the children and be ready to do whatever was needed next. We called her son Robert 'Wobs' when he was little and he had ear trouble sometimes. Mum put him in with Harry to sleep the first night, and Harry was just dozing off when Wobs said: 'Hey, Harry.'

'What is it, Wobs? What do you want?' And the little five year old asked 'Have you got any cotton wool for my ears?' Harry assured him he would get some in the morning and he was satisfied then. He used to stand just outside the kitchen door if Dad had gone for a mob of sheep and watch for his Grandfather to return, sometimes for over an hour, and then he would run over to the yards which Dad would be filling with sheep. He was Grandfather's shadow while he was there.

He really loved being at Mt. Pleasant but he began his career after school in the bank, then abandoned that for bookmaking, then had a pet food shop, and finally in later life he indulged his love of horses by buying some land near Tweed Heads, building a ranch-style home and running polo horses on his acres. Some he breeds himself and others he has on agistment for other people, but Robert is amongst horses, caring for them, riding them in polo matches and doing what he loves best.

With Jack in mind, and knowing he would need his own place when he left the Army, Dad had bought a place at the back of Mt. Pleasant called Bundala. To get there one had to cross Flagstaff, which was an extremely high hill. There was no formed road and it was very steep in places. Bundala itself was rugged country and dotted thickly with blackberry bushes, but most of us had not seen it yet, so Dad decided to take us there.

Horses were much the best mode of transport, but there were not enough for all of us, so W.B. drove the truck, with Nana and Mum in the front with him, and Gwen, Bill, Mel and I on the back. Jack, Harry, June, and Dick rode the horses. I pleaded with Dad to let me ride too, but to no avail.

It was a hairy trip; I think we would have been safer on a horse. Dad ground the gears, and sometimes the truck would slip backwards. We who were on the back would give a squeal or two and Mum would say 'Oh Wilf, be careful!' Finally we arrived on flatter country and pulled up at the old deserted house. We all scrambled out, the riders dismounted and tied their horses up, and Nana and Mum spread a cloth under an old apple tree, and put out the sandwiches and cakes and some drinks. I started to sing 'In the Shade of the old Apple Tree' and Gwen joined in, as it was a popular song of the time.

After lunch we explored a bit, and were amazed to see kangaroos leaping through the scrub, and there was even one with a Joey in her pouch. I asked Dad, 'Why don't we see them at Mt. Pleasant?'

'We see an odd one up in the hills, but Mt. Pleasant is mostly cleared country,' he told me. 'The 'roos seem to hang about in scrubby country.'

Just then a big red kangaroo leapt over the high orchard fence as though it was a foot high.

'You know kids, they can kill a dog. If a dog attacks an old man kangaroo, he can rip the dog down the middle with the claw of his big toe,' Nana added some information. 'And I've been told of a case where a kangaroo held a dog under the water in a dam until it drowned!'

Gwen shuddered, 'They look such gentle creatures in zoos and parks,' she commented.

'They are really,' Dad told her, 'but if they are threatened, then they can be dangerous.'

Jack told us: 'We aren't far from the Macquarie River here.' We were surprised but decided to investigate that another day so we looked through the old dilapidated house and then, taking a billy each, picked blackberries, eating a few as we picked. Dad made the old joke that we should all be whistling and then we each found a tree for a toilet, and finally, as the evening shadows started to creep in, we boarded the truck for the trip home.

I didn't give up easily so I suggested Dick take my place in the truck and I could ride his horse! Dad compromised and said I could ride behind Harry until we reached Flagstaff but then I had to climb back on the truck. I can tell you that coming down Flagstaff was worse than going up it, with more slipping and sliding, a few more squeals from the back of the truck and Lady June riding Byng and looking as if she was in a fox hunt in England! It was an absolutely fabulous day and I would love to have done it again when I was older, but it was a treat we never repeated.

Mum made the most delicious blackberry jam the next day, which we ate with our own fresh cream and I expressed the hope that Jack wouldn't get rid of all the blackberry bushes. 'Surely he can leave one or two just for us,' I said, tucking in.

'Not a chance,' Dad replied. 'When he comes home for good, his first jobs will be getting rid of the blackberry bushes and the rabbits, if he wants to run sheep, which he will.'

The holidays ended, Gwen and Bill went back to Wagga, Harry and Jack returned to camp, June returned to her nursing post in Sydney and Dick and I went back to school. For me it was the beginning of my final two years at Perthville. It was 1945 and the war was escalating. Nana and Grandma remained at Mt. Pleasant with Stella and W.B.

I don't know how Dad managed without any of the boys, and labour was short. But he did, and Mt. Pleasant continue to prosper, despite the drought that had struck so badly in 1944. The Hubbard family at Mt. Top, over the hills from us, employed two or three Italian prisoners of war to help with the work as, like Jack and Harry, Claude and Ted were in the Army and Air Force and only Robert was there to help his father. Salvatore Mollo was one of these prisoners of war, and you will be surprised when and where he reappears in this story much later.

CHAPTER 8

CHILDHOOD ENDS

My return to school after the summer holidays marked the beginning of my last two years as a student of St. Joseph's College, Perthville. There was one very pleasing change at the college, for me at least. There had been a change of staff, and Sister X had been replaced by a beautiful nun, Sister Catherine, and this caused my last two years to be the happiest of my life there. We all hugged and kissed each other and asked, 'Did you have a good holiday?'

Sisters Catherine and Sabina were like mother hens, showing us our new dormitories and, as there were only seven of us going into 4th form and on to the Leaving Certificate the next year, we were given a small room with only seven beds in it. The other change was that our classroom wasn't with the other classrooms, but over at the novitiate and we had to walk across the lovely front garden to get to it. Immediately we began to feel our childhood slipping away.

Among my classmates were my friends Carmel Sheridan, from Coolah, Bake, (Margaret Baker) from Cessnock, Philomena Gearon from Oberon and Shirley Ryan from Lithgow, while through the wall in the Novitiate section, were two more of my friends, Kath Dwyer from Alectown and Joan Morrissey from Granville. They had made the brave decision to test their religious vocations and had entered the convent during the holidays, continuing their studies through the wall from us.

We could hear Mother Kevin teaching them, but we were not allowed to speak to them as they were in the process of 'giving up the world'. It was hard not to communicate, especially as we were at such close proximity to each other. However, we respected this edict and obeyed it, but once or twice, a whispered, 'How are you?' slipped out as we were passing. We could however, approach Mother Elizabeth, the Mistress of Novices, and ask permission to visit them occasionally for a short visit on a Sunday. Mother allowed this once in a while, but later in the year when I asked her, she refused, 'No dear, why don't you give them up to God now?'

As well as my studies, I continued my piano and singing lessons in preparation for exams later in the year, and piano practice was very time consuming. Sometimes I had to get up at 5.00am and practice for an hour before Mass, and it was strange on a cold Perthville morning to be breaking the silence with a bracket of scales to get my cold fingers working, and to know that not many others were about.

There were other piano practice periods during the day but they had to be fitted in with school lessons and the myriad other things on the agenda. Hence the early morning rise, especially close to exam time. I had such good teachers in Sister Agnes Mary, for piano, and Sister Veronica, for singing, and I loved both of these activities so much that I didn't get below Honours for either the whole time I studied them.

Not so with Maths, though! At Maths I was a real dunderhead, and though I tried very hard, I could not grasp the concept of Trigonometry. Finally, Sister Mark had to admit defeat and she and Sister Sophie decided I should drop Maths altogether and do Honours English, and Honours Music, resulting in a very relieved Margaret. At this time, the Sacristan, Mother Kevin, approached me to be one of her assistants. In the dictionary, sacristan is defined as 'the official in charge of vestments and sacred vessels in the church'.

So I added this to my chores, and with basketball training, Bjelke Peterson Physical Culture training once a week, my daily sweeping of the front veranda, music and singing lessons, piano practice, school lessons, study periods twice a day, Mass every morning, meals of course, the recitation of the Rosary with the school, choir practice and my typing lessons with an elderly Sister Margaret Mary. If it's true that the Devil finds work for idle hands, he must have had a frustrating time around Perthville!

Every Sunday night there would be Benediction in the church, which was in the grounds of the college, but the Perthville parishioners came to Mass on Sunday there as well and to Benediction at night. We all loved Benediction for its reverence and the atmosphere created by the candles with which the Sanctuary was aglow. The organ throbbed, while the congregation sang, 'O Salutaris and Tantum Ergo'. The white-clad altar boys swung the crucible to and fro, the incense wafted upwards taking our prayers to God, and our senses were assailed by the pungent odour of the incense.

All was very still and very reverent, and then the moment I waited for arrived when the priest put on the big flowing cope, clasped the monstrance firmly with both hands and holding it high with the Blessed Sacrament inside, blessed the congregation, first on the left, then on the right and finally straight ahead. I would fix my gaze on the small, white host encased in the monstrance, believing it was the Body of Christ, and as the altar boy pealed the bells, I, and I guess most of us, would say in our hearts, 'My Lord and my God!'

In the deep hush that pervaded the church, I would ask God to bless my absent family and would name them all. The priest would then take off the cope, and kneel and intone the Divine Praises which we would repeat after him . . . 'Blessed be God, blessed be His Holy Name, Blessed be God, true God and true man' and so on until the end. Then we'd sing the final hymn:

> 'Sweet Sacrament of Peace, dear home for every heart,
> Where restless yearnings cease, and sorrows all depart
> Therein Thine ear all trustfully, we tell our tale of misery,
> Sweet Sacrament of Peace, Sweet Sacrament of Peace!'

Like many other Catholics, I regretted the 'axing' (if it is not too strong a word) of Benediction as it was then, in favour of the watered down version that we experience today. The feeling of deep reverence, that feeling of God speaking to you and you relating to Him, the consciousness of His actual presence, are mostly missing today, but I should add, that is just my opinion.

It almost seems a shame to shatter the illusion of this serious, ostensibly religious, 16-year-old praying so earnestly in the chapel, but in the interest of truth, I must tell the story of the beret. Despite my recent maturing, I was still a scatterbrain in some areas. One of my most common faults was that I could never keep track of my black beret, and on Sunday nights it was compulsory to wear it to Benediction.

Unfailingly, I would hear the bell for Benediction, look wildly around for my beret, and not finding it, grab Bake's spare one from her desk, jab it on and break the 4-minute mile to join the other ninety-nine beret-clad girls filing into the chapel. That night I knelt with bowed head, and, among other things, thanked God that I had found Bake's beret in the nick of time for Benediction, completely unaware that I had the offending beret on inside out, and starkly embroidered across the top was MARGARET MARY BAKER, clearly visible to all.

I was in default on two counts: one, not having my own beret when ninety-nine other girls had theirs, and two, borrowing someone else's when borrowing was forbidden. So you see the halo had a habit of slipping!

Something that happened most nights at Perthville in winter was that our recreation time before study was spent dancing. I still played by ear despite Sister Agnes Mary's tuition, and I played foxtrots, one steps, waltzes, and so on while the girls danced with each other or with one of the nuns. Little Marie Hanrahan would play then and I would dance. It was good fun and good exercise.

Sister Mark loved these dances and she would be in there with one of her pupils with her veil flying, gaily dancing and enjoying it. Speaking of Sister Mark, she loved 'Rustle of Spring,' a piece of music I had to practice, and always when I was playing it, she would come running in, breathless and flushed, and gasp 'Oh I was down in the laundry and I heard it,' or 'I was in the kitchen and I just had to come.'

Debating became one of my interests and I enjoyed the cut and thrust of it, and the challenge of thinking on the spur of the moment. When I married, my husband told me that he had found 'attack was the best form of defence' and he certainly used this strategy when we disagreed, so I was grateful for the experience gained in my days in the debating team. Sometimes, in disagreements, when I thought I was stating my case calmly and succinctly, he would throw his arms up and declare, 'no one should ever marry a debater'.

That year my singing examination results were good, and one day Sister Veronica was on the front veranda, clapping her hands and waving a white paper at me. I ran up and could see my teacher was excited. 'You've won the State Medal,' she exclaimed, 'Congratulations Margaret,' and she clasped me in a warm embrace. Everyone was pleased to have this honour coming to the college, and my family at home was thrilled, too.

I continued to sing in the choir, which was of a very high standard under the baton of Mother Elizabeth, who seemed to draw our voices out with her hand as she would stand in front of us with her arm up and then curve her hand and bring it towards herself in a beckoning motion, saying as she did, 'To the front dear, throw your voice to the front.' It sounds crazy but she certainly produced some amazing harmony in that choir. I particularly loved 'O Jesu Mi', 'Panis Angelicus', and 'Regina Coeli', and sang these for many years in the Parkes choir, in several parts.

Retreats and Missions were held every few years at the college, and these were conducted by a priest from an order, such as The Redemptorist or Marist Order, and sometimes even a Jesuit priest would come for the few days. The Mission was attended by the parishioners as well and was mainly of the fire and brimstone style, spelling out the very real possibility of us going to Hell for eternity if we disobeyed the laws of the church, or died with mortal sin on our souls.

These sessions added to my disquiet about the condition of my mother's soul and the precarious situation it may be in, but because of my youth, I said nothing to anyone, not even my best friends who had nothing of like nature in their families, at least as far as I knew. Sometimes I lay awake at night though, worrying about it, and this had dire consequences later.

During the three day Retreats, we had to observe silence as this was conducive to us looking into our hearts to see where we were offending God and to help us absorb what the priest lecturer was telling us. We could walk about outside and meditate, or find a good spot and read a religious book. One night after the priest had been telling us about sudden death, and likened it to 'a thief coming in the dead of night', and added that we might, 'wake up and find the Angel of Death standing at the foot of our beds', we all crept up to our dormitories in the mandatory silence, and the Sister in charge of our dorm whispered to us that an elderly nun, Sister So and So just through the wall from us, had died.

We only just coped with that, and then one of us looked out the window and saw two gravediggers over at the nuns' cemetery digging the grave by the light of a lantern! Someone giggled nervously, then another, and finally there was mild hysteria, causing Sister to come in and scold us and to urge us to be more mature. I maintain to this day, that if a team of footballers had listened to what Father had been telling us, and then heard what we heard, and had seen the grave diggers carrying out their grisly task in the eerie light of a lantern, and all of it *in silence*, they would have reacted as we did!

Another auburn-headed Dwyer girl had come to Perthville and her name was Delia. She had a beautiful, light mezzo-soprano singing voice and began lessons with Sister Veronica, and later with Sister Fidelma. She was entered in a section of the Eisteddfod in Bathurst and I was asked to accompany her while she sang 'On Wings of Song'. We were both nervous but it went off well and Delia sang it beautifully, as she always did whenever she sang.

The war brought many casualties and a few of the girls at school lost brothers or cousins. In August of my last year at Perthville, wonder of wonders, the great news came . . . the Japanese had surrendered and the war was over. Our closest contact with it had been the large air raid shelters that had been carved into the hill behind the college to which we had to hasten when the air raid siren sounded loud and clear from Bathurst, five miles away. We all had a designated escape route, some down the cement stairs, some had to use the spiral stairs and the remainder were directed down the fire escape. We had to wait in these deep trenches until the All Clear sounded.

However, many of us had brothers at the war, or in camps, and, some like the Dykes girls, had their father being held a prisoner of war by the Japanese, so there was much rejoicing when we heard the news, and the nuns turned a blind eye to the shenanigans we got up to. Some one climbed the flagpole, others climbed down the fire escape and still others had always wanted to go down the spiral stairs from Holy Angels' Dormitory to the nuns' quarters, so grabbed the opportunity when the guard was down.

Over the years we had all enjoyed our weekly sessions with Mr. Allen who came once a week on the train from Sydney from the Bjelke

Peterson School of Physical Culture to teach us. Mr. Allen was of average height, and resembled George Formby, but he was much nicer looking. (For the benefit of those not of my vintage, George Formby was an English comedian, who sang, among other things, 'When I'm cleaning Windows'.)

We had to go to the local village hall for our exercises, which were set to music and followed a pattern. First we marched around the hall in single file, and because it was 'deportment', it was 'toe-heel, toe-heel' all the way, backs straight and arms swinging.

Just as a matter of interest, when we marched in Bathurst on the Feast of Christ the King in the march in which all the Catholic schools competed, we had to march military style, and it was 'heel-toe, heel-toe'. When we practiced for that, it was a soldier from the camp at Bathurst who trained us, and we would march up and down the village streets with him issuing instructions military style. We always did well in the march and often won it.

But back to Mr. Allen! When we finished our deportment, we lined up in rows, the music was changed and Mr. Allen would face us from the stage and instruct us in all the exercises. These were very invigorating and have remained in my memory, so that even now, nearly seventy years later, I amuse my family greatly by giving them a demonstration, humming the music to help my rhythm, arms flying in all directions. Mr. Allen told us often, 'belts in, brooches out' and I began to realise that this encourages a flat tummy, and once in the habit of holding the 'belt' in, one soon does it subconsciously.

One day (I think it was his birthday and the nuns found out), we put on a little concert for Mr. Allen at the end of the lesson and sang in harmony an English folk song called 'Barbara Allen'. I remember he was touched and wrote down the name, and then walked over to the college where the nuns always gave him dinner before he caught his train back to Sydney. Some time passed and then one day before commencing, he faced us with a big smile and announced the arrival of his daughter, BARBARA ALLEN! We all clapped and congratulated him individually before we left, and that would be a wonderful story for him to tell his wife that night.

Mum wrote that Grandma had suffered a fall and broken her hip so she was hospitalized for some time. Eventually, the hospital staff couldn't keep her in any longer, so Mum had arranged for her to go to a private nursing home, run by a Miss Bullard. She wasn't entirely happy there as she developed a phobia about her bowels and was afraid of having 'accidents' in the bed so she wanted a pan left near her.

Miss Bullard must have had her reasons for refusing this request, and I can think of some too, but it was a source of great distress to my gentle grandmother. Because of this, it was a happy release when she died peacefully in the nursing home. So that left only one grandmother at Mt. Pleasant. Harry was back from the war and working at home, Dick and I would soon be there too, and so life at Mt. Pleasant would change again with workers being family members.

I don't like writing this part, but I am determined to write a truthful story, at least as I saw what happened in my life. As the time for the Leaving Certificate approached and we concentrated more on our study, I began to have bad nightmares. I sailed through my music and singing exams, and had Sister Veronica calling me up to the front veranda again while waving a white paper at me, to tell me once more excitedly, that I had been awarded an exhibition to the Trinity College of Music in London. However, she added regretfully that I was unable to take it as we had done the wrong theory, A.M.E.B. instead of Trinity College of Music theory.

I wrote the news of the award to my family, and received the only phone call that I had ever received in my six years away from home. It was from Dad, who congratulated me and asked for details so he could explain it to his friends, 'when he stuck his chest out' were his words! I was so pleased to hear him say this, as it was the closest he had ever come to saying he was proud of me.

But those nightmares . . . I honestly don't remember complaining of these but the nuns knew, so I must have shown signs of distress. The dreams were always about planes crashing near me, on the garage near Mt. Pleasant, or somewhere equally close, and in retrospect, I can only link them with the movies we saw of the war when there was violence with planes crashing everywhere.

I remember the nuns brought a doctor out from Bathurst and he asked me a lot of questions and gave instructions that I was not to attend any more of the Leaving Certificate exams in Bathurst where we had been going to sit for them. I was to stay in bed, and on no condition was I to study!

It is all a bit vague, almost as if I have blocked it out, but I know I was upset because I missed the spelling exam which had a bearing on whether or not one got a scholarship, and I knew I could handle it easily, but worse for me was that I still had Honours English and the theory side of Honours Music to do. I didn't do these of course, and I can remember being scolded by a very cross Sister Catherine (who was never cross with me) for studying with a book under the sheets.

As a result of all this, I got a mediocre pass in the Leaving Certificate despite being awarded a prize as Dux of the class at the end of the year. When I had been home a couple of weeks, Mum took me to the hairdresser in Orange to get a soft perm in my hair. I was sitting in the chair and the lass got everything ready and then a plane flew very low and very loudly above the street. Immediately, I, who had always been self-contained, burst into tears, and when Mum explained 'she hasn't been well', the nice girls scheduled it for another day. This was the final episode of 'nerves', if that was what it was, though I have retained an uneasy relationship with aeroplanes to this very day.

The day of departure from my alma mater finally came. It was sad in many ways as I loved the college, the nuns and my friends, but we all said a tearful goodbye and I boarded the train for home as I had done for the last six years. The person I became was firstly the result of my happy and secure childhood, and for that I thank my parents, though belatedly, and secondly, and more importantly, it was my years at Perthville which brought to fulfillment any talents I had, enriched me and brought my dormant spirituality to life . . . and for that I have always been grateful.

I am especially grateful for the friendships that were forged there, both with the nuns and my friends who are still special to me today.

CHAPTER 9

LIFE IN THE BIG WORLD

When I left school I was seventeen years and eight months old, and though I had learnt a lot and matured as well, I was as innocent and naive as a newborn baby. I had read many books, but they were from the school library, and therefore selected very carefully, and, as Catholics, we were forbidden to read books on the banned list. These included books like 'Forever Amber' and 'Lady Chatterley's Lover' which I must confess I still haven't read!

Our Religious Studies course had changed greatly in the last two years at school, and, up until fourth year we studied Apologetics, Bishop Fulton Sheehan, and Church History, and we could have defended the Catholic Church against all comers. But in the higher classes it was all about dating, and not placing yourself in the occasion of sin by parking in cars with boys, and also about being considerate to your family and not coming home late and disturbing their sleep etc. There was a segment on the correct use of make-up; moderation was the key, and of course modesty in dress was stressed.

I didn't make my debut as countless other girls have done for years, but I did attend my first ball. Mum bought me a pretty blue dress with a boat neckline, which had a frill around it, and it had hand-painted flowers on a band around my waist. Frank Stanford, who was a neighbour and had gone to Store Creek School with me, was my partner and I couldn't have wished for a nicer one, so I enjoyed the night. I eventually had that soft perm which was aborted the first time due to my nerves and my hair was shiny and curled softly around my face.

Like lots of young girls, I was insecure about my looks so I wasn't vain, as I thought my face was too long to be pretty, and no one in the family ever said, 'You look lovely to-day,' or 'that colour makes you look pretty' so I didn't give my looks much thought, except to start using make-up.

As soon as I arrived home from Perthville, I started to do the housework for Mum, but we hung washing together, pulled the sheets between us to get them nice and straight and after we had folded them she would iron them slightly. Nana was still with us, but she missed Grandma who had died the year before, aged eighty-eight, and she often spoke of her. Nana still wheeled her barrow to and fro from the woodheap, she still fed the dogs when Dad would prefer her not to, still raked up the leaves in her old felt hat, but her deafness was increasing and she still spoilt the boys.

With the boys home, she resumed her task of cleaning their shoes, the only trouble was that now she would sometimes put black polish on brown, and vice versa, bringing a shout from the boys when they were dressing to go out. The bedsocks grew longer and more pointed in the toes, but she still continued to make them. I would wash her hair and put it in the bun each week and she appreciated any little thing I did for her, but I felt sorry for her as most of her friends had died.

The tennis court had been a family project a few years before, and because the homestead was on the slant of a hill, we had carried lots of rocks to build it up one end. The boys and Dad had searched for, and carted, ant-bed sand for the top layer of the court and after much activity there, it was finished. Now, with some of us home permanently and the others occasionally, Dad had lights put around the court, and the era of night tennis emerged at Mt. Pleasant.

We had some great tennis days that stretched into the night, and Hubbards, Braziers, and various young friends from other families would converge on Mt. Pleasant and enjoy some great tennis and some equally great food. Mum and I would prepare lunch and then she would say to me when we were washing up 'Margaret, your ice—cream is low, you'd better make some more!'

It was always 'my' ice cream to be made, 'my' piano that wasn't dusted, but these were minor irritations which bugged me a little, and I generally reacted favourably.

The evening meal was the same as lunch, mostly salads and meat, and I guess people used to bring a contribution, but I can't remember. Of course, the Hubbard family would take their turn, and the Braziers, so it wasn't a one-way street. I remember after the evening meal, I would attempt to go into my room to freshen up, and some young mum would say, 'Oh, don't go in there, my baby's asleep!'

After the tennis was over, and the babies still sleeping, I would sit at the piano and community singing would start. They all loved to sing around the piano, especially the younger ones, while the older people listened and chatted. Finally, the young mums and dads would wake their sleepy children and carry them to their cars, and they'd all go home.

With Harry, Dick and I now at home, life at Mt. Pleasant resumed its former routine of chasing rabbits, bringing in sheep for shearing, crutching, dipping, or lamb—marking. Dad kept a sharp eye out for Bathurst burrs which he hated, and I've heard him say to the boys after returning on Byng, 'There's a big Bathurst burr near a dead tree on the south side of Lanky-one', and I couldn't believe my eyes when I first rode with Frank Dwyer over his property and saw Bathurst burrs along all the fences.

He explained to me that, if they had seeded, he sprayed them with a boom spray and killed the seeds, and if not, he ploughed them in. A farm was vastly different from a grazing property.

At Mt. Pleasant I was often called upon to help with all activities, either I was needed, or Dad wanted to keep me busy and take my mind off what he feared, that I might be wanting to go back to Perthville and enter the convent. I did have a strong attraction to the religious life, but knowing how he would feel about it, I started to join in social outings with my brothers, and we went to dances, balls, cricket matches, football, and of course tennis.

My home duties soon extended to cooking for the family and I was learning as I was doing it. Stella still made the special cakes and sponges and also the scones, and she was a joy to watch as she trotted in and out from the pantry to the kitchen, her hands busy with the pastry and singing happily as she worked. When I say my mother 'trotted', that is just what she did. Always, while cooking, she would not walk, and she didn't run, she really trotted!

She would say to me, 'Mard, why don't you make a nice curry for dinner?' or, 'What about an apple pie for dessert, with cream and ice-cream?' Even though electricity had come through our area when I was about eight, we still made our own ice cream as we were a good hours drive from Orange and there were no Eskies in those days. Mum had actually had enough of cooking by the time I left school, after rearing a big family and having so many extras to cook for always, so it was a load off her shoulders when I was happy to take most of it over.

I sometimes felt I looked like a shearers' cook when my glamorous older sister, June, came from Sydney and brought her friends with her. We always cooked nice meals, though our taste was unsophisticated, but each meal was well presented, and our guests always enjoyed the country food. It was 1946, and we were unfamiliar with instant coffee, I doubt it was even on the market then, and our introduction to wine with meals was only just beginning.

One night, dinner went off extremely well, June had arranged the wine, and then she asked her guests if anyone would like coffee. Of course they all said they would, so Mum and I were in the kitchen trying to work out how to make it! We had no coffee percolator, and as I said, instant coffee wasn't an option (we always drank tea in our family anyway) and if we had coffee we made it with milk, so feeling embarrassed, that is how we served it. Nothing was ever said, but Mum and I made sure we bought a percolator so it wouldn't happen again.

Everywhere the boys and I went, Kevin Peters came, too. He lived at his property, Mangoplah, which was a couple of miles from us, with his parents and his sister, Marie. Manny (Emanuel) and Alice were a delightful couple, and Marie was a great cook, so I asked her advice on many occasions. I consider myself very, very, lucky that I had Kevin to shepherd me around when I left school, as I was so naive and inexperienced in the ways of the world.

In time, he became like a big brother to me and, when he eventually told me he was very fond of me, I told him I was considering being a nun. Though he was disappointed, he respected my feelings and treated me like a piece of porcelain.

However, this didn't stop him speaking of marriage occasionally, and asking if I had changed my mind. I still felt an attraction to the life

I had been witnessing for six years, so I always said 'no' and yet Kevin stayed on in my life, taking me everywhere and expecting nothing in return.

I was very immature, and I should have urged him to get on with his own life, but it didn't occur to me then. As I said, he was an absolute gentleman at all times, so imagine how I felt when I learned that Jack, my incorrigible older brother and Kevin's best friend, said to Dad, 'Aren't you worried about Margaret going everywhere with Kevin?'

Dad said, 'Not at all, I haven't a worry in the world about it, I trust Kevin implicitly!'

Jack's reply was very like Jack, 'Well, she'll need a forky stick!' I never did.

I played my piano every day if I had time, and usually sang along with it, singing all the popular songs of the day, and if Dad was in his office, I would include his special favourites. I would hear his door open so he could hear me better, and sometimes he would offer a suggestion for improvement. Here I was, with certificates at all levels in my exams, and with a State Medal and an Exhibition to boot, and he would call out, 'Your mother used to sing it like this' and he would give a little demonstration of where Mum used to put the emphasis on the words, 'TELL me, that you LOVE me, tell me softly, sweetly As of yore,' and I didn't have the heart to disagree with him, which I did, privately.

Two of the Hubbard family were getting married in Sydney churches and they asked me to sing at their weddings. Margot was married on my 19th birthday to Brian Mulvey, in a large church with a huge organ and I sang, 'Keep thou my heart and make it strong and pure'.

Then Claude and his fiancé, Helen Ross, were married in St. Marks Church, Darling Point and for their wedding I sang, 'Still as the Night, Deep as the Sea, such is my love, my love, for you'. Another couple, Bill and Rose Brazier, were to be married in Melbourne and they had been at Helen and Claude's so they wanted 'Still as the night', too. We travelled to Melbourne via Albury and it was in Albury that Mum and I bought our outfits for the wedding. Stella wore clothes well, and her outfit, hat and all, was violet, and it looked lovely with her soft white hair. Mine was a nice shade of green and I remember we both wore feathers in our hats.

About this time I decided to brave Dad in his den to tell him that I had thoughts of returning to Perthville for good. I didn't choose my time well at all, as Mum was in Dudley Hospital being stabilized with her diabetes which had reared its ugly head during the previous summer. We were shopping in Sydney and my mother couldn't pass a milk bar without buying a drink, and this led to a visit to the doctor, and the diagnosis was mature-age diabetes.

She unfortunately had to have insulin by injection every day and occasionally go to hospital to bring it under control. It was during one of these hospitalizations that I, quite insensitively as I realised later, chose to broach what was always on my mind, to my father.

I can't remember what either of us said, perhaps I've blotted it out as I have another instance in my story, which is really strange because everything else I have written about is very clear in my mind in every detail. I do know I slept well that night, so I was amazed and sad when Gwen, who was visiting at the time, told me next day, and I'm quoting her, that 'Dad cried all night!' I was very upset so of course I put it to the back of my mind again and we carried on as usual.

I noticed in the local paper that the Orange Choral Society was auditioning for The Mikado, so I up and tried out for it, singing an absolutely inappropriate song, which was about as far from musical comedy as it could be. It was far too serious, and not what they were looking for, so I missed out. However, a couple of months later, the Society contacted me, and offered me a solo part in Merrie England, so I drove in each week for rehearsals, and the show was a great success.

Most of it was in four parts and there were a few bars where the sopranos had to sing up very high, 'She's a witch, she's a witch, she's a witch! She's a witch, she's a witch!' I was practicing it one day and Harry passed through and sang, 'She's a bitch, she's a bitch, she's a bitch, she's a bitch, she's a bitch!' That was Harry.

When I came home from school, I joined the Euchareena branch of the Red Cross, and now was about the time I was elected president. Mum and I would drive to Euchareena for the meetings, which were held at the hall. I was young, and more or less a figurehead for the experienced and capable members of the committee, but there were a few occasions when I had to welcome VIPs, and so I was glad of my experience in the debating team at Perthville.

What a wonderful organisation Red Cross is, and how far reaching into every corner of the earth where there is tragedy on a grand scale.

I would have been a far better president then if I had known what television has shown us today.

Mum asked me if I would drive her to Orange each week to meet with Father McGuin at the Presbytery. Ostensibly we were going shopping, so Dad didn't question it at all, and on the way in, Mum simply said that it was to fix things up so she could go to Communion again. Typically, I didn't ask any questions. I'm beginning to realise I wasn't a good communicator as a young girl. Where were the follow-up questions, the feedback questions, the 'How do you feel about it, Mum?' question.

No, my recollection of the weekly sessions is that I drove her to the Presbytery, waited for her for half an hour, and then drove her home again, chatting about inconsequential things all the way. How lonely for her to be with someone who didn't appear to realise what a monumental thing she was doing, and ultimately, what a courageous act! I'm berating myself as I write this, and actually feeling quite disappointed in myself. However, I'm forgetting one thing, and that is I was only nineteen and my experience of life was negligible, so I have to forgive myself and move on.

These meetings went on for a few weeks, and then one day Father McGuin said, 'Well Stella, will we go up to the Church now and you can make your confession?' So Mum went to confession and we returned home. This was Christmas week, and on Christmas morning, Dad took Mum in her usual cup of tea and piece of bread and butter. In those days we had to be fasting to receive communion, so Mum put the cup of tea under the bed. We drove to Stuart Town to Mass, and as communion time approached, I wondered would Mum have the courage to go up to communion, no longer the excommunicated one, in front of the 'pillars of the church' and all who knew she *never* went to communion.

I needn't have worried, for my gallant little mother followed me up to receive her God. And that is the first time I've told that story. The procedure by which it was allowed, bears a resemblance to the Pauline Privilege, but whichever process brought it about was approved by the Bishop of Bathurst, probably Bishop Norton. I will just add that Dad continued to take Mum her cup of tea every day, including Sunday, for the rest of their lives together, and Mum continued to put it under the bed every Sunday for the rest of their lives!

At this stage, Jack, Mel, Robyn and Stephen, lived in their home, Woodlands, about six miles away. Their property was the Bundala that we visited in an earlier chapter, but Jack lived at Euchareena, and travelled to Bundala to work his property. Harry, Olive, Lesley and Pam, lived on their property, Avoca, about eight miles towards Wellington, and Dick was still living at Mt. Pleasant. Gwen, Bill, Jayne and Robert (Wobs) were still in Wagga, and June either at the Royal Hospital for Women at Paddington or doing private nursing in Sydney. They visited us quite frequently, Gwen and Bill every school holidays, the married boys and their families now and then on a Sunday and everyone would come for Christmas.

These times when all the family were home were very precious, but it is the winter visits I remember most vividly, when Mum would light the lounge fire as well as the dining room one and Dad would bring in a huge log and we would all sit around it talking and there would always be music and laughter. Dad had a sense of humour, but he was fairly circumspect. He would sit on the floor in front of the fire with his back against a chair, reading the Sunday paper, and one night as he got up and the room was totally silent, W.B. farted.

You could have heard a pin drop; we were all sitting like stunned mullets, no one looking at anyone else. Dad made a dignified exit and we all exploded, but into our hands to try and muffle it, then Dad poked his head inside the door and said aggrievedly, 'You don't let a fellow get away with anything, do you?'

In summer, as at Christmas, with no air conditioning, we would sit out on the front veranda, as Mt. Pleasant was so elevated there was always a breeze there. I would be sent to bring out Granny Smith apples and a knife, someone would sing out to bring the salt shaker as we seemed to like to sprinkle that on our apple and we would stay there talking until bedtime . . . and even though I still thought God might be calling me to a different life, I sometimes wondered how I could leave these very dear people.

Then out of the blue I received an invitation, which was to ultimately change my life.

CHAPTER 10

I MEET THE DWYER FAMILY
OF ALECTOWN

Carmel Sheridan, Margaret Baker and Philomena Gearon, three of the class of seven with whom I had done the Leaving, had entered the convent at Perthville (no wonder my Anglican father was a bit concerned!). Kath Dwyer, who had entered the novitiate after we did the Intermediate, struck some ill health and had eventually returned to her home, Derrymore, at Alectown.

I was, therefore, pleased to receive an invitation from Molly Dwyer to her 21st birthday party as I was keen to catch up with the two girls again, and had heard them speak of their home so often I was anxious to see it. I took the train to Parkes, and Mollie met me at the station and drove the 18 miles to Derrymore along a dirt road, known today as the Newell Highway.

When we arrived, the family was all on their knees in the dining room, saying the Rosary. We joined in, and I cast a few, surreptitious glances around me and saw Mrs. Dwyer very devoutly kneeling, then Kath was there and gave me a smile and a wave, but continued praying. Next, my eyes lighted on Delia, who also recognised me, and then three lovely little auburn-haired girls who turned out to be Maureen, Margaret and Rose-Marie and they appeared to be about 12, 10 and 7 years old.

Then I noticed a young boy of about 17 or 18, who I guessed must be the younger brother, Pat, and finally the older brother, Frank, who

I had been told had shouldered the burden of farm work since his father died in 1942. They, and their mother, had one thing in common: this amazing auburn hair.

The Rosary finished, introductions were made, and almost instantly there was a cup of tea in the large farm kitchen, where I noticed a wood stove with a kettle boiling on top. There was also an open fire burning brightly beside the stove and as it was July. This made the kitchen warm and gave it a very homely look. Rose Dwyer, the mother of this family, welcomed me very warmly, holding both my hands in hers for quite some time.

I slept well that night with the anticipation of seeing around the farm the next day. I had never been to an actual farm before, even though I had been reared on the land, and it was to come as a revelation. I only lived 80 miles away, but no one owned or lived on a farm there, as our places were always referred to as properties, there being little or no actual growing of crops, nearly all sheep and cattle and with Dad growing the occasional crop of oats with which to feed the stock in dry times. At home there were flats along the creek, which were sometimes sown with Lucerne, again to graze sheep on, so I was interested to see Derrymore, a real farm, in daylight.

Frank saddled two horses the next day and we rode around some of the 3,000-acre farm, which was as flat as Mt. Pleasant was hilly and undulating. The recently sown wheat was coating the paddocks very evenly and I could sense Frank's pride in how well the crops looked. I couldn't believe how big the sheep were as they were Corriedales and bigger framed than the Merinos at home, and the cattle were Shorthorns, a deep red colour with a big Shorthorn bull in attendance.

We came to a large house and Frank said, 'We'll go in here and you can meet Aunty Mai, Uncle Pat and Grandfather. This is their house, Maivin.' Uncle Pat was Frank's uncle, his father's only brother, and his wife, Aunty Mai, was Irish and spoke with a touch of brogue. They seemed pleased to meet me and made us a cup of tea. Grandfather was a tall man with white hair and a moustache, and we found him sitting on the veranda, reading *The Bulletin*.

Frank spoke to him with great respect and introduced me as a friend of Molly and Kath's. Aunty Mai then said, 'We will see you tonight at Molly's party,' so with those words she waved us off and we cantered the short distance home. On the way Frank told me his grandfather had come out from Ireland as a young man with an equally young wife and through hard work had made a success of his life. He also said he was eighty-eight and still rode a spirited horse. He added that he didn't seem to have much of a sense of humour, as every time he told him a joke, or a funny story, he would listen attentively and after Frank had delivered the punch line, nearly killing himself laughing, Grandfather would look up and inquire, 'Waal?' (Well?).

Preparations for the party were happening when we reached the homestead so I joined in and helped a bit. The atmosphere at the party was very happy and I met several more aunts, uncles and cousins of the Dwyer family as well as some neighbours. The party was in full swing when suddenly the lights went out. I thought it was just a blackout, but someone said, 'Oh no! There was no wind today so there's no power!'

I didn't know what that meant, but Frank hurried out and then the lights came on again. Apparently, bulk electricity hadn't come through the Alectown district yet, and Derrymore and Maivin were powered from a free-light, like a small windmill perched on top of a 60-foot tower, which relied on wind. No wind, no power. Frank had turned on the generator, which took over and voila! Light!

The week passed with me being introduced to farming the Derrymore way which involved large tractors and trucks, a combine with which they sowed the crops, disc ploughs and a McKay header. We played tennis, and attended a dance in the Alectown hall, maybe causing speculation as to whether or not I was Frank's girlfriend! I was introduced to Willie Klein who lived in a small cottage near the house and worked on the farm. He was a gentleman in every way, with a round face, snow-white hair and a mild manner. He had gone to school with Frank's father, Will, and Uncle Pat, at Coobang, and though his family lived at Bumbery on a farm, he came to live and work at Dwyer's when he wasn't needed at home.

He would come to the house for meals, and I was amused when the younger members of the family came in dribs and drabs for breakfast, found Willie just finishing his meal and after saying: 'Good morning Willie,' each one would begin saying grace with, 'In the name of the Father, and of the Son and of the Holy Spirit,' and Willie would bow his head each time until the grace was finished. All right for one, but three or four times as each one arrived at the table! As I said, he was a gentleman, and I suspect one or more of the children did it out of devilment!

It was a pleasant week spent catching up with the girls and their news, and meeting their relatives, and I returned refreshed to take up my duties at Mt. Pleasant. A bit later I invited Molly and Kath to visit me and they were a great hit with my family. Dad in particular was impressed with their social skills and Harry and Dick enjoyed them, too. Kevin came over and we played tennis and the girls showed they were no strangers to the tennis court.

Molly announced her engagement to Jack Sheridan from Coolah and he was Carmel Sheridan's brother, so Molly arranged for me to help out in a concert at Coolah. I visited Carmel and her family at Collie Blue, and sang in the concert. Carmel had made arrangements to enter the novitiate at Perthville so Molly and I dressed her as a bride, put on evening dresses ourselves and had someone take photos of the bride and bridesmaids. We even picked flowers and had bouquets. Carmel was a very pretty girl with straight, shiny black hair and a rosy sort of complexion, but she couldn't sing a note. This didn't stop the nun coaching us for competitive choir work from placing her in the front row, 'only because you look so nice dear,' but added, 'Don't sing though dear, only mime!'

Time flew by and there was to be an Empire Ball in Parkes run by the Catholic community as a fundraiser, and Frank asked me to go with him. I wore the only dress I possessed, the one with the hand-painted waist, and the girls and I dressed at Derrymore in great excitement. I noticed Frank was interested in me and felt I should tell him of my desire to be a nun in the St Joseph's order. I wasn't so insensitive as to tell him at the ball, but as soon as I could, I told him.

Naturally, he was disappointed but clung on to the hope that I would change my mind. I didn't run around telling everyone this, only the two men fate had brought into my life. I returned home after this visit feeling a bit confused and uncertain where my life was heading.

Kevin knew nothing of Frank Dwyer's existence at this stage, and why would he, as there was really nothing to tell. However, he became serious one time when we were alone, and asked me again to marry him and I guess I tried to fob him off with the old nun story. However, this time he wasn't satisfied with that and asked me point blank, 'Margaret, if you were not going to be a nun, would you marry me?' I really loved

Kevin, but as a brother, and this I was forced to tell him. This ended our very close association, because we didn't see much of him after that.

Eventually, and it should have happened sooner if I had been thinking more of his needs, and less of my own, he became engaged to a very nice girl whom he had known for a long time, Kath Devenish, from Stuart Town, who had been working away for a few years and returned. I will always remember Kevin's devotion to me, his humour and his kindness, and being human and honest, the pang of loss I felt the day of his wedding!

Harry's wife, Olive and I were very good friends, and she arranged for me to go on a week's holiday with her two younger sisters, Jessie and Amy Dunlop, from Ardlethan. They were fantastic girls, full of fun, and they were good for me as I sometimes looked at life too seriously. We booked in at a holiday resort at Bundanoon, and travelled there by train. They brought a friend from their hometown as well, a nice girl called Gwen Jeremiah. It was the first time I had been on a holiday without Mum and Dad, and it was the best week I had ever had.

The place, Rosnel, was full of young people and they catered for that age group exceptionally well. We were seated at a table in the dining room and there were four of us and four vacant seats. We were curious about who they were for, when four very nice young men were led to our table, and introduced to us. These boys became our companions for the week and we did everything together which made it most enjoyable, but no romances came out of it.

There were tennis courts, and a tennis match was arranged in which we played. I didn't shine, but I think the Ardlethan girls did very well. There was also a golf tournament, and I drew one of our tablemates to play with me. I had never played golf before, and learnt all about replacing the divets if you dig out some grass when you hit the ball. We played in a bowls match and I was put with the three boys from our table, and once again I had never played, but wonder of wonders, we won the bowls and I was presented with a cup, saucer and plate as my prize.

The three girls and I hired bikes and rode six miles to Exeter where we looked through a beautiful, historic church. Another day we hired horses and rode to a farm where we were served Devonshire tea with lovely homemade scones and strawberry jam and cream. It was embarrassing for me as my horse was an awful old nag who wouldn't lift his head off the ground no matter what I did, and I was supposed to be a rider!

Now I'm casting my mind back over sixty years and I remember there was a fancy dress dance and we all had to dress as a song title. I went as 'The Chatanoogie Shoe Shine Boy' and darkened my face with shoe polish and danced around with a shoe in my hand polishing it. Jessie put on a large black hat she borrowed from someone, wore a black dress, very red lipstick, and carried an empty whiskey bottle, and she waltzed around to 'Cigarettes and Whiskey and Wild, Wild Women.'

The last exciting thing we did was to go on a moonlight hike to Glow Worm Glen where we saw these little lights clinging to the rocks in a cave, and they were the glowworms. We sat on rocks and sang a few songs to a guitar one of the young people played, and ended with Silent Night. It was magical.

Imagine fitting all that into one week! All would have been well if there had not been a little coffee shop on the premises, and after we played Table Tennis, another activity, we would have a milkshake, or an ice cream, or a coffee with cake. I went home a stone heavier, and my mother was horrified as Molly's wedding was coming close and my dress wouldn't fit me.

However everyone, especially Dad, was pleased I had such a wonderful time—Dad, because he thought the more I enjoyed life in the world, the less likely I would be to want to leave it! He definitely didn't understand the concept of a vocation and the pressure it brings while one is considering it.

I travelled over to Molly Dwyer's wedding by train and, as I had an hour to wait at Molong, I walked up to the convent to see my former singing teacher, Sister Veronica, who was stationed there. She was pleased to see me, and I poured my heart out to her about telling Dad about wanting to return to Perthville and his upsetting reaction to it. She listened carefully as I shed a few tears during the telling, then finally she spoke the words that turned my whole life around, 'Margaret,' she said, 'I've known your Mum and Dad since we were all young together and they have been through so much. This will cause trouble between them. I THINK YOU SHOULD GO OVER TO PARKES AND MARRY FRANK DWYER!'

I couldn't believe my ears, here was a nun, of all people, advising me in just the opposite of what I expected her to say! I had much thinking to do on the train between Molong and Parkes, but I remember my over-riding emotion was relief, and with it came a feeling of freedom.

Molly's wedding was in the beautiful Holy Family Church in Parkes and she was a lovely bride, and Jack a handsome groom. I finally ended up in a black taffeta dress but I was conscious of it being a bit tight after my wonderful week at Bundanoon. Molly had asked me to sing Ave Maria at the wedding and it was the first of many times that I sang in that church, at weddings and funerals alike. There were quite a few guests staying at Derrymore because of the wedding and it was decided that we should all go to the Wellington Caves a couple of days after.

I travelled in the car driven by Frank, and as we chatted, he asked casually, 'I don't suppose you have changed your mind?' I hesitated a second, and then said carefully, 'I might have.' It is the absolute truth that Frank swerved and nearly ran off the road, so great was his surprise.

I think I might have burnt my boats at that moment because it seemed to give Frank great encouragement, and when we were in the Cathedral Cave, I felt his arm steal around my waist. Everyone voted for driving up Mt. Arthur, which stands like a sentinel over Wellington, so after dinner at a cafe, that is what we did. Frank and I sat up there overlooking the lights of Wellington, and more or less came to an understanding . . . we would begin corresponding!

I returned home but said very little and after a while when the letters started to arrive, conjecture began to grow within the family. Harry was there one Sunday and he ventured the remark, 'I really like that red Irish fox', referring to Frank in that way because of his curly red hair. He said it again later, and I know all the family really liked Frank and his special brand of humour.

There was not a lot of romance in the letters I received, as I was informed which paddock he was ploughing, or sowing, or working-over (a term I had never heard before) and he would describe the paddocks as 'the 150 acres' or the 'the 270 acres' as only an odd one had names. One was called Watson's, and there was also the Bull paddock, where the big red Shorthorn spent his lonely days until the time was ripe for him to have some company.

I understood Frank's interest in the farm work, almost to the exclusion of anything else, as he had been only sixteen when his Dad died and he assumed control of the farm. The family had bought their first tractor in 1938, but Frank's grandfather never drove it, as his farming life had revolved around the two teams of Clydesdales, which pulled all the machinery, and Uncle Pat only drove it occasionally. So when Frank left school in 1942, he and his father did the tractor work.

His father contracted pneumonia in July that year and sadly died on 3rd September, leaving eight children, the youngest Rose-Marie was 18-months old. Frank often said, 'I was thirty when I was born', and as we weave our way through the rest of this story, there will be episodes where we will see that he was a lot older than his years.

During the next few months, I made a couple of visits to Derrymore, and Frank came now and then to Mt. Pleasant. The first time we were expecting him, Mum suggested to me, 'Why don't you make a rhubarb and apple pie for Frank?' Then she added, 'And we'll have it with cream and ice-cream.' Yes, I thought, everyone likes rhubarb pie and cream.

I couldn't have been more wrong! The only two things Frank hated in the food line were rhubarb and cream! In fact, he would never eat either of them at home, but guess what? He ate them both and didn't say a word. The girls refused to believe it and they laughed and said, 'It's amazing what people will do when they are in love.'

After returning home from college, I had resumed singing lessons with Sister Lucy who taught music at the Stuart Town Convent, which was about eight miles from home. This necessitated a horse ride to Store Creek and a train trip to Stuart Town.

This is always what happened: I would be working with the men, lamb-marking, drafting sheep or shifting sheep or cattle, and at a certain time Dad would say, 'You'd better go and get ready now, Mardie.' I would shower, and put on jodhpurs and ride my horse, Midget, over to the post office where Joan Peters (Kevin's sister-in-law) would allow me to change into a dress or a skirt in her room. My children will be amazed at this, but this was 1947 and 1948 and, where we lived, a nice girl would not travel on a train in trousers of any description let alone go to a convent dressed like a man! I know today it seems bizarre, but that was how it was. But to proceed with the saga of my weekly lesson . . .

Once suitably dressed, I would walk down the steep hill to the railway station and wait for the Express, which twenty minutes later would arrive at the Stuart Town station. I then had another steep hill to climb up to the convent and then I had an hour's lesson. After the lesson, it was the nuns' dinner hour, and I would be given a roast dinner in the parlour which was cooked by Sister Basil. Then, after thanking the nuns, I would walk in the dark back down to the station, and wait for the mail train, which deposited me back at the Store Creek station! Up the hill again in the dark to the post office, where I changed back into jodhpurs and began the two-mile ride home over the hills.

I was never nervous riding along in the dark, but Mum always got Dick to ride to meet me and, after I left the post office, I would begin singing with all my heart, 'The hills are alive with the sound of music', 'At the Balalaika' and whatever song came into my head. Picture me riding along on Midget, who must have been the most musically educated horse anywhere, singing happily, and then here comes Dick.

Didn't I say earlier in this story that I was spoilt by my brothers! Dick would tell me what soup Mum had kept for me, because my meal at the convent was hours ago, as the mail train arrived at Store Creek about 9pm. I always looked forward to my mother's homemade celery soup. The trip was worth it though, because Sister Lucy proved as capable a teacher as Sister Veronica, and helped me gain high Honours in the seventh grade singing exam, as well as success in the Bathurst Eisteddfod.

Just before I leave this segment, I will tell you that I am nostalgic now, thinking of those nights, riding along in the dark with a song in my heart and on my lips . . . and I treasure the memory.

On each of Frank's visits in the next few months, he saw quite a lot of Nana, as I was fairly busy, and so he would sit and talk with her. I would be cooking or cleaning and I'd notice they were having a lovely chat. Frank has often told people that he nearly married Nana, as he saw more of her when he came over to visit me than he did of me!

One day, Nana was telling him: 'You know Frank, we were in NSW just this side of the border, and my sweetheart lifted me over the fence and said, 'Philippa, now you are in Queensland.' Just then, W.B. passed through and he said to Mum testily, 'What is Mother telling Frank?' As he closed the door, the wind caught it and it slammed noisily. Nana looked up, and said, 'Huh, what's wrong with the Bishop!'

So this chapter ends with W.B. being W.B. and Nana most definitely being Nana.

CHAPTER 11

A WEDDING IN THE FAMILY

News came from Wagga that Bill was accepting a position as Teacher in Charge at Bogan Gate, and there was general rejoicing, as this would bring Gwen much closer to home. June wrote from London that she had a great job caring for Mr. Cohen, an elderly man of ninety-two, and he and his wife, Maude, were very kind to her. Harry was 'making a good fist' as Dad said, of managing Avoca, running Merino sheep, cattle and doing some farming. He and Olive worked very hard there and their two small daughters proved to be very bright and did very well at the Stuart Town school.

Jack had got rid of the rabbits at Bundala to a certain extent, and also most of the blackberries, which provide a haven for rabbits and his children, Robyn and Stephen, were attending school in Euchareena. That only left Dick and me, and we were both working at Mt. Pleasant. Nana often went in to Orange those days to stay with her second son, Uncle Poss, who was a butcher and occasionally she went to Bathurst where her youngest son, Uncle Barney, lived.

Dad's office had a large roll-top desk in it, and he had bought a typewriter years before but he was a one-finger typist, so I did a lot of typing for him. He liked a vase of flowers on his desk, and above the sink in the kitchen there was a ledge between the kitchen and the breakfast room, and he would say to me, 'A vase of flowers would look nice there.'

So I would arrange some flowers in a vase and put them above the sink, and he was right, they did look nice there! It's funny how one memory invokes another. All our lives Dad would be up very early riding around sheep or doing something away from the house, and when he came back we would be finishing our breakfast. Unfailingly, he would get the porridge saucepan, add milk and sugar, and eat the left over porridge from it while he was standing, and I remember him doing that right from my childhood.

One day when I was dusting Dad's office and he was searching in his iron safe he exclaimed, 'Oh Margaret, look at this.' He produced a child's exercise book and showed me a story I had written when taught by Bill McCloughan. It was called: 'A Conversation between a Motor Lorry and a Horse.' The gist of the story was that Mrs. Draught Horse met Mr. Motor Lorry out on the lane, and he politely asked after her health. She told him she was all right now, but she had been unwell and recently had a baby foal. Not to be outdone, the Motor Lorry told her he hadn't been well either, as he had just had a baby Austen! Apparently my teacher brother-in-law was very amused by this and gave it to Dad, who had put it in his safe. I thought women were supposed to be the sentimental ones!

Frank and I had been corresponding since Molly's wedding in the autumn, and he finally popped the question in August. I was visiting him and we had called at Maivin to see Aunty Mai, Uncle Pat and Grandfather, and I was riding a big black horse. After we passed through the gate on the way home, Frank was closing it and my horse became restless and eager to be off. I was only used to quiet horses and I probably didn't control him properly, for the next thing I knew we were flying.

The horse was bolting, with me, totally shocked, on his back. I thought, 'Well if that's what you want fella', I'd better do my best to stay on,' so I really rode him. By the time we were close to the house there was quite an audience outside, as all my future family were there with their collective hearts in their mouths. The hairiest moment was when a mob of rams ran across in front of us, and that was when Frank, cantering behind, became concerned. I received a great welcome from a very relieved group and that must have been the catalyst for what happened that night. Frank proposed!

There was much excitement at Derrymore over our unofficial engagement, and equally so at Mt. Pleasant when I went home. Dad and Mum were going to Sydney, and it was arranged for us to go too and look for an engagement ring. We stayed at the Metropole Hotel, which was where many country people stayed when in Sydney, and the night we arrived, Frank and I took a stroll into the CBD and we spotted 'the ring' in the window of a prestigious jeweller's shop.

There was no late night shopping in those days, so the next day we visited the shop, found it was in our price range, and Frank bought it! It has been much admired over the years, with its beautiful, dark blue sapphire set between two diamonds, and I couldn't believe it was mine. I had never owned or worn a ring, and it was like being given one's first watch and hoping someone would ask you the time so you could show it off.

After Frank bought it, we walked across Hyde Park to St. Mary's Cathedral, and knelt in one of the front pews and then he put it on my finger. As we were both practicing Catholics, it was our way of simply asking God's blessing on the huge step we were taking and for further blessings down the track. Believe me when I tell you we were going to need all those blessings during the long years of our married life!

Sister Veronica was delighted with our news, and, deep down, my own Aunt Marion, Sister Kostka, was pleased too. But Aunty could be sometimes a bit forthright, in a teasing sort of way (that's the only way I can describe it), and Frank didn't altogether appreciate the reaction he got when he called to see her at Manildra on his way back to Parkes after the announcement of our engagement. She congratulated him of course, but one might say the sting was in the tail, for she added, 'But you've stolen her from God!'

Imagine Frank's reaction to that, as he had his fair share of Irish corpuscles in his blood! During our married life he often referred to her as 'Kosygyn', the name of the Soviet President at the time, and as her religious name was Sr.Kostka, you can see what prompted the nickname.

There was more excitement, when June wrote from London to say she would be heading home in time for our wedding, which was planned for May the following year. I immediately wrote back asking her to be one of my bridesmaids, and I chose Kath Dwyer, Frank's sister, as the other. My two eight-year-old nieces, Jayne McCloughan, and Robyn

Edwards, were thrilled to be junior bridesmaids, and Frank asked his brother, Pat, and Kath's fiancé, Neville Freeth, from Gilgandra, to be his groomsmen. So we were all set and began the necessary steps for a wedding in Orange with a Nuptial Mass on 6th May 1952 at 10am. In those days, Nuptial Mass was always celebrated in the morning because of the law of fasting from midnight.

As the time of my departure from the family home approached, Nana was spending more and more time in Orange with Uncle Poss and Aunty Elsie, and June was planning to stay on at Mt. Pleasant when she returned from overseas, so I wasn't concerned about leaving Mum to manage on her own. For some time, Dad had been hiring a lady from Store Creek to help us once a week, so she came on washing day. After the sheets were blowing on the long clothesline, which was held up by poles and stretched across the paddock outside the garden fence, this lady would use the water from the copper to wash the kitchen, pantry, breakfast room, bathroom and laundry floors.

Doreen was small and dark-skinned, of island extraction, with straight black hair, which she held in place with a very large bobby pin. She always wore men's trousers as she rode her horse over from the village. She wasn't young, or married, so we were mildly surprised when she announced she was pregnant. The whole district knew she was someone's mistress, but a baby, and at her age!

In due course, a dark-haired boy was born, and very soon after the birth, she arrived on the horse with baby David held in front of her in a shoebox! W.B. offered to drive her home so the baby might be safer, but she refused, saying it was all right as she didn't take the horse out of a walk.

When he was about two, David had bright, brown eyes, a mop of curly dark hair, was as brown as a berry, and used to ride behind her with his arms around her waist all the way over to Mt. Pleasant. One day, she was washing the floor and had left the bucket, with the mop in it, across the doorway. David wanted to get past so said to his mother, 'Shift the buddy stick!'

Stella's merry laugh rang out, and we were all amused. After this incident, it was quite common to hear one family member say to another, 'Shift your buddy chair!' or 'Pick up your buddy shoes!' Remembering now, I can only admire Doreen who was so used to adversity, that she didn't let a little thing like the lack of a vehicle stop her from working to earn money for her family. Have horse, and baby, will travel!

June spent time with fellow Australians whilst in London, most of them doctors, and some had wives. They ran short of money because they wanted to go places and see things and took a trip to Europe together. Just before she came home, she loaned one couple £15.00 (a lot of money in 1951) and another young doctor needed a loan of £7.00. As a result, June borrowed money from the Purser on the ship, so Dad received a telegram which she sent from Perth, 'Arriving Woolloomooloo Wharf Sydney, 10am. Thursday. Owe Purser money.'

When Dad had greeted her, he said, 'How much do you owe, and where do I pay?' She sent me her diary a few years ago and after writing about Dad meeting her with the money, she wrote 'What a wonderful Father!' She had so much to tell us, and I could fill a whole chapter on June and her travels, but there is no room for it in this story. Suffice it to say, that between her arriving home, and preparations for our wedding, time just flew.

Most weddings bring a few tensions and mine was no exception. Dad was unfamiliar with the Nuptial Mass and, never having been to one, was unsure how his Protestant friends and colleagues would react to one, especially in Latin. On the other hand, I could not conceive of being married without the full blessings of the Church on my marriage, so for a short while we reached an impasse. Dad, as usual, finally agreed, and he was told after the Mass that one and all declared it 'the most beautiful, and meaningful ceremony' they had attended.

Another bone of contention was the colour of the bridesmaids' dresses. Kath was happy to have any colour, but June wanted white. My dress was cream satin, and I thought white with cream would be too insipid, so I preferred a colour. June dug her toes in a bit, and, though I was used to deferring to June's superior knowledge, especially about clothes, I uncharacteristically asserted myself and we compromised, settling on pale grey ninon over pink taffeta.

The dresses were delightful, with the pink visible under the shimmering grey. The bodices were covered with large white wax medallion flowers, which made them very unique, and the girls wore small Dutch style caps on their heads. Their flowers showed the florist's expertise, as they were pink gladioli, with blue delphiniums pushed up through their centres. Jayne and Robyn wore the same coloured frocks, but their full skirts had small pink bows dotted around the bottom, instead of the medallions, and they carried a basket of flowers. Frank and his attendants wore navy suits, white shirts and grey ties. I thought all our bridal party looked great and were colour coordinated very well.

The afternoon before the wedding, we were preparing to leave for Orange as we had booked into the Canobolas Hotel for the night and the wedding was at 10.00 am next morning. I was in the bathroom, cleaning my teeth, when Gwen came in, shut the door and leaned her back against it. She had a slightly exasperated look on her face, and said, 'Dad's walking up and down the hall out there asking, 'Does Margaret know all she's supposed to know?!'

Margaret didn't, as it happened, but I didn't wish to have a lesson on sex from Gwen at this late stage, so I said: 'Of COURSE I do!' with as much emphasis on the 'of course' as I could manage. A very relieved Gwen must have bought it, because she left. Thinking about it now, that would be the closest reference to the word 'sex' that I, or possibly any of us, had heard Dad make. When any of us were going out with a boy, or girl, he mostly told us 'to mind our P's and Q's!' and that was the extent of our sex instruction!

My Parish Priest from Wellington, Father Corcoran, married us, and Frank's father's cousin, Father Laurence O'Dwyer, who was stationed at Branxton near Newcastle, said the Mass. He was assisted by Father Corcoran, Father Fitzgerald from Newcastle, and another relative of the Dwyer family, Father Cecil Patterson, from Yass. I'm sure I won't have as many priests at my funeral as I had at our wedding!

Delia Dwyer sang Gounod's Ave Maria, beautifully, at the signing of the register, and as we were processing out, I spotted some of my teachers, nuns from Perthville, who had brought Aunty Marion to Orange to see me getting married. I got so excited that I'm told I swept out instead of walking demurely as is expected of brides. (Today, my aunt would have been invited to our wedding, plus Sisters Marie Therese and Veronica, but before Vatican Two, this was not permissible.)

When we arrived at the Canobolas Hotel for the wedding reception, we were told that Mr. Sweet, the manager, had just been taken off in the ambulance as he fell down the stairs and broke his leg. However, everything was in readiness for us. The Reception was buffet style and people could mix freely instead of being anchored in one spot at a table, so it was very convivial.

At one stage, we were entertained by Gwen, Delia, and my cousin, Ailsa, who all sang delightfully. And then, to everyone's surprise, Frank and I sang 'This is the Happiest Day of all my Life,' which had been made famous by Joseph Smidtt. Frank had been coached by his sisters and he acquitted himself very well.

Dad made reference in his speech to the house we were moving into after our honeymoon, Wancurra, and he said, 'At the front of the house is a large Kurrajong tree and that one Kurrajong is what gave the house its name, Wancurra. I think of Frank as being like that tree, standing sentinel over his family, protecting and supporting them since the untimely death of his father.'

I thought that was beautiful, and I didn't know my Dad could be so eloquent. We were both lucky to have our ninety-two year old grandparents there, Grandfather, Michael Dwyer, in a dark suit, and Nana, so special to me, in a smart suit and with a tam-o-shanter beret on the side of her head.

They all waved us off on our honeymoon from the steps of the hotel, and I carried the memory of the much-loved familiar faces with me, as well as those of my new family. Mt. Pleasant, with its rolling hills, meandering creeks and oh so much-loved landscapes would be, from now on, not my 'home', but 'where I used to live'. My life, from this day forward, was entwined with my new husband's, and it was scary, but thrilling as well, and I looked forward to it.

W.B. Edwards (Dad)   Stella Edwards (Mum)   Nana (Edwards),
Harry Edwards and
Grandma Sloane

Dad and Nana   June, Jack and   Margaret Edwards (me)
Gwen Edwards as children   striding out purposefully

Margaret (me) on Molly   Margaret and Dick, the youngest
Edwards children, at Mt. Pleasant

Harry and his father, W.B.,
at Mt. Pleasant

Jack in his AIF uniform

Harry in RAF uniform

Gwen sets out for Gumly Gumly
to teach sewing in Wagga

June modelling hats for the
Lady Gowrie Appeal in Orange

Dick Edwards on his horse

Margaret (me) with
my horse, Midget

Jack and his girlfriend,
Melva Whitehead

June on Dad's horse, Byng

Gwen McCloughan
(Edwards)

A young Margaret Edwards

June modelling for
charity in Orange

Gwen and Bill with Robert (Wobs)
and Jayne at Mt. Pleasant

Jack, Mel and little Robyn
at Mt. Pleasant

Sisters, Gwen McCloughan
and Margaret at The Entrance

June as a trainee nurse
at Maitland

Young friends, Gwen and
June Edwards with
Margot Hubbard (centre)

The Rugby Union team with Harry, Dick (in front) and
Kevin Peters, fourth from the end, singing Macnamara's Band
at the Ball in Orange

Harry and Olive's wedding, with left to right, Harry and Olive,
Jack Edwards and Olive's sister Gladys, and Dick with her sister,
Amy Dunlop

Dick and his bride, Maree, dancing at their
wedding reception in Orange

It was a wedding in uniform
for Jack and Mel

Gwen and Bill were married at
St Mary's Cathedral in Sydney,
also during the war

Dad poses with June at her wedding at
St. Canice's, Elizabeth Bay

Margaret (me) and my attendants, my sister June, and Frank's sister Kath Dwyer, with flower girls, my nieces, Robyn Edwards and Jayne McCloughan, at my wedding in Orange in 1952

Frank Dwyer and bride, Margaret, shake hands after singing at their wedding reception

The Lanz Bulldog tractor

CHAPTER 12

I BECOME A FARMER'S WIFE

After our honeymoon in Uncle Tom's Cabins at Surfers Paradise, we returned first to Mt. Pleasant, and then to what was to be our home, Wancurra. It was only two miles across the paddocks from Derrymore, and a week or two before our wedding, we had painted the exterior of the house with Linseed Oil. This was necessary because it hadn't been painted for years, and we hoped this would stop the paint from soaking in when we finally did paint it. Because of heavy rain, the road across was impassable by car, so Frank got the sulky out (I had never ridden in a sulky before) and off we would go every morning clad in our painting gear.

I had bought some sweet-pea seeds, and I suggested to my then fiancé that he might dig up a section, and I would plant the seeds. Imagine my surprise, and it was a portent of what was ahead of me, when he just bent down and pushed each seed into the mud at regular intervals with his thumb, and, at my urging, hammered in two steel posts and strung a couple of wires between them. No fuss, job done! I was far from satisfied, but said nothing.

When we arrived back as newlyweds, we couldn't believe our eyes as every seed had germinated and there was a row of healthy sweet pea plants, which had literally been pushed into mud. They were actually the best we ever grew, and we picked sweet smelling bunches of them for ages and proudly took some over to Derrymore and Maivin.

The crops, which had been sown hurriedly so Frank would be free for the wedding and honeymoon, had got away to a good start and they looked great also, so Frank was free to come and help me buy some furniture as we had been sitting on bee boxes. One day while I was painting at Wancurra, I had called to see Aunty Mai, Uncle Pat and Grandfather, and the latter gave me a shock when he handed me a cheque for £100. I raced up and showed it to Frank's mother and she said, 'That would be for furniture', so we bought a red Laminex table and four red chairs for the kitchen, a bed and twin wardrobes, and a china cabinet for my lovely wedding gifts. That was a good start, and though the £100 didn't cover it all, it went a long way towards it in 1952.

I was in a quandary as to what to call Frank's mother, and a lovely lady though she was, I knew I could only call one person mum and that was my own mother. She left it entirely up to me, so I stuttered and stammered a bit and finally settled on Ma, which I didn't like much, so I was glad when Molly's two little boys, John and Peter, converted her legitimately into Grandma. I was to learn in the next twenty years what a wonderful woman my mother-in-law was, and I had a loving relationship with her right up to her death in 1972 at the age of 71.

Before we were married, Frank's mum had given Frank the money for a car, an English Wolsley sedan, so I was able to come and go and do my shopping, and Frank rode his horse to work at Derrymore and Maivin. The name, Maivin, was chosen for Aunty Mai and Uncle Pat's home which was built in 1926, as a combination of their names: Mai for Aunty, and Uncle was Patrick Vincent, hence Mai-Vin. It was written up on the front of the house, and I had never seen that on a house before.

It was strange at first to be living with just one person after six years at Perthville, surrounded by girls, sitting eight at a table, and at Mt. Pleasant there was always the family, plus Nana and Grandma and lots of visitors. Suddenly there was just Frank and me, and at last I learnt who my husband really was.

As we ate our meals, we talked, and he told me about how his father seemed to be over the pneumonia and had a mug of Milo, but had died by morning from a heart attack. Frank was down at the shed milking, and when he returned to the house with the milk, Alba Wild, a neighbour who always looked after the children when their mother was in hospital with a new baby, met him at the gate with the sad news of his father's death.

I could only imagine his grief, having just nine months working with his Dad after leaving school, and he had probably been looking forward to it for years. I realised, for the first time also, how overwhelmed he must have felt with his grandfather being eighty-two years of age, and his uncle not always well, as he suffered with bad sinus trouble. And it was now up to him. Sitting at the red Laminex table, I heard how Grandfather only relinquished the reins slowly, and Frank would be ploughing in one paddock and Grandfather would arrive on his horse, and say, 'Don't be killin' yerself now,' and in the next breath, 'We'll do the 100 acre paddock next!'

Then there was his mother with eight children, Frank being the eldest at sixteen, and Rose-Marie the youngest at twenty-months, and six others in between. I heard how the day of his father's death, Reg Nock, who owned a garage and usually kept the Dwyer car in going order, came out with a family member and drove that car in to his garage where he cleaned it, and then came out and drove the family to the funeral. He also arranged for Frank to get a restricted license at this early age, as his mother didn't drive, and the family had to be able to get about.

Frank also told me he wasn't always popular during the war years, when petrol was rationed, and he had to balance the farm requirements with the social needs of a growing family of girls, and some excursions had to be vetoed. No wonder he had told me he was thirty when he was born!

There was shearing shortly after his father's death, and this was followed by hay-cutting, with his grandfather on the binder, and Frank, Len Cook and Bob McLean (two local men), carting the hay straight into ensilage pits in the Bull paddock down near Maivin. His eighty-two year old grandfather cut 200 tons of hay that year with his horse team. Hay-cutting ran into harvest, and Willie Klein returned from working on the place he share-farmed at Bumbery on the Orange road, to sit on the header and work the levers of the old McKay header, which was pulled by Frank on the tractor.

Uncle Pat, having recovered from pneumonia he contracted 'from the shock of his brother's sudden death' as Aunty Mai told me, carted the grain to the Alectown silos in the truck, so they coped with their grief and just got the work done. Shortly after this they bought a new header, which was still pulled by a tractor, but Frank could work it on his own as he pulled the levers from the tractor. It was about this time that I met Molly and Kath when they came to Perthville and into my class.

There were humorous stories as well, Frank being who he is, and I was gullible and believed him implicitly. So I told the ladies at Red Cross how surprised I was that Frank had learned dancing and tap-dancing when young! Their astounded faces told me the truth, and everyone knew Frank, so we all had a good laugh.

A true story though involved Alan Somers, a very well known and highly respected member of the Parkes community. He and his two brothers, Arthur and Peter, played in Frank's cricket team known as the Nelungaloo team. One Sunday morning, Alan picked Frank up after 10am Mass in an old, one-seater utility, and they were headed for the cricket field. As they veered down past the old post office in Court Street, Frank asked Alan, 'Are you worried about the brakes on this vehicle, Alan?' Alan was concentrating on driving, but his reply was, 'You don't worry about anything you haven't got!'

The following story is also true. Frank went to Marist Brothers, Campbelltown, for his education, and he was travelling home for holidays on the train, when he decided to try smoking! He smoked a full packet of cigarettes, between Central Station and the Blue Mountains, and was, to quote him, 'As sick as a dog!' The humorous part of this true story is that his mother told everyone that 'Poor Frankie was terribly sick from train sickness on the way home!' The consequence of this was good though, as it turned 'poor Frankie' off smoking for life.

Each morning I noticed a distinctive sound that I had never heard before. It was the Lanz Bulldog tractor starting up in the morning two miles away at Derrymore. Frank would have breakfast, milk the cows, separate the milk, and ride over to start work. Then I would hear this 'Boom . . . boom' and for five minutes or more it would go on, 'Boom . . . boom . . . boom . . . boom' and so forth. Of course I asked Frank and he said, 'Come over tomorrow morning and I will show you how I start the Bulldog.' So I drove over and saw my husband, holding a blow torch under the front of the tractor, and it was hissing away, then suddenly the tractor came to life, and it was 'boom . . . boom . . . boom . . . boom' just the way it sounded from Wancurra. Then he would lift the steering wheel out and put it in the side of the tractor, turn it back and forth and the tractor would roar into life. And I had never seen that before!

For the uninitiated, people who milk cows usually lock the calves up overnight, so that when they milk the cows in the morning, they haven't been sucked dry. I was used to doing this on the horse at Mt. Pleasant after school, but I was terrified of the big Hereford bull, and when he was running with the cows, I would ride out in fear and trembling and as I rode closer, he would put his head down and sometimes paw the dirt. I said Hail Mary after Hail Mary as I rode towards him, considering, 'Do I go around him and bring him in with the cows, or do I cut him off, and just take the cows?' Common sense told me it was better to have him in front of me than coming up behind me following his lady friends, so that is what I usually did.

When I drove them into the orchard, there would be Stella, on foot, with her pinafore in her hand and she would walk behind the bull, HITTING HIM ON THE RUMP with her pinny, and saying, 'Go on old fellow, get in there,' right down to the cow yard. Then the calves would run into their small yard, she would close their gate and my ordeal was over for another day. My hair turned prematurely white in my forties, perhaps the process started then! There was no bull with our cows at Wancurra, so I would walk around them and bring the calves in each evening, and Frank would milk the cows each morning.

Using the separator, he would separate the cream from the milk before going to work and my first job was to wash the separator. To my surprise, no one seemed to buy butter, and Rose, Frank's Mum, made gallons of it. We used to make butter at Mt. Pleasant and I was a dab hand at it, but we didn't depend on it, and bought most of our butter. We always had lovely thick cream for our scones and cakes and when there was cream left over, Mum or I, would make a pound of butter.

My problem now was that the cream had to go in the refrigerator to keep fresh, and as there was no electricity through the Alectown district yet, we relied on a kerosene refrigerator, and everything that went into it would freeze solid. Maybe there were ways to regulate it, but Frank couldn't seem to fix it, and I knew nothing. The result of course was a young bride in tears struggling to whip frozen cream in order to convert it into butter. I tried heating it slightly . . . disaster! I tried leaving it to thaw out . . . again disaster, as it would turn all milky and wouldn't respond properly. Finally my husband took charge and when in Parkes one day, brought home a packet of Daffodil margarine, and that was the end of the saga of making butter at Wancurra.

Although I had been reared on the land, life on a sheep and wheat farm was entirely different. At home we had very busy times like shearing, dipping, crutching, lamb-marking (no mulesing at that stage) and drenching, after which we moved the sheep to a different paddock to prevent re-infection, lots of mustering and bringing them in to cull them.

There were specific jobs to do with cattle too, but when I became a farmer's wife, it seemed that the combination of sheep and cattle with the actual growing of crops and all that it entailed, was never-ending. There was stubble burning, spraying of the burrs, ploughing, working over, scarifying, sometimes harrowing, and the very time—consuming maintenance jobs, and in the case of breakdowns, repair work. The next cycle began with carting fertiliser in to the farm and sowing it with the wheat, oats and barley using the Combine. Oats and Lucerne were also sowed in chosen paddocks just for stock to graze on.

Where did I fit into all this activity? With all the enthusiasm of the newly initiated, I threw myself into making sandwiches and cakes, packing a tucker box as I had seen Dad do so often, filling bottles with hot tea and taking it all to the men wherever they were in the paddock. I can see the raised eyebrows of my children, re the bottles.

Well, we didn't have a thermos, and Frank's mum showed me what she did, so I did the same. We heated the bottles carefully, then filled them with hot tea from the teapot, then rolled them in a few layers of newspaper. When I finally went to buy a thermos that wouldn't break, I was sold a stainless steel one, the first I had ever seen, and the words of the vendor were, 'Mrs. Dwyer' (yes, I was Mrs. Dwyer then, though only twenty-two!) 'This won't break even if it is dropped from an aeroplane!'

I thanked him but thought it just sales talk, but would you believe it? Before harvest was over, someone ran over it in the tractor and put a big dent in it. I was upset, but decided to fill it anyway, and today, fifty-nine years later, it still keeps liquid very hot, and is probably the best thermos we own!

The interior of Wancurra was in need of painting, and I couldn't wait to have it nice, so I started on it and painted the rooms, one at a time. Frank seemed to be affected by the smell of paint, so he was happy to fix up a chook-yard, and do other jobs. One day I asked Grandfather Dwyer to come for lunch and Frank drove to Maivin to pick him up. I was a bit nervous to be having him for a meal for the first time, and when Frank pulled up, I went out to the car and in a voice equally as Irish as Grandfather's, I squeaked, 'Hello, Grandfather,' and then, 'Come in out of the hhhhheeeeaaaaatt!'

If I had been inviting someone in 'out of the heat' in an Irish play, I couldn't have sounded more Irish! He didn't seem to notice, so I sat him down with Frank at the red Laminex table, with a pretty cloth on it of course, and started to serve the meal. I made the mistake of looking at Frank, and the result was disastrous. We both 'got the giggles', as we would say at school. We made a huge effort to control ourselves, by pretending we were coughing, and then I said something funny so we really could laugh, and oh, it was awful. It just goes to show what nerves can do to you.

Finally, after the meal, I showed him the house with the new furniture, and told him we had bought it with the money he gave me, and I showed him where I had been painting. Frank took him home and his only comment to Aunty and Uncle was, 'Maggret has got the plaice looking like a little palace!'

At shearing time, the arrangement between Frank's Mum and Aunty Mai was that Rose would give the shearers their midday meal, and Mai would send up their morning and afternoon lunches. The men all lived locally, so there was no breakfast or dinner provided as at Mt. Pleasant. It was decided that I would assist Aunty Mai with the lunches, so I would help her make sandwiches and cut up cake, and then take it up to the shed in the morning by 9.30am and in the afternoon by 3.00pm. Sometimes, I would take a batch of scones over for a change, and I always had lunch with Aunty, Uncle, and Grandfather during shearing.

Nobody had been living at Wancurra for quite some time before we moved in, and it was in need of repair. This is when I was introduced to Rhinehold Boehm, always known to us as Ryan. He was of German descent as is evident from his name, a man of rugged features, but one of the nicest men one could ever meet. He became our builder, mechanic, tractor and header driver, but most of all, our friend.

The first project he and Frank undertook to build was a garage to house our precious car. After that, we looked at the house with him, and it was most definitely in need of 'jacking up' as he and Frank described it, as the four corners of the house had sunk because of the heavy black soil it was built on. This gave it a bowed look, so they built each corner up with bricks and cement and it made an amazing difference. This was all that was done to start with, but as this story unfolds, Ryan appears in it many times as we had to close in verandas to accommodate our family, and he was always available to help us out.

About this time I visited Dr. Lorger, and he confirmed that I was pregnant! He was a kindly man and when he asked, 'How many children would you like, Margaret?' I didn't need to think: 'Six, Doctor,' I replied. Well, that dear man has been in Heaven many years, so I didn't get the chance to tell him, sixteen years later when my seventh child was born, that I was never good at Maths!

Frank and I were delighted of course, though Frank thought it was a bit soon, and there was excitement at Derrymore and Maivin and jubilation over at Mt. Pleasant, and indeed in the whole district.

I wrote to my family telling them what instructions Dr. Lorger had given me (after all, I had never had a baby before!) and I concluded by telling them I was continuing with tennis for a few months but would give it up when I was six-months pregnant. This led to a few jibes from June about 'wrapping yourself in cotton wool,' but I was too happy to be bothered by that. There wasn't too much cotton wool around, as I continued painting the interior of the house, and only finished the bathroom a couple of weeks before the baby was born.

It was Easter Saturday, 4th April, and my contractions started about 4.00pm. We decided to go to the hospital via Derrymore so we could tell the family. Frank went in, and they all came running out to the car, very excited, none more so than the soon-to-be Grandma. She said, 'Margaret, you sit up like a doll now . . . Frank, you open the gates, and Margaret, you sit up like a doll!' Isn't it funny how some remarks one never forgets?

Luckily it wasn't a false alarm, and on Easter Sunday, at 3.00pm, Mary-Ann Dwyer was born, a bonny baby girl weighing 8lbs 4ozs. Every first-time mother will relate to my emotions when they laid her in my arms; I know I cried with joy and I knew the feeling of 'my cup runneth over'.

Frank came in half an hour later, as the custom then was for the fathers to go home and wait for the phone call, and when he came in the door, I literally couldn't see his face for the Easter Daisies in his arms. Apparently, the altar in the Church at Alectown was adorned with a profusion of these special flowers for Easter Sunday Mass, and the ladies gave them to him to bring in to me.

Where would we be without our memories? The birth of each of my children brought great joy, but this was our first, and I thanked God for guiding my life to this moment. As I gazed down at my precious little daughter, I knew I was meant to be a mother, but little did I realise then I would never again know a moment without worry. This sounds dramatic and God tells us in the Bible that we should not worry, but suddenly I was responsible for a new life, and the carefree life was gone forever. But that's how it is for most of us when we have children.

In 1953, new mothers were kept in hospital for fourteen days, and on the tenth day we were allowed to put our feet to the ground to go to the toilet, and have a shower. This meant calling for a pan and being bed-washed for ten days, and we were healthy young women in our early twenties! Constipation was often a problem because of the inactivity, and I found my legs were wobbly at first, and my feet felt strange too. Imagine the number of staff needed for all this to happen, and compare it with today when new mums go home a day or two after giving birth.

In 1960, when I had my fifth child, I enjoyed a shower as soon as I had breakfast, and when my last child was born at 8.00am in 1969, I had a warm shower immediately, but it was very different in 1953.

Because of this I was still in hospital for my twenty-third birthday on 15th April when Mum and Dad came over to see me. Dad had the biggest surprise for my birthday, a second-hand grand piano! Mum said he had fretted a bit that I couldn't play and sing anymore, so he came up with this generous gift. As June said, when he paid her debt as she came home from England, 'What a father!'

This gift went a long way towards keeping the song in my heart alive, because it provided a release from worries and stresses, as well as the opportunity to keep on singing and playing. So Mary-Ann and I came home to a proud Daddy, and a house where there was always music.

June couldn't wait to get to know her new niece, so she and Mum came over for the first week I was home. I was so thin that I hardly cast a shadow, so Stella took over the cooking and June was never far from Mary-Ann. She couldn't believe how placid she was, and one day she declared that she was going to put a burr in her nappy to see if she could cry!

This 'good' baby syndrome caused Mary-Ann to have a little setback when she was just a couple of months old. I used to breast-feed her, at 6.00am, 10.00am, 2.00pm, 6.00pm, 10.00pm and 2.00am (in the middle of the night). I was so proud of my baby when she started to sleep through the 10.00pm feed, then the 2.00am feed, and only seemed to need the early morning drink, and I was amazed when the clinic Sister weighed her and she came in light.

I spluttered, 'But she doesn't wake so she must be getting enough.' The Sister explained that some babies sleep, even when they are hungry, and I was to wake Mary-Ann for those night feeds as she had lost weight. So I did, and we were back on track.

At this time in history, King George VI had died, and we had a new, young Queen on the throne. Frank chose her Coronation to tell me that he was a twin of Her Majesty's, having been born on the same day, the 21st April, 1926, but in Dubbo, not London. I cautiously believed him, and he went on to say, 'You know, the bells rang in London the day I was born!'

This coincidence was, in his mind, his only claim to fame, and eventually, most people learned about it. Did I think it was his only claim to fame? No way . . . there was far more to Francis William Dwyer than his date of birth. I saw him, even before our marriage, get up very early, even after working on the tractor all night, and drive in to 7.00am Mass while the rest of us could go to a later Mass. He did this unfailingly. And when he played cricket, the team knew they had to wait for Frank to go to Mass first.

I saw his devotion to his Donnelly uncles, and when Uncle Tom Donnelly was dying, it was Frank who sat with him all night, giving him sips of water. Uncle Jack often came to Wancurra and stayed the night whereas his son Brian would go to Derrymore, as Pat was more his age, and I noticed Frank had a great rapport with his elderly uncle.

I witnessed many times his gentlemanly acts to help elderly people, or women with children, and I marvelled at the respect he showed when driving past a cemetery or a church and he would lift his hat. His dedication to farming was absolute, and he left nothing undone if he could help it, even if it sometimes meant missing a function that he would enjoy. If it came to a choice between an outing, and something that needed doing on the farm, in Frank's eyes there was no decision to be made. I learned to accept that very early in our marriage. Conscientious is how I would describe the man I married.

Mary-Ann added a new dimension to our lives and was as amenable as a toddler as she had been as a baby. When I bathed her each morning, I would sit her on her potty chair out in the sun and give her an orange, divided into quarters, and she would sit there with her golden curls glinting in the sunlight, eating her orange, and waving to anyone passing in the lane. To her biased parents, and to Stella, W.B. and Aunty June, she was a curly-headed princess, and I loved dressing her up and taking her wherever I was going.

The 'three little ones' as we called Maureen, Margaret and Rose-Marie, would drive the runabout car over the paddocks to see us when they were on holidays from Perthville, and they just loved their little niece. Grandma also enjoyed having a grandchild so close, as her other small grandchildren lived at Coolah and Gilgandra, and she was very generous in having us over for meals at times and when the married girls were home.

Just before Mary-Ann was born, Gwen and Bill moved to Boggabri to a new school where Bill was to be Headmaster. Gwen had made all the beautiful vyella nightgowns, and matching jackets, for the baby, embroidered by hand on the bodices, and she had even embroidered her little singlets in grub stitch. She was such a generous, devoted sister and was very disappointed to be leaving Bogan Gate just when her new niece was born. As for me, I was devastated, as I was looking forward to having my motherly sister so close. We picked Mum up at Mt. Pleasant when Mary-Ann was three months old and drove to Boggabri so Gwen and Bill could meet her, and they fell victim to her charms as well as everyone else.

Dad was conscious of Frank not having his father to do fatherly things for him, so he took to coming over in his utility to give him a hand. He asked Frank to call him W.B. or Wilf, but Frank always called him 'Dad', right up to the day he died. Mum would come too of course, and when they were expected, Frank's Mum generally gave us the leg of lamb instead of the shoulder to cook after a sheep was butchered. My folk enjoyed the meat from Derrymore, and Dad said that the Crossbred meat was more tender than the Merino meat at home.

He arrived one time limping from a sprained ankle and had advised Frank to have cement, sand and the cement mixer here, and sprained ankle notwithstanding, he and Frank put in some cement paths. Frank said to me, 'Thank God for his sprained ankle or I wouldn't be able to keep up with him!' These paths were an absolute godsend as the soil over where our house was situated was black and rich, and anyone arriving would sink into mud as soon as they got out of the car.

Another time he brought the necessary pipes, and did some plumbing under the sink so I would not have to empty a heavy bucket of water each night. Of course, he was a great believer in grease traps, so he put one outside the kitchen window with instructions for us to put a hose down it every three weeks, not easy as we didn't have water connected to the garden. However, that spurred us on to do just that and Frank bought a pump for the dam, and built a little corrugated iron shelter over the pump, and voila! I could start a garden. You might be getting the idea that I had a high regard for my father . . . well, I did, and Frank also thought the world of him.

While all this work was going on, I found opportunities to play the piano, as I knew Dad would enjoy it and know that I was using it and appreciated it. My adjustment to my new life was an ongoing thing, but having the paths down was a huge help as I hated the mud being walked into the house, and the plumbing made life a lot easier too.

Aunty Mai had a sister in Sydney, Beatrice Linnane, and when Aunty received the news that she was in a coma, Frank offered to drive Aunty and Uncle down to be with her. They drove through the night, and every time they saw a house with a light on, Aunty, in her Irish brogue, said, 'Oh they must be having a party!' They were a couple that retired for the night fairly early, hence her remark. The day Frank was driving back happened to be Mothers' Day and it was my first, as Mary-Ann was born in April. He arrived home late, and he has never been one to give presents, so I was touched and delighted when he handed me a small box of Winning Post chocolates! It was also our first wedding anniversary, so our first year of marriage ended on a high.

CHAPTER 13

LET THERE BE LIGHT

Christmas 1953 was a worrying one for us, as our little girl became sick with projectile vomiting. She was only eight months old and I had just weaned her, and with the advice of the Clinic Sister, started her on cow's milk. Dr. Lorger saw her a couple of times and as her weight had dropped from 20 lbs to 16 lbs, he thought she might have gastroenteritis, and made arrangements with the Children's Hospital at Camperdown in Sydney for her to be admitted.

When we rang Mt. Pleasant, June insisted on coming with us, so we drove via Molong where Dad met us with June. It was dark by this time and we travelled down at night, with June sitting in the back with Mary-Ann, who lay in her big baby basket (no capsules then, girls). We had arranged with Dave and May Lynch, who were life-long friends of Frank's family and owned the Brooklyn Hotel in George Street in Sydney, to stay there overnight and take Mary-Ann to Hospital next morning. While we were having a cup of tea in their lounge, I laid the baby on a rug on the floor, and everyone was amazed at how lively and bright she was. She kicked her legs, and literally thumped her feet on the floor and laughed, and didn't seem sick at all.

At the hospital next day, she was put in Wade House in an isolation ward, where she had to stay until she passed a stool, and it could be tested to see if she had gastroenteritis. She was in there for a day, but the stool proved she wasn't infectious so she was put in the children's ward. In all, Mary-Ann was in hospital a week and discharged without any real diagnosis.

We brought her home to Mt. Pleasant, as June was there with her many years of nursing experience, and I can still see June sitting in the cot with Mary-Ann, feeding her with a spoon. We were all so worried about her and the idea was to build her up. Frank had to go home, but Mary-Ann and I stayed a few days and then June drove us back to Wancurra. I gradually came to the conclusion that she had a fat intolerance and the cow's milk was aggravating it. Even after we got home, she would vomit every few weeks, mostly at night and for no apparent reason. She grew out of it eventually, but that curly head of hair was often washed and dried in the night after an episode of sickness.

A couple of months passed and our little girl was now well and thriving, and I realised I was pregnant again. Oh well, I did tell Dr. Lorger I wanted six! We were thrilled and excited as September drew near, and Michael Wilfred was born on 25th September 1954. He was 9lbs, with a mop of dark hair and so different from the dainty baby his sister had been, that when Sister Jean Sense brought him in to me, I said emphatically, 'Oh no, that's not my baby!'

She assured me he was, and then it was, 'Oh come here you beautiful boy', and I stretched out my arms for him, marvelled at the size of his back and inspected him all over, as new mothers do. As this was my second pregnancy, we were allowed to go home on the twelfth day, so we did. I was feeding him the next day and he started to cough and his nose was running, so we took him in and Dr. Lorger put us both back into hospital. Apparently, Michael wasn't the first baby from Niola Hospital to present with these symptoms that week and Elvie Dumnesy's baby boy actually died. The nursery had been sprayed with Mortein, so that was suspected to have caused respiratory problems in the babies, but it was only a suspicion.

We were in for another two weeks, so that meant June and Mum had Mary-Ann for a month altogether. Not that they minded, as she was at an adorable age, and June loved babies anyway. When they brought her home, June said, 'I'm afraid she has a nigh-nigh now Mummy.' This was a silk scarf June had given her at bedtime, and she would say, 'Nigh-nigh darling', and Mary-Ann would put her thumb in her mouth, rub the scarf between her fingers, and go to sleep.

Back home, the little one would go and get the scarf if she was feeling tired, and say to me, 'Nigh-nigh Mummy', so that is what it was called for four years! It was a large scarf, probably from France or somewhere during my sister's travels, but I made four out of it, so we could always find one, and so I would have a clean one always on hand. I can hear a chorus of mothers' voices as I write this: 'Yes, my baby had a nigh-nigh, it was a special handkerchief, or blanket, or favourite toy.' I have a few tiny great-grandchildren now who's nigh-nighs are their bottles, so it carries on down the generations.

When Mary-Ann was four and a big sister to Michael, Philippa and newly-born Libby, I said, 'Now you are four and such a big girl, perhaps you had better give up your nigh-nigh.' She totally agreed with me and allowed me to take it away but as I was leaving the room, I noticed her thumb oscillating between her mouth and the sheet, but I hardened my heart and said goodnight. Next morning she raced into my bed and exclaimed, 'I didn't have a nigh-nigh Mummy,' and I said, 'Good girl!' but she exclaimed triumphantly, 'I used the sheet instead!'

Mary-Ann was nearly too kind to her baby brother. I was introducing Farex (baby porridge) to him when he was a few months old and he started to choke. Mild patting on his back didn't bring any relief, so I panicked and ran outside with him, tipping him up and hitting his back a bit harder, while half-crying and saying, 'Dear God, he can't choke!' Suddenly, out popped a SIXPENCE! My relief was enormous, and when I told Frank that Mary-Ann must have put it in his mouth, he said, 'Um, possibly, but I think we'll keep him anyway. It might be lucrative.'

Harvest was upon us again, and the sound of tractors and headers grumbling all around us, Jack Wild opposite, Austie Helm on the other side, and our own machines filling our eardrums all day and well into the night. I still packed lunches and took meals to the paddocks, and this was before seat belts or restraints for children came into being, so I would sit Mary-Ann beside me in the front of the Wolsley and put Michael in his basket on the back seat. Frank and Ryan Boehm were usually working together and would come and eat at the car, but Frank's younger brother, Pat, and Uncle Pat, were carting grain to the silos and would take their lunch with them.

Frank still had chores to do at Wancurra before work each day, as there was always the milking and separating and wood to chop in winter and bring in. Where, oh where was Nana? Speaking of Nana, I took Mary-Ann to Orange so she could see her when she was a baby, and received my last letter from her after that in her always-illegible handwriting, which only her daughter-in-law Stella could really read. In it, she said she was thrilled to see the baby, and added, 'Oh, those beautiful blue eyes!' Shortly after that, when Mary-Ann was six months old, this wonderful, unforgettable woman died peacefully in her sleep at the age of ninety-four.

The minister asked Mum if Nana had a favourite hymn, and Mum replied, 'Well, I have heard her sing 'Nearer my God to Thee,' and 'Abide with Me,' so these were sung and she was carried out by her four grandsons (my brothers and a cousin) to the haunting strains of the latter, reminding me forcibly of the two old ladies singing it at Mt. Pleasant and me playing for them as a child. We stayed for a few days after her funeral, and on Sunday, Dad drove quietly down to the little Anglican Church at Euchareena to attend the Sunday Service, the one and only time I had known him to 'go to church.' Perhaps, in grieving for his mother, he felt the need to return briefly to the faith she had instilled in him, in the church where she taught it, seeking consolation.

In September 1955, Stella and W.B. left for a world trip on a ship called the Orsova. They travelled with friends, Howard and Gladys Carr, and Uel and Eve Oates from the Orange district, but didn't stay together for the whole nine months. After England, Scotland, Wales and Ireland, Mum and Dad took a Cook's tour of Europe, and Dad took pleasure in telling Frank that he had his wallet stolen in Italy at the opera 'by one of your mob!' After Europe, they returned to London and boarded the Queen Elizabeth for America where they had to 'dress' for dinner each night. Mum told us Dad looked so handsome in his dinner suit, and some of the ladies on board said jokingly to her, 'Your husband can put his shoes under my bed any time he likes!'

In America, their most scary trip was on a plane from Vancouver to Calgary in Canada when there was a violent storm and coffee cups were hitting the ceiling. Mum and Dad were separated by an aisle, and Dad was sitting beside a woman who, at the height of the storm, was fervently saying the Rosary. He told us he would have said the Rosary himself if he had known it. Mum saw the lightening flashing on the wings of the plane, and as I mentioned in an earlier chapter, her thoughts flew to Harry and his work on rivets during the war. They had to turn back and take a later flight to Canada, where they visited the Yosemite Park and saw black bears rummaging amongst garbage bins. They also had an overnight stay at Banff where they stayed at Lake Louise, overlooking the spectacular lake with the glaciers shining in the distance that we often see in advertisements on television today.

A highlight for them was being garbed in yellow mackintoshes and walking under the Niagara Falls. We saw photographs of all these claims, but the marvel to me was that for the whole nine months, Stella the Valiant gave herself an insulin injection every single day, no matter how early the start was. They hadn't wanted to spend money on a trip, but we, the family, insisted, and told them we would prefer they did this than what they intended to do, and that was to leave money to us.

We had not told them I was pregnant again, and Elizabeth Stanford had not told her mother, Gladys Carr, that she was either. They were all staying at the Metropole Hotel the night before sailing, so imagine their surprise when Frank and I arrived to farewell them, and me in a maternity smock! Mum wrote to Margot, a mutual friend, who sent me the letter years later: 'Margaret was a shock, but she's as happy as a sand boy, and I'll just have to leave her in God's Hands.' I was thrilled to read that, even though it was many years before I received it, and Mum was gone then.

Just a few weeks before this baby was due, something of importance in the Peak Hill District occurred. Father Michael Heath, who had come to Peak Hill in 1912, and was Parish Priest there for forty years, died in Sydney. He was an architect before becoming a priest and designed the very beautiful Catholic Church in Peak Hill, even getting on the roof sometimes to help with the tiling. He was a close friend of Grandfather Dwyer's, and as his body was being brought back to Peak Hill for burial, it was thought fitting for the hearse to stop at the Alectown Church.

He made fortnightly visits to both Alectown and Tomingley during his forty years as Parish Priest, to say Mass, and had prepared all the local children including the eight Dwyers, for Confirmation, so the short stop at Alectown was to be a special mark of respect. Imagine the shock and horror of everyone there when a utility pulled up, driven by the undertaker, and on the back, Father Heath's coffin! The driver, who was not from Parkes, had collected the coffin from the train and proceeded to Alectown. Grandfather's sense of propriety was outraged, and he walked about, very distressed, saying, 'Where's Frank? Where's Frank?' As if Frank could have done anything at this stage!

My parents were in Oslo when Philippa Frances arrived, a healthy 9lbs 4ozs, with a round face and rosebud lips. She was born at 3.00pm on 29th June 1956, and Frank sent a cable immediately, 'It's a girl, Philippa Frances, both well.' I thought it was strange when Jean Sense, the Sister, brought the baby in to show me, but kept her in her arms. When I asked if I could hold her, she said, 'Oh no, you had a long, difficult labour this time, so we want you to rest. You can have her tonight.' Grace Armstrong was in the room with me, so we discussed it briefly, and then I dozed off.

About 9.00pm, I noticed Dr. Lorger walk briskly past my door, and about half an hour later, I saw Sister Sense escorting him out again. She came into my room, looking harried, and said, 'These doctors! They leave the unpleasant things for us to do.' I was looking puzzled, so she added, 'The baby turned blue so we got Doctor up. He checked her thoroughly, and thinks she must have swallowed some of the amniotic fluid during birth and it got on her lungs. He assures us she will respond to the oxygen we are giving her, so don't worry.'

Of course it was like telling me not to breathe. Grace and I were still looking dumbstruck, when Jean came back in with a sleeping pill in her hand. I swallowed it, and she was just leaving, when she turned around and said casually 'By the way, what was the baby's other name? Philippa what? In case we have to baptise her in the night!' I stammered, 'Frances,' and then she left, leaving us in turmoil.

Next morning a hungry little baby was brought to me to feed, and I was very relieved, as she looked well and quite rosy. There was a great welcome at home from Frank, hugs from my little girl and boy, and Frank said, 'I think I'll ring Ryan Boehm to come up. We might have to close in a veranda for some of these kids to sleep in.' I was so happy and grateful for my little family, and so relieved Philippa's setback was short-lived.

A funny thing happened when I brought her home. Margaret, Frank's sixteen-year-old sister, came to help me until I felt stronger, which was lovely. I had expressed milk and I put it in a blue jug in the new refrigerator on the back veranda, but I neglected to tell Margaret what I'd done. Frank, Pat, George Rankin and Ryan Boehm came for their morning lunch and I was feeding the baby so she got it for them. I finished and came out to show them the baby, and noticed with horror, the blue jug on the table!

I was very calm, and just picked up the jug, took it back to the fridge and got the proper milk, and talking all the time about being home etc., placed it quietly on the table. They didn't notice a thing. Margaret meanwhile, was splitting her sides laughing around the corner when she realised what had happened.

Just before Philippa was born, we were absolutely delighted when the electricity came through the district and we were connected, hence the new fridge. I had done battle from day one with flat irons, which always seemed to carry smudges of dirt from the fuel stove, which invariably ended up on Frank's shirt collars, then later with a petrol iron which hissed away and terrified me so I really could not bring myself to use it. The kerosene fridge was an ongoing battle for me with frozen milk, frozen eggs, frozen everything, and with three babies, a washing machine loomed large on my wish list.

The Aladdin and kerosene lamps were a challenge too, especially when seeing someone off from the door and a gust of wind would cause them to flare, or go out, and even more importantly, when there was an urgent cry from a child in the night, and I would be scrabbling with matches to light the lamp.

We take so much for granted today when our world is controlled by the flick of a switch, the radio, the TV, the computer, mobile phones, electric stoves, cookers of all description, the toasters, electric jugs—the list is endless. Electricity made our lives so much easier, and we today should spare a thought for those women in third world countries who still, in the twenty-first century, are without its benefits, and while doing so, thank God for our own blessings. I am only going back about fifty-five years, so imagine what it was like when Stella and W.B. were very young.

When Philippa was three months old, my parents returned from overseas, so we drove to Mt. Pleasant to show them their newest grandchild. They loved her of course, Mr. and Mrs. Hubbard came from Mt. Top to see her, and for evermore, Frank Hubbard referred to her as 'the pretty one.' This was the year when the three Edwards girls all had a baby in the same year. Gwen started it off by giving birth to her third child, Gerard Edward, in January. My Philippa Frances arrived in June, and June, who had been a late starter in the marriage stakes, gave birth to Lynne Louise, or Lindy Lou as she came to be known, in December.

A bit later, Frank, Bill and Lester were instructed by W.B. to chip the tennis court when we were all there in January, and Frank called out to Dad, 'Hey Dad, it's very hot out here, why don't you just take us into the office and give us a good talking to!' There was much hilarity from the men, especially from W.B. All my family enjoyed Frank's sense of humour, which was never coarse, just usually spot on, and very funny.

Philippa was seven months old when the thyroid condition which doctors had been keeping an eye on during all my pregnancies, flared up in the form of a large swelling in my throat, as well as increased agitation in my behaviour, such as a rapid pulse. I was referred to a Sydney specialist, who advised me to distribute my children and present myself at the Mater Hospital, Crows Nest, by a given date. Kath and Neville Freeth, our bridesmaid and groomsman, took Mary-Ann, Jack and Mel opted for Michael, and Olive and Harry were kind enough to take Philippa for the duration of my stay in hospital.

This proved to be three weeks instead of the six days I had been promised, as the gland was much deeper than was expected, and during the operation I had to be given ether to keep me under, on top of the pentathol which I had initially been given. When I came out of the anaesthetic, I had my arms spread out in the form of a cross, with glucose going into one vein, and a blood transfusion taking place on the other side. A very worried Frank accosted Dr. Rundle outside, and asked worriedly, 'How's my wife, Doctor?'

The Doctor's reply alarmed Frank a bit as he said, 'Well she lost a lot of blood but I think we can pull her through.' Frank came back with, 'Don't think Doctor, make bloody sure!'

I was in the Mater for so long because a haematoma had developed, and blood had seeped down past my breasts, and up to my chin on both sides of my face. I looked an absolute fright as the incision under my neck was swollen up like frankfurts under my chin, and each day they drained the blood out. All I wanted to do was sleep, but that was a big no-no, as they feared a clot, so were constantly urging me in daylight hours to walk, walk, and walk. At night, I had to sit bolt upright in bed with a pillow each side of my face. I know thyroid operations, especially the post-operative nursing methods, have changed for the better, but that was my experience in 1957.

Enter good old Dad. As he had for Gwen and June when they each had a thyroidectomy, he arranged for a nurse to special me for the first three days. Normally one would not have been needed, but because I was so nauseous having had the ether and had complications with the haematoma, she was a great consolation to me. When I returned and gathered up my little brood, Frank's Mum had contacted a young woman named Roberta Martin, from Dubbo, to come and help me and this proved a lifesaver.

Roberta told me she was a bit disabled 'from being held back at birth,' to quote her, and I noticed she had to wear special shoes with supports in them so she could walk. Despite her early disadvantages, Roberta was a wonderful girl who helped me tremendously and the children adored her. I have seen her down on one knee so she could be at eye level with Michael, explaining something to him, not talking down to him, but telling it so a little boy of five could understand it. She would say, 'You see Michael, it's like this etc,' and then go on to tell him. From time to time she went to other members of the Dwyer family helping out when needed, came back to us when Gemma was born in harvest, in 1960, and is still today very special to me.

In January 1957, Frank's brother Pat married Kittie Crowley from Trundle, so Rose Dwyer and the younger girls moved to Dubbo, and Kittie and Pat made Derrymore their home. Towards the end of that year their first child, Jacinta, was born, so four-year-old Mary-Ann, three-year-old Michael, and 16-month-old Philippa were excited about a new 'bubby' in the family. The Volkswagen made its way across the paddock often for picnics on the lawn, and the children enjoyed having a little cousin to play with.

During the next three years, we added two more children to our family, Elisabeth Maree in 1958 and Gemma Louise in 1960. Elisabeth soon became Libby, and when we were expecting Gemma, I suggested the name Yancee Elisabeth to Frank, but he scoffed at the idea, and said, 'And if it's a boy, we'll call him Ah Wong.' He was quick with the repartee was Frank. I remembered a dear little nun at Perthville, who used to look after the elderly nuns, and her name was Sister Gemma, so I found out a bit about St Gemma, and that's how our Gem got her name. We also liked Louise, but when we asked twenty-month-old

Libby to pronounce Louise, she said 'Do wees'. So we settled on Gemma Louise, and then Libby called her 'Gemma-do-wees.' Sometimes you just can't win.

Meanwhile, Ryan Boehm was kept busy with extensions at Wancurra to house our ever-growing family. Uncle Jack Donnelly said, 'It's funny up there at Wancurra, Ryan's only just keeping in front of Margaret and Frank,' and Dad was telling people at home that I was his 'incubator.' They were busy years, with babies, toddlers, a couple of bed-wetters who used to pray every night that they wouldn't wet their beds, but they always did, and then suddenly we had a little schoolgirl.

Mary-Ann started school aged five at Beargamil, on the Wellington Road. I noticed that Gwen Nugent drove her boys past my gate to school every day, so I approached her about a roster and Gwen, Vilma Wild and I took the school run in turn. Michael started the following year and everything went well for a while, but then a young teacher came who was a bit irresponsible, so we three families shifted our children in the opposite direction to Alectown school.

The good news came that Bill McCloughan had been promoted to South Dubbo as Principal and that meant Gwen would be living closer to us again. She had Gerard, a young child then, so she gave up golf and started playing bowls. She also bought a dress shop in conjunction with a friend, Leah Laws, and they called it the Gwenda Lea, and their clothes and hats were extremely smart.

Jayne went to school at St. Mary's in Bathurst, as Gwen had, and then did her nursing training at Royal Prince Alfred Hospital in Sydney, while Robert, and later Gerard, attended St Joseph's College, Hunter's Hill. June and Lester, Lindy and Philip were living in Brisbane, and Stella and W.B. drove up every couple of years to see them, and they came down occasionally too, but I've always hated the tyranny of distance. My brothers were going along well but Jack was having trouble with a bleeding ulcer. You would ask him how he was and his reply was always the same, 'Crook,' he'd say, but he kept on working and ignored it, so I suppose we did too.

Dad didn't go much on our pit toilet down the back, so he made enquiries about one that didn't need much water to flush, and it didn't have an elbow, but went straight down to a tank underneath. He ordered it and came to help Frank install it on the end of the back veranda. We were thrilled not to have to go out in the weather to go to the loo and it was so much better for the children. To be honest, it wasn't a great success, but better than going outside.

We didn't have to put up with it for too many years, because Aunty Mai died, and after a few months of being on his own, Uncle Pat told us he was going to Ireland for a couple of years and now would be as good a time as any for us to move to Maivin. We were pleased for a couple of reasons. Most of Frank's work was at Derrymore or Maivin, and he was always coming or going, and it was a more spacious house than ours. We had lived at Wancurra for eight years and had five children while there but we didn't want to spend any more money on it.

Frank couldn't get Ryan as he was working elsewhere, so he hired Keith Edwards, another farmer who also did some building. When this work was finished, Frank told me we would be shearing in a couple of days and we had to be installed at Maivin by the time we started shearing.

I decided to leave all the clothes in the wardrobes and just take out the drawers, but leave the clothes in them, as there was no way I could pack everything in such a short time when my eldest helper was only seven. Frank, his brother Pat, and a couple of the workmen came with a truck to shift the furniture, and unloaded it all at the house, then hot-footed it to the shed to get ready for shearing the next day. I followed with the children in the car, and imagine my dismay when I found the wardrobes were unloaded all right, but with the doors facing the walls! I made up whatever beds I could, including the cot for Gemma, who was nine months old, and gave the children their dinner and we all fell into bed exhausted.

Next day being Saturday, and no shearing, Frank and I turned the wardrobes away from the wall, and I continued unpacking and sorting out where to put everything. I told my husband that I was never moving again, and do you know what, I didn't, at least not for another fifty years! But at least we were closer to the action, we were young and had been told by Aunty and Uncle for years that we would be moving to their home eventually, but, like any young couple, we were wondering 'When?'

We had plans for the homestead within our limited recourses, the first being to rename it, and that is the first thing we did. So Fana came into existence in Australia as well as in Ireland, and I wondered if Grandfather could see from Heaven and thought how pleased he would be.

CHAPTER 14

FANA AT LAST

A new phase of our lives was beginning. We had left our bridal home in much better order than we had found it, and we needed to renovate again. There were seven of us, at this stage, and we knew Uncle Pat would return in due course to make his home with us, and Fana only had three bedrooms.

Frank did not want to close in verandas to make dormitories as we had done at Wancurra, so he surprised me by designing the renovations, which I still think are worthy of an architect. There was a veranda around three sides of the house, so Frank kept the front and back verandas, and extended the roof over the one facing north, and planned two new bedrooms with a new bathroom in between.

The existing bathroom was very small, so he extended the hall through that, and the result was four bedrooms opening off the hall, and the living area (kitchen, dining room, lounge and family rooms) was at one end of the house, and the sleeping quarters at the other. We also added an outside shower-room with wash-basin and toilet, just near what we thought would be the boys' room, and did away with the louvers on the southern side of the house, replacing them with sliding glass windows from Wancurra, thus creating an office for Frank.

I had always liked the idea of Grandfather's home in Ireland, Fana, and his wife's home over there, Derrymore, being replicated in Australia, so we talked it over and decided to rename the house Fana. It was good to have the two homes only a mile apart, having the same name as their Irish counterparts. We didn't mention it to Uncle Pat though when speaking to him while he was still in Ireland, thinking it would be better to tell him when he came home.

When he eventually arrived, we had quite a few surprises for him, mainly our newest addition to the family, another son, who I'll always believe arrived as a direct answer to Michael's prayers for a little brother. When he made his First Communion, Michael approached me and said wistfully, 'You know Mum how I've always wanted a brother?'

'I certainly do Mike. You hung Gemma's baby clothes in your wardrobe for six months, so I sort of got the idea!' But I added, 'Don't get your hopes up though, if we had a new baby, it might be another girl.'

'No it wouldn't,' he said earnestly, 'because when I made my First Communion someone told me that what I asked for on that day I would receive, and I asked God for a brother.' What defence have you got against faith like that?

Well, I did fall pregnant, and yes it was another 9lb boy who we named David Francis. It's a wonder he didn't arrive early as I got such a shock just before he was born. Frank's brother, Pat, arrived to take 10-year-old Michael with him to bring in cattle and it was looking stormy so Pat told Mike he should wear his raincoat, and they called out to Mary-Ann to bring it.

Mezzie, as we often called our eldest child, took the raincoat down to the gate and Michael said, 'Don't throw it.' She thought he said, 'Throw it.' It flew through the air and startled Michael's horse, Silver, who shied, throwing the young rider off balance and he came off, but with his foot caught in the stirrup! I came running out when I heard children screaming, and with my heart in my mouth, saw, unbelievably, Silver going round and round in circles, trying to shake Michael off.

Finally, the stirrup slid out of the saddle with Mike's foot still in it, and Silver just stood there! For a long time after, my blood ran cold when I thought of what the result would have been if the horse had done what others have done in that situation—galloped off with the child still attached.

I had taught my children to say a prayer to their Guardian Angel each night, and that was one time, as there have been many, when someone says, 'Someone must have been looking after you, or him, or her,' and I think to myself that I know Who it was. I know skeptics will doubt it, but in this story there are too many examples of a similar nature for me not to believe in Divine intervention. Later, God was to ask something huge of us, but in these smaller matters, I have always felt his loving Hand.

In 1961, the Radio Telescope, which had been rising majestically on our immediate horizon for a couple of years, was officially opened by the Governor-General, Lord de Lyle, so we all attended the opening. The site had been chosen for various reasons, one of them being that the area had low wind velocity. On the big day, the wind velocity was so high that the operators chose to leave it in an upright position, (resembling a huge teacup), deeming it unsafe to move it. It became a landmark as well as a place of interest for people from all over the world from that day on, even playing a major role in the first moon landing. I even refrained from planting trees that would have obstructed my view of it from my kitchen window, and on nights when it was floodlit, I loved it.

David was born in August 1963, and that was the year the world heard the devastating news that President John F. Kennedy had been shot in Dallas. I can remember how shocked everyone was, including us, and we welcomed our new baby boy realising how lucky we were, as Jackie Kennedy was left with two fatherless small children.

So with Davy here safely, now we had to accommodate them all, because Uncle was arriving home fairly soon. We put a partition in the large 16ft by 14ft family room, creating another hall for us to pass through to the bedroom area, and the other half made a perfect room for the two boys. I wallpapered one wall with a pattern featuring trains, and David's cot and Michael's double bed fitted in quite well. Later we replaced the cot with a single bed and they still had plenty of room, so when Uncle returned, he had his own bedroom. Not knowing his long-term plans, we put his furniture and possessions over in the cottage so he could dispense with them as he wished on his return.

While Uncle was in Ireland, the Club House Hotel which he and Frank's mother jointly owned, was struggling because the Clubs had taken a lot of the bar trade from the hotel, so Nella Dakers, the proprietor, approached Frank about selling it. Frank consulted the family solicitor, Michael Maguire, and he advised Frank to see Toohey's Brewery in Sydney and ascertain how much beer the Club House was getting from them, so Frank flew down and saw Toohey's.

The result of all this was that Meaghers bought McGlynn's store, the Club House Hotel, the Paragon Cafe, and Nippy Goodwin's barber shop (the last three which Uncle also owned) and turned it all into a large store named Meaghers. Some wag put a notice on the door, 'Gone to MARS!' Frank cabled Uncle Pat the news and received a very happy cable back, saying how relieved he was and how grateful to Frank for his input into it all.

Uncle Pat's return was marked by our nervousness at how he would view the very necessary changes we had made to his former home, so Frank showed him around while I prepared a welcome home meal and attended to the children. In the course of their inspection, Frank pointed out the ramp which we had found it necessary to install because of the amount of traffic between Derrymore and us, Frank and Pat still being partners and my sister-in-law and I sharing the school run.

Uncle's only comment was a mild, 'I never liked ramps,' something which of course we knew when we built it. Frank assured him the sheep hadn't tried to cross it, and they came in for dinner.

After Uncle had retired for the night, and was probably asleep, we heard a strange noise like something, or someone, violently thrashing against metal. Alarmed we got in the car and followed the sound, and horror of horrors, Uncle Pat's big grey horse, Smokey, who had never once come down from his paddock or gone anywhere near the ramp, had galloped into it! This is the first time in this narrative that I've used four exclamation points, so that will give you some idea of how we felt.

What to do now? The first thing of course was to tell Uncle, so poor Frank knocked on his door, and asked, 'Are you awake, Uncle?' After a while, Uncle said, 'Oh, yes Frank?' with a question in his voice. Frank then told him, 'Uncle, Smokey's in the ramp!' Uncle came out, and there was a bit of discussion as to what to do, perhaps ring Norm Watt, or Jack Wild, to bring a sling, but we finally decided to go down first and view the situation. It was only a couple of hundred yards, and the child in me who used to pray in emergencies behind doors, surfaced again during that short drive and I prayed with all my heart, 'Please God let Smokey be all right, help him get out and not be badly hurt.'

We were approaching the ramp, and we could see and hear poor Smokey thrashing about and trying to get traction, which of course he couldn't, as the soil was too far from his feet, when, to our absolute amazement, this wonderful animal heaved himself out and stood quivering. How he did it no one knew; it seemed to be miraculous, but it was a great relief to all of us, especially Frank, and I guess Uncle, as it was his horse.

Frank opened the gate nearby into the paddock with the dam in it, and Smokey quietly limped through. Next day we awoke to find him waist deep in the dam and he stayed there for three days, and Uncle told us that was nature's way of healing him. That night we made a cup of tea back at the house, and to Uncle Pat's great credit, he didn't say a word of recrimination, not then, not ever.

David was only three months old when Uncle returned to live with us, but when he was a toddler in about twelve months time, he was Uncle Pat's shadow. When Uncle was filling the barrow at the wood-heap, Davy would be there putting little sticks in 'helping him'. I remember Uncle would go to town on business and when he came home, he would produce about six or eight bananas. These were a luxury for the children, and after they had one each, Uncle, who was childless, would say in amazement, 'They didn't last long.'

Before we left Wancurra, Frank had bought bikes for Mary-Ann and Michael so they could ride the six miles to school. They would set off with their schoolbags on their backs, aged six and seven, and I can still see Mary-Ann's straight little back as she rode over the rise near the house. Sometimes, they would ride home via Derrymore, and Kittie would give them a drink, and sometimes I would put Philippa, Libby, and baby Gemma in the car and drive to meet them, putting the bikes in the boot.

After we moved to Fana, they continued to ride but it was only three miles from there. One day they raced into the kitchen all excited, and both talking at once, 'Mum, we rode over a snake at the ramp,' but it was garbled, as they were each anxious to be the one to tell me. I said, 'Steady on, I can't listen to two at once.'

'But we're both telling you the same thing,' they insisted.

Philippa turned five in June, so we waited until she was five-and-a-half before starting her at school and then it was back to the school run again as she was too little to ride her bike. By this time, Kittie had another son, John, and our David was five months younger, so I would drive to the mailbox on the lane, pick up Leslie, Elizabeth, and Heather Watts, then collect the Derrymore children at their gate, and deliver them to school. Of course, Kittie and Rae Watts took their turn too, so we only did it every third week.

At weekends, the cousins from Derrymore, Jacinta, Cathy, Bill and John, would spend time with ours at either place and have great fun together. Then later, they were joined by Bernard, who was Kittie and Pat's youngest child, and as soon as he could toddle, and with Davey as well, we just about had a cricket team.

One day, I heard some excitement coming from the back garden, and when I went to investigate, there were several little upturned faces, gazing up at the sixty-foot tower which was a relic of the pre-electricity days, and still had the free-light on top. To my horror, two-year-old Gemma was well on her way to the top, and Michael on his way up to rescue her. We watched with bated breath until the adventurer was safely down and then we hailed Michael as a hero, and as usual, scolded the intrepid climber, 'Don't you ever do that again, you naughty girl!' Sound familiar?

David was an allergic child who had more loose motions as a toddler than firm ones, so we bought a goat, called Nanny, a beautiful white goat with huge amber eyes. We tethered her to the back fence and Michael milked her each day, as David was allergic to cow's milk. We were training Davy to do wee and, as an incentive, if he was a bit reluctant, we would urge him to go out and 'show Nanny'. He was happy to do this, and while Mike was milking the goat, Davy would go to the edge of the veranda, pull his little peanut out, and say, "Ook Nanny,' and do his wee (If David comes looking for me after reading this, I have definitely left for Siberia!).

I certainly had tots and teens, as Mary-Ann, unlike her mother, developed early. I had explained to her about her periods when she was ten, and shown her the 'where—with-all' and what to do with them, and just as well I did, because one day before school, when she was not even eleven, I had David in the bath after one of his little accidents, the other children waiting to go to school, and Mary-Ann poked her head around the door and announced brightly, 'Mum, I've got my periods!' Stunned, I said, 'Well darling, do you know what to do?' and this sunny-tempered girl replied, 'Sure', and that was that. Because of the lack of privacy afforded by the schoolyard toilet, I arranged with the teacher's wife for Mary-Ann to use her toilet at the house, if necessary.

When there was a drought, and that seemed fairly often, the hand feeding of stock was a daily chore. Frank, Michael and Mary-Ann would get on the back of the truck to push the hay off to the sheep following behind, and for some reason, Frank would put David, who was *two*, behind the wheel, put the truck in low gear and let him steer it. It would only go at a snail's pace, but I always thought of freak things that might happen, and didn't approve. One day, Davy was out of sorts, and he steered all right, but whined and grizzled all the time and it looked quite humorous, so I captured it on our little movie camera.

We seemed to be busy every day, but come what may, we always took the children to Mass every Sunday, clad in their best clothes, and the girls in hats and gloves. It seems ridiculous now that they were so dressed up, but it was what was done then. I took my turn at cleaning the church at Alectown, and preparing Father's breakfast, and I would make sandwiches and cakes, pack a basket with my nice china, fill a thermos with tea, and he would have it on the front seat of the church after Mass, which was sometimes at 11 o'clock.

Fasting that late wasn't easy when one was pregnant but we just did what we had to do. To keep the children occupied during the sermon, I would peel apples, put a piece of string through them and when the smaller ones got restless, hang one around their neck and they would eat without dropping it.

One Sunday, a little Irish priest got testy when he saw Frank say something to me during his sermon, and he stopped and said in his Irish brogue, jumping up and down a bit, 'I come all the way out here to preach the word of God and you don't appreciate it', or something in that vein, then he turned on his heel and resumed saying Mass. Kath Cook thought it was her young Paul who was the culprit, but I knew it was Frank, and it was just an innocent aside, something like 'he must have got that from Ireland'—harmless, but not an appropriate thing to do during Mass. I said to Kath Cook, who had taught Frank when he was seven, 'I'll know whose neck to hang the apple on next time!'

When I had the children settled in their own rooms, I had a conscience about not hearing their prayers at night. To be honest, I was too weary sometimes to do that individually, so I started the practice of standing in a central position in the hall and I'd intone, 'In the name of the Father, and of the Son and of the Holy Spirit', and then I'd lead their prayers in a loud voice so they'd hear me. Then I'd say goodnight to them, tell them to go to sleep now, and I'd leave.

Then I would hear shades of The Waltons, the show they loved on TV where the kids would sing out goodnight to each other, and I'd hear: 'Goodnight Mikey Boy' . . . then from another room, 'Goodnight Phips' . . . 'Good-night Lib' . . . 'Goodnight Davy-Boy' . . . 'Goodnight Mezzie-Pooh' and 'Goodnight Gem-Gem.' They were funny kids, and mostly that would be the end of it and they would go off to sleep.

One night though, I heard sort of farting noises coming from some of the rooms, and realised someone had learnt to make those noises with their hands under their arms. Craaaaaak! There was a succession of them, the boys winning by far. Suddenly Philippa's little voice came loud and clear. 'Listen everybody, no hands . . . Craaaaaak!' The laughter started out muffled, but ended up in a crescendo of mirth which none of them could control. Wisely, I didn't investigate, but heard about it next day when they were still laughing about Phips and her 'no hands', and of course giving their father a demonstration.

Time marched on and Mary-Ann was in sixth class and we intended to send her to Perthville, but just before we made the arrangements, everything there changed. Classes at the College ceased as the Diocese built a new school in Bathurst—MacKillop College—and it was staffed by a couple of orders of nuns. St. Joseph's College, Perthville, my alma mater, became just where the boarders lived. None of that worried us, but neither Frank, nor I, was keen on our daughter catching a bus in and out every day to Bathurst. I had been at Perthville when the senior girls were involved in a serious bus accident, and the driver and three of the girls were badly injured and hospitalised, and it still haunted me a bit. Ironically, in later years we had to organise a bus service to divert from its regular route, in order for our younger children to go to High School in Parkes, as we could no longer afford boarding school, but that was later.

Having reluctantly decided against Perthville, Frank and I took Mary-Ann to Sydney where we had arranged for interviews at a few colleges. We were most impressed with the Sacred Heart College, Rose Bay, with its beautiful, Gothic buildings made of sandstone, and the magnificent art throughout the college, but most of all we liked the quiet atmosphere and its air of refinement. So we settled on that and came home to face harvest, and then buying her clothes, marking them and sending her off in early February. It was a heart-wrenching thing to have to do, to send your first-born eleven-year-old child away for three months at a time, but we had no alternative at that stage.

Mary-Ann, at twelve, could be described as an attractive child, on the verge of womanhood. She had light-brown curly hair, grey-blue eyes, and classical features, and it was remarked by many as she grew older that she resembled Grace Kelly. There was a fancy dress dance at Alectown one night and I decided to dress her as the young Queen Elizabeth. She had been a junior bridesmaid for her Aunty Margaret Carolan in Dubbo not long before, so we decided she should wear the long lemon dress she had worn for that. I made a blue sash to go over her shoulder and across her chest, pinned my silver, star-shaped Child of Mary Medal on the sash, and that made a great Order of the Garter. I had kept the pearl tiara I had worn as a bride, and she wore that on her head, and with long white gloves, and a tiny evening bag hanging over her arm, she looked a miniature of the Queen.

What impressed us all though, was the regal way she walked in the parade for judging; she was every inch a queen with a straight back and royal bearing, and even lifted her gloved hand a few times in a wave as she had seen the Queen do, so no one was surprised when she won first prize.

Now she was a boarder at The Sacred Heart College, Rose Bay, and she wrote about her teachers, the music lessons, the friends she was making (who included Gai Smith, now Gai Waterhouse) and loved the position of her school near the bay where the flying boats landed. She usually flew back to school, but once we took her by car when Davy was not quite two. He started to cry when we said goodbye to her at the college and cried non-stop for an hour, all through the city, saying between sobs, 'I want Mary-Ann, I want her here', and there was no consoling him, until exhaustion set in and he slept.

Frank and Pat missed Michael when he in turn left for boarding school, as he was invaluable, carrying fuel out to the paddock when they needed it and helping with sheep work. He was a good little driver and as Frank said, 'As handy as a pocket in a shirt.' When they were dipping sheep, I had to run him down to school at the eleventh hour as he was needed for as long as he could stay. It was the same at shearing time if it wasn't during school holidays and he would be at the shed as soon as he was home from school, penning up, taking sheep back to the paddocks etc. He could drive the Ferguson tractor from a very early age, and did a lot of work on that.

The decision to send him to a college near Goulburn, St. Michaels, Inveralochy, was made with the help of our dear friend, Father John Kelly, who researched a few agricultural colleges for us and came up with this one run by the Christian Brothers. It was set on 1,000 acres fifteen miles from Goulburn, on the Braidwood road, and ran Romney Marsh and Suffolk Cross sheep, had a piggery, poultry, a market garden and a dairy. The boys were formed into groups of eight (Mike was in charge of one group) and the groups would work for one week in each section.

When they were on the dairy, they got up each morning at 5am to milk the cows mechanically on weekdays, but on Sundays because of Mass, they rose at 4am. Goulburn is one of the coldest towns in the State, and our 12-year-old boy must have wondered why we sent him there when he had to get up at ungodly hours to milk cows in freezing conditions on a regular basis. But he actually loved it, and wrote to tell us that they started schoolwork early and knocked off at 2.30pm, when they changed into work clothes to do the physical work of the Agricultural College.

Once when we visited we saw many of the boys with long scarves around their necks to stave off the bitter winds, which blew off the snow, and were told they had each knitted their own. At a later date Michael was joined by his cousin, Laurence Crowley, Delia and Bernie's boy, and that forged a friendship between the cousins which I feel still exists today, though they don't see each other as often as they would like.

We went to see Mike another time, as there was a function on that night and the Bishop from Wagga was to be there, and Mike was playing football next day, so once again we took David. The problem he caused this time was that he wouldn't go to sleep in the back, and jumped around all the way. It was before child restraints, of course, and I tried everything to get him to sleep, as I knew he needed to be fresh and not cranky that night. I even smacked him thinking he might cry himself to sleep, but no way, and do you know when he went to sleep? Just as we turned into the driveway of the college.

When we pulled up, there was Mike with his friends, wanting to show off his one and only baby brother! As Stella sometimes said when

Nana tested her patience, 'I'm to be pitied', and as we pulled up at the college, I felt a bit like that.

The years flew by, as they do when you are busy. Sadly Uncle Pat developed renal cancer, and died in Sydney on 31st December 1965. He was a thorough gentleman, and his nephew, Michael Byrne, said to me only recently, that he hadn't ever known him to raise his voice. I lived with Frank who could be a bit testy at times and we had our feisty moments in our marriage, but I can't picture Uncle ever having an outright row with Aunty Mai. They were a lovely couple, who, because they were childless, and because Frank's father had died so young, were exceptionally fond of the eight children he left behind. There was no competition as there might have been if they had also had a family, just this very strong affection, and they extended this same affection to me as Frank's wife.

During these years Frank was involved in the community in many areas. He was President of the Alectown Hall Committee for several years and before that, worked alongside Bill Nicholas and Lloyd Westcott in their endeavours to improve the Memorial Hall by adding toilets, extending the hall to provide two supper rooms and a better kitchen, and with these two stalwarts, doing general maintenance.

The committee wanted to put septic toilets in the hall, but the Shire Council wouldn't give permission because they were afraid we would run out of water for the toilets, and they would have to provide it, so Frank made a trip to Sydney to the office of the Minister for Halls and Recreational Affairs, the office where my Uncle Jack, Ailsa's father, worked. He was told to go ahead, and if they ran out of water, to close the hall until water was available again, so they built the toilets that are still functioning today.

Also, as Vice President of the Parents and Citizens Committee, he filled in for Lloyd when he was in hospital or unwell, chaired the meetings and dealt with whatever came up, some of it as it turned out, of a confronting nature, which caused us some grief because of a clash of interest between the ambitious teacher and the parents.

He was elected Captain of the local Rural Fire Service, and held this office for twelve years, and I can vouch for how seriously he took this position. He was vigilant in times of fire bans, causing Ryan's wife, Jess Boehm, to extinguish her little rubbish-burning endeavours as soon as she saw him coming. She was always careful, standing there with a hose in her hand, but Frank made no exceptions. Jess would say to me, 'He's tough Margaret.' Frank was also involved with the St. Vincent de Paul Society and the Knights of the Southern Cross in Parkes, which necessitated trips into town and once even a trip to Nyngan in a truck to collect furniture for Vinnies. With the constant work on the farm, this made for a very busy life for Frank, as it was all extra-curricula. Nothing diverted him from the necessary farm work.

Frank and his brother, Pat, went to a Knights function at Trundle once, and as Frank was driving, Pat was free to have a couple of whiskeys, that being the drink the doctors favoured for diabetics. Later in the evening, Frank was amused when Pat took Ted Day around introducing him, saying, 'Jim, or Jo, have you met This Day Tonight?' TDT was a TV show that was on each night.

We had trips to Mt. Pleasant each Christmas, and I felt sorry for the children having to leave their few Santa Claus things behind and pile into a hot car for the trip over. Next day being Boxing Day was Grandma Dwyer's day to have all the families at Quin Street in Dubbo, so we travelled up there and celebrated Christmas with all of Frank's family, as we had the day before with mine.

During the year Frank's Mum sometimes came to Fana and Derrymore, and she would bring everything she needed to make what are still called 'Grandma's biscuits'. One day she was stirring a huge mixture in the large mixing bowl she had brought with her, using her hands, and she said, 'Margie, you can see why I take my watch off when I'm making these.' I looked at the enormous mixture rising and falling in the bowl as she stirred it around and I said, 'I'm only surprised you don't have to take your glasses off, too!' She threw back her head and laughed heartily and that was something Rose Dwyer did often, laugh heartily.

Now she rolled the mixture with a rolling pin, pressed the cutter down, and soon, tray after tray of pale circles were sliding in and out of the oven, until she had made a monumental pile of crunchy, golden biscuits. While my mouth was watering, she said, 'I used to bake a KEROSENE TIN full of these biscuits when my children were young, and I'd be having a rest, and I'd hear the plop of the tin on the floor as they pulled it out of the cupboard, in order to help themselves.' I remembered that tin well when she lived at Derrymore; there were always biscuits in it, and it had a wooden lid which Willy or someone had made to fit the tin. The biscuits themselves were not a gourmet's delight, as they only had butter, sugar, eggs and flour in the ingredients, but they were 'more-ish', meaning everyone came back for more, and children loved them.

David was only four-and-a-half when he started school at Alectown as the numbers were down, and they wanted to keep the school open. I regretted sending him so early as he had to repeat first class later, being too immature to go up to second. The year after this, a few things happened in quick succession. Philippa was finishing primary school, and with high interest rates of 17 per cent our mortgage was climbing dangerously. We couldn't afford to send her to Rose Bay with Mezzie, so I spoke to the Sisters of Mercy in Parkes about the possibility of her being a weekly boarder. Sister Sheila Crowley accepted her, and said weekly boarding was a possibility later, but not at the moment, so we packed our second daughter off to boarding school, only this time locally.

We actually saw a lot of her as she did come home often at weekends, and she was very happy, especially when the boarders were moved to a brand new building in Want Street, with special little cubicles of their own which had a bed and desk in them.

So that was Phips set up . . . and then a few of us arranged an extension of the existing bus run to pick up at Alectown and along our lane, so Libby, Gemma and David, and the Derrymore, Watts and Wild children caught the bus into Parkes to their respective schools. Libby and Gemma were enrolled at Our Lady of Mercy Primary and Davy at the Infants' School, where he repeated first class. It was tiring for them as they were picked up first in the morning, and dropped off last in the afternoons.

David made his First Confession in preparation for his First Holy Communion, and just before he did, Frank was cranky with him because he hadn't put the calves up. This is how it went: Frank pointing up at the cows in the paddock, berating the little five-and-a-half-year-old for not doing his job, Davy making excuses, and then Frank pointing to the scrap bucket for the chooks and saying 'And take these over to the chooks', giving the bucket a kick as he spoke. Result, the bucket tipped over. So Davy's first confession went something like this: 'Forgive me Father for I have sinned.' Then more explicitly, 'I forgot to put the calves up and Dad was cranky and kicked over the bucket of scraps.' I'm not sure whose confession David was making, his own, or his father's, and I can only wonder at what the young priest, Father Ged Fitzgerald, thought.

We had Mary-Ann at Rose Bay, Michael at Inveralocky, Philippa boarding in Parkes, Libby, Gemma and David travelling by bus each day to Parkes schools, and then this forty-year-old suspected she might be pregnant again. I told Frank, and saw Dr. Waddell who had taken us on when Dr. Lorger died. He was a fatherly man, and I remember he told me consolingly, 'Well, it's not so bad. You will be tied up for ten years rearing this baby and it will be a great interest for you.' I hastily assured him I really wanted another baby, and that this wasn't an accident, and moreover, the rest of the family would be thrilled to bits to have a little sister or brother. Doctor told me he would ring me that night 'if the rabbit died.'

I picked up Philippa as she was coming home that weekend and we drove home. We were all watching TV when the phone rang. I answered and Doctor Waddell said, 'It's positive!' I said meekly, 'Thank you John', and replaced the receiver. It was the shortest conversation on record. I returned to the family, Frank looked at me enquiringly, I just nodded, and Frank raised his eyes to Heaven. Later that month when I told Phips our exciting news, she said, 'Oh, I knew Mummy (she was the only one who continued to call me Mummy into high school). I asked her how she knew, and she said, 'You know that night when you answered the phone, and when you came back, Dad looked at you, you nodded and Dad raised his eyes to Heaven? I knew then.' Philippa was always as sharp as a tack.

My children were excited to hear the news, and when Mary-Ann came home in early December just before the baby was due, she came in to where I was resting, 'to have a talk.' Mezzie knew how short money was at the time, and she started off by saying that she wanted to do nursing after she left school, and questioned the necessity of her going on for two more years at Rose Bay. She said she would be accepted at the Mater Hospital at Crows Nest with the School Certificate and she would be finished in two years, thus saving two more years of school fees for Dad. It made a lot of sense, and I knew Frank would be relieved, so I agreed.

After talking with her father about it, she went ahead with the arrangements, and the hospital said she could come in the September intake of students. Until then, she would be home with us and could be a help to me. She arranged at the TAFE to do a sewing course, so that occupied some of her time too, and of course, she could make her debut in May, so this, with the baby as well, was going to make an exciting year for us.

It was a momentous year in history too, as it was in 1969 that the world was stunned again to hear of the shooting of another Kennedy, this time the former Attorney-General, Robert Kennedy, the father also of a large family, and President Kennedy's brother.

David was six when I was due to have the baby, and he was interested in the movements, which were often obvious on my tummy. One day I was making sure he had washed his ears in the bath, and he looked at my big stomach, and asked me, 'How is the baby going to get out?' I assured him the doctor would help me when the time came, but he wasn't satisfied, and asked, 'But HOW is it going to get out?' I told him, 'You have been with Daddy when a sheep has been having a lamb, haven't you?' A look of absolute horror passed over his face, and he said incredulously, 'Out your backside!'

I looked at my hair where the tell-tale grey was inching along the part yet again and I confided to my husband that I thought I might let my hair go grey and just grow old gracefully, as I would be too busy with the new baby to keep putting colour in. Frank agreed, and added, 'You have put up a mighty battle so far!'

When my hair was quite grey later in the pregnancy, Gemma, who was eight, came to me and asked worriedly, 'Mummy, will the baby have grey hair?' I assured her it wouldn't, and when Marguerite Estelle arrived at 8.00am, on 17th December, while my family were having breakfast at Fana, she had lovely dark hair and 'a face like a crushed pansy', to quote my friend Roma Condon. She was off to a good start at 9lbs 6oz, and the family all came in at 10.00am to see her. I was showered and dressed and they thought she was beautiful and the girls already had her ear-marked as a flowergirl. Mike and David wanted a boy beforehand, but fell in love with her on sight. Everyone was home because of school holidays so Father Kelly (Ned) baptised her in Alectown Church on Christmas Day when she was six days old, with Mary-Ann and Michael as her godparents.

Not long before Marguerite was born, W.B. suffered a stroke while driving, and his station wagon broadsided into a tree. He was in a coma

141

for a couple of weeks and had been in hospital for a few months, then in Apex House in Orange for rehabilitation. Here he learned to dress himself again and was able to talk, but he had to rely on a walking frame, and was actually still in Apex House when my last baby was born.

My brothers brought both Mum and Dad to Gwen's in Dubbo for Christmas, as it was easy for me to slip up to Dubbo and show them the baby, so after she was baptised, we took her there. We then spent Boxing Day with Frank's family as usual, so everyone in both our families met Marguerite when she was eight days old. So on the cusp of 1970, we have Mary-Ann leaving school, a brand new baby, and a debut planned for 1971.

CHAPTER 15

LIFE BRINGS CROSSES
AS WELL AS ROSES

Marguerite was four weeks old when Gwen rang and told me she and Bill were going on a short holiday in January and that Dick and Maree, who lived close to Mum at Mt. Pleasant, would also be taking their children for a break. She asked could I manage to have Mum, as she certainly could not stay at Mt. Pleasant on her own. Of course I was delighted to have my Mum and I had Mary-Ann's help, so we met Gwen at Tomingley, halfway to Dubbo, and brought Mum to Fana for what turned out to be her last visit.

Stella would watch Marguerite lying on the bed and kicking her legs, and she would pick each leg up in turn and sing the 'leg' song, as I termed it, pushing the tiny legs up and down as she sang, 'Round the bend, round the bend, three wheels round the corner.' The baby was only 4 or 5 weeks old, but she was an early smiler, and she gave her grandmother so much pleasure by responding with lovely smiles. Mum remarked to me: 'She's a very shapely baby, isn't she?' I've often thought Stella would be able to say the same thing still about our Margie today, who, though always a bit anxious about her weight, is definitely 'shapely!'

While Mum was with me, she became sick, so our doctor put her in hospital in Parkes with pneumonia. I put Marguerite in her carry basket and drove in every day to see her, without realising I was putting a lot of strain on my back, still weak from carrying such a big baby. When she came home she received a letter from June from Brisbane, and I was alarmed when she didn't seem to be able to read it. I remember getting the large magnifying page out of the phone book for her, but it didn't make any difference.

During her illness she had one bout of incontinence in the night, and Mary-Ann was so good at helping me with it that I knew she would make a wonderful nurse. Frank was marvellous and hosed it all down before putting everything in the washing machine, and I went in to Mum and said, 'Well, everything's nice and clean again, and the sheets are blowing on the clothes line,' knowing how mortified she must be, and trying to make light of it. I was worried when she replied, 'Well they weren't really dirty, were they?' Suddenly, she became disorientated and thought she saw things moving under the other bed, and I felt afraid for my Mum and didn't know what was happening to her. Gwen was home so we arranged again to meet at Tomingley, and Gwen took her to her home in Dubbo.

Dad was still in Apex House 'learning to walk again', to quote him, so Gwen and I took Mum to have her hair permed softly as she wanted to look nice for Dad who was being brought up to see her at the weekend. The male hairdresser put her under the dryer and as all women know, one can't hear a thing under that. He sat down and lit a cigarette when he had Mum under the dryer, and Mum said with a raised voice because of the noise of the dryer, 'He's going to leave me under this now while he smokes a cigarette!' I suppose it was embarrassing, but Michael laughed, so we did too.

The doctor in Dubbo put her in hospital again and I can see her now, walking up the steps into the hospital carrying gloves and handbag. Frank and I drove up to see her on Sunday. She didn't seem sick but was talking to her sisters who had all died except Aunty Marion, the nun, and remarked on the pretty curtains, but her words were indistinct and running together.

On Tuesday night, Bill, Gwen's husband, was sitting with her. At about 2.00am, Stella, our wonderful mother who had worked alongside Dad to forge a secure future for the six of us, and who had created a happy home for her mother and mother-in-law and all of us for so many years, went peacefully to receive her reward.

Ten-year-old Gemma was the one Mum called 'Saucers' because of her big eyes, and she was very upset, as were all the children. After the funeral, and we were all back at Fana, I had plenty of time to think about my mother, as my back, always a bit touchy, just gave out and I was confined to bed with a board under the mattress for a couple of weeks. Mary-Ann had just been picked up to go to her TAFE course, the children were at school and Frank was out working. The two-month-old baby was in her basket in the lounge and I knew she had to have her bath and I had to feed her, so I rolled out of bed onto my feet, and my back promptly gave out and I couldn't stand. In all the years, it was about my darkest hour and I looked at Mum's photo on the wall near my bed, and the tears just came. Marguerite was a very contented baby and just lay happily oblivious in her basket in the lounge, and I just sobbed.

Suddenly, I thought I heard someone in the kitchen, and after a while, a young woman from Alectown came up to my room. Her name was Maralyn Boehm and she was Ryan's daughter-in-law. Apparently Ryan had said to her 'Why don't you go up and see if Margaret needs a hand?' and she did. She was marvellous, got the baby bath and bathed Marguerite, then brought her in for me to feed. If there was ever an angel in disguise, she was it, and I have never forgotten her kindness. She brought me a cup of tea, and I asked her to bring the baby's basket in close to my bed, and then I could manage until Frank or Mary-Ann came home.

Frank began to take an interest in community affairs and attended meetings at the Alectown Soldiers' Memorial Hall, the local Rural Fire Service, the school Parents and Citizens' committee and the Knights of the Southern Cross in Parkes. As a result, he became president of the Hall Committee, vice-president of the P and C, and captain of the Bush Fire committee, as it was called then. He held these positions for many years; in fact, he was captain of the Fire Brigade for twelve years. These positions all called for leadership and were time-consuming, but like other farmers, Frank knew the importance of building a solid community. He also, I was told, provided comic relief many times at these meetings with his special type of humour, sometimes easing a tense situation with one of his comments.

We had become friendly with Frances and Vince Flannery who owned a general store in Parkes and were the parents of seven great sons, so at Christmas after Mass we would go to their home where a great Irish Craic would be going on. Once again I would be on the piano and all comers would be up dancing, and everyone singing and not a drop of liquor in sight. One morning, Mary-Ann was the life of the party as usual, and dancing with one of the boys, when a couple of men who were also friends of the Flannery gang came to the door. Mezzie, who would have had no idea that one of the men was gay, sang out, 'Hello you two, grab a poofter and sit down!' Of course, all chairs were taken and she meant to say pouffe pronounced 'pouffay' which of course is a large, round cushion. Oh Mary-Ann!

Bernard Flannery was about eighteen, and Mezzie was sixteen, so she asked him to be her partner at the debutante ball that was approaching. They became good friends and made an attractive couple at the ball. Her frock was Swiss cotton with a silk thread running through it and she chose a girlish pattern with a gathered skirt, short, slightly puffed sleeves and a neckline at which she wore her grandmother Stella's cameo brooch. Her hair was drawn back behind her ears, combed high at the back and fell in short ringlets, and we thought that she looked just how a debutante should look.

Others must have thought so too, because at a later ball where 'Deb of the Year' was judged, Mezzie was pronounced winner and was awarded the sash by Jenny Gill, the winner from the previous year. I had a walk down memory lane when I found the photographs of Bernard and her together. He was a lovely young friend, and when she went to Sydney to train as a nurse in September, he was doing Graphic Arts there. Their friendship continued, but not the romance.

When September arrived, Frank and I took Mary-Ann to the Mater Hospital at Crows Nest to begin her nursing training. She was excited and full of hopes for a future in nursing, and her letters were interesting, telling us about the lovely girls with whom she was training. There were two from the South Coast, Anne and Sue Heffernan, and she became very friendly with them and brought them home to Fana once or twice. She also visited them on the coast and got her driver's license while she was there. We received great reports from Sister Barbara, who was the nun in charge at the Mater, about Mary-Ann and the progress she was making, saying she was a very amenable girl.

Then disaster struck. Out of the blue one day when Frank was under a machine doing maintenance, and I was hanging clothes on the line, the phone rang. When I answered, a voice said 'Mrs. Dwyer, it's Sister Barbara from the Mater Hospital, and I regret very much to have to tell you that Mary-Ann has hepatitis.' I was shocked, but not unduly worried, as I knew people who had this and recovered very well. She went on to say that Mezzie was in Prince Henry Hospital out at Little Bay in the Infectious Disease building, and would be there for about fourteen days.

I went over and told Frank and I sometimes wonder was his answer prophetic. He crawled out from under the machine and said flatly, 'Well that's that then!' We spoke to Mary-Ann on the phone and she was cheerful and said she was feeling a bit better, so we were looking forward to bringing her home in a couple of weeks. When the two weeks were up, I rang Sister Barbara and asked when we could pick Mezzie up, and her reply scared me a bit. She said: 'Oh Mrs. Dwyer, I think you had better ring Professor Davis,' which I did, and that is when the full impact of what had happened to our daughter struck me.

Professor Davis said, 'Mary-Ann was unfortunate in the type of hepatitis she contacted as it was viral, in fact, Hepatitis B, and was much more serious than thought earlier.' He added she would be in Prince Henry longer than at first projected, so of course we drove to Little Bay to see her, this time taking Marguerite who was eighteen-months old. The baby was not allowed in to the Infectious Diseases area, so we each visited Mary-Ann separately and one stayed with Marguerite in the car.

Eventually, after three months, Mary-Ann was allowed home and she insisted on getting work in Parkes, as nursing was now out of the question. She still suffered from nausea, and when she was hired to manage a small boutique called 'Fleur,' she had to have a container handy at work each day because of the nausea. She also rented a large flat in a Heritage-listed building, called Balmoral, and about this time Jim O'Donnell offered her a position in the Ladies section of the store of which he was manager, called Howards, so she happily worked there and continued her convalescence.

This was the early seventies and the rural recession had set in, making life tougher than usual for the farming community. Michael passed the School Certificate at Inveralocky with a 6 A level pass, and was all set to do the Higher School Certificate there, but St. Michael's was an Agricultural College and most farmers couldn't afford boarding school fees, so it was forced to close.

We brought Michael home, and it was fortuitous that Mike and Philippa were both needing accommodation in order to finish their education when Mary-Ann started renting a flat in Balmoral, so of course they moved in with her. We provided them with meat, milk and eggs, and she paid the rent out of her wages, so once again our unselfish girl came to the rescue. She loved their company too of course, and I know both Phips and Mike have wonderful memories of that special time with Mezzie-Ann. They were intrigued to find there was a cellar under the house, but with a girl who wasn't allowed to drink, and two students, it was wasted on them.

About this time Frank's mother, Rose Dwyer, lost her battle with renal cancer, and died peacefully in Dubbo Hospital on 3rd July, in the very room in which my mother, Stella, had died, seventeen months earlier. We were all with Grandma when she died, and the Matron arranged for a large pot of tea and many cups to be brought in to the next room. While the family was saying the Rosary and the priest was there, I slipped out and brought each of them a cup of tea. Little Marguerite was eighteen-months old, and Frank's Mum was propped up almost in a sitting position, so Marguerite said, 'Mummy, what about Grandma?' and pointed to her grandmother in the bed, not knowing that wonderful lady was no longer with us, but was already meeting her God and reaping the rewards of a life lived for Him and her family.

After the Requiem Mass in Dubbo, Rose Dwyer was brought to Parkes Holy Family Church where a second Mass was celebrated, after which she was laid to rest beside her husband, Will, in the Parkes Cemetery, where he had been buried over thirty years before. Mary-Ann hosted a lunch for all the family and anyone who wanted to come at Balmoral in Hill Street, assisted by Michael and Philippa, and as these occasions do, it turned into a happy family gathering.

Though not entirely well, Mary-Ann and some of her friends decided to support the Show Society and entered in the Show Girl competition, the Show always being at the end of August. They were all excited and chose their outfits with great care. Mary-Ann bought a fine check grey skirt, teamed it with a yellow blazer and added a tie of the same check as the skirt.

One day she said to me 'Mum, I was thinking a really nice parasol would improve my outfit.' I agreed with her, and thought privately, 'Yes, that would make her stand out,' as of course, after all she'd been through, we thought it would be wonderful if she could win the competition. How great was my surprise then, when I heard her telling some of the other contestants, 'What a great idea it would be if we all had parasols!' But that was Mary-Ann.

The judging was spread over a couple of days, but finally the day arrived when Miss Show Girl 1971 was to be announced. I made sure all my brood were dressed warmly, and as usual, dressed warmly and casually myself as I've never considered an agricultural show to be a 'dress up' occasion. None of our family really expected Mezzie to win, as the winner had to be knowledgeable about rural affairs, as well as fitting all the other criteria required, so our surprise was genuine when she was pronounced the winner from amongst all those lovely girls.

We were all delighted of course, and then my habit of dressing *very* casually let me down, for one of the Committee came and invited Frank and me into the Secretary's Office for champagne and delicious food, and I looked a bit like Eliza Doolittle before the Professor took her on! I didn't have any idea that was on the cards, or that Mezzie would win, or I might have still dressed casually, but a little more elegantly! Still, it was a great thrill for her and we were proud of her.

Shortly after this, she had her regular check-up with Professor Davis in Sydney, and he suggested she return to Sydney so he could measure fortnightly, among other things, her enzyme levels. He told her they had made great strides in America with liver transplants, and I think his aim was to bring her to the point where she would be a suitable candidate for one. It was early days even in America for transplants, but it was mentioned.

The timing of her return to Sydney was fortuitous as her place of work in Parkes, Howard's large store, had burnt down overnight, so she would have had to look for work elsewhere. Incidentally, Gemma, who was eleven or twelve, had left her guitar in one of the dressing rooms at Howards and Mezzie was keeping an eye on it while she went to netball training, and of course it was burnt in the fire. She had forgotten to pick it up before coming home on the bus, but fortunately, insurance covered the cost of a new one.

Gemma was a funny little girl by now with her pigtails, freckles and big blue eyes, and one day I found her in front of the bathroom mirror with steel wool in her hand. She was intent on scrubbing off her freckles! When I stopped her, she told me some of the girls at school had been teasing her about them. I explained to her that some people considered freckles to be a sign of beauty; they were sun kisses, and those who had them as children usually had beautiful skin when they were older.

She still wasn't convinced, so I added, 'You'll see Gem, when you're fourteen you will be beautiful.' This seemed to satisfy her, but in the interest of truth, I have to confess that not long before her fourteenth birthday, she asked me, 'When is this wonderful transformation going to take place?' The humorous adult Gemma was emerging with her particular sense of humour.

That story about Gemma reminds me of one involving Philippa when she was about ten. She was washing up and she complained that she couldn't get the saucepan clean. I was busy so I just said, 'Use some elbow grease, darling,' meaning of course, scrub harder. When I came out of the laundry, she was on her knees looking under the sink, and when I asked what she was looking for, you've guessed it, she replied, 'The elbow grease!' I've often said everyone should write down the humorous things their children say, as one forgets over the years.

While I think of it, I may as well record for posterity the story of, not David and Goliath, but David and Diabolo! Frank and I were going into Parkes to have dinner with friends, and Michael and Mary-Ann were the babysitters. As we were passing the post office in Alectown, Mr. McLean ran out and flagged us down, telling us, 'You have to go back, the horse has bitten the little fellow.' Alarmed, we drove quickly home and were met by Gemma at the gate who dodged the question, 'Where did Diabolo bite David?' with the reply, 'He'll tell you!'

We found David sitting on the veranda, a bit tear-stained, with blood trickling down his leg, and he told us it was Coppertop who had bitten him, not Diabolo. This was a white lie to protect his horse, Diabolo, but Mike told us that Davy was feeding the horse some hay and he was a bit slow, and the horse turned his head and nipped him ON THE PENIS! I ran to the phone and rang our doctor, John Waddell, and when I told him what had happened, he said, 'That is the third one this week, only one was a cow!

John told us to sit him in a bath with some ice in it, that it might sting a bit when he tried to do a wee, and that it would probably drop off in about a week! Of course he meant the tip of it, but I didn't impart that piece of information to Davy. Michael said, 'You go off to your dinner, Mum, he'll be better with me anyway. I'll put him in the bath.' So with his assurance he would ring us if anything went wrong, we proceeded to Parkes with a tale to tell at the dinner table.

Twenty years later, at David's wedding reception, there was a telegram from Diabolo, wishing him a happy wedding night! And you can guess who was responsible for that!

CHAPTER 16

CUPID STRIKES AND WE BECOME GRANDPARENTS

On her return to Sydney, Mary-Ann got a job as a receptionist with the Daihatsu Company in Alexandria. She lived in a bed-sit in Cook Street, Randwick, and walked to work each day past the racecourse. Her visits to Professor Davis took place at his rooms in Prince of Wales Hospital, also at Randwick, so as she had to walk everywhere she secured accommodation in the area. How I wished that our hard work at Fana could have resulted in our being able to buy this brave, chronically ill girl a car, so that in wet weather at least, she could have driven to work and to all her appointments.

It was while Mary-Ann was living in Cook Street, Randwick, that she prevailed on us to let Gemma live with her and go to school at the Brigidine Convent there. This worked very well, as Gemma loved being there and Mary-Ann got to practice her motherly skills on her much younger sister, and Gem no longer had to battle with the dust on the bus.

Mary-Ann eventually bought herself a pushbike and used it to ride to work, but in all the ten years before she married, and had a car, I never once heard her complain about having no wheels. She knew the struggle we were having with droughts, high interest rates and four children still to educate, and she tried at times to assist us financially, not ask for help from us. She did this by having Michael and Philippa with her at Balmoral House in Parkes, and then later by urging us to send Gemma down to her so she could go to Brigidine College, and avoid the allergies which were plaguing her at home on the dusty bus run. The only money we had to pay was to the College for Gemma's education and her clothes; Mary-Ann somehow managed the rent and food, as she did in Parkes.

For a girl who was far from well, Mary-Ann crammed a lot into her life. She renewed contact with my cousin, Claire Garty, and her husband, Denis, and my Aunty Glad and her daughter Judy; and rang any Parkes people who were living in Sydney to invite them to a picnic in Centennial Park. She also invited the staff from the Daihatsu office where she worked, and arranged for her cousin, Pam Carpenter, who was proficient in the Japanese language, to come as well so she could act as interpreter. This happened a couple of years running and I think gave a lot of people pleasure.

When Marguerite had started school and I was about forty-six, I took a job for the first time in my life. The rural recession of the seventies was biting deeper, people were being retrenched, and Australia's unemployment level was close to 10 per cent. Add to this, interest rates of 17 per cent, and poor commodity prices, and we were battling to make ends meet. We had to destroy sheep as they were only bringing in $15 a head, and it didn't pay to cart them to the saleyards at Forbes. The worst thing a farmer has to do is to destroy stock, or see them starve. I thought by going to work, I could at least earn enough to buy groceries each week.

It was a menial job, working for Home Care, and after I put Marguerite and Davy on the bus each morning, I drove to Peak Hill, a distance of 30 kilometres, to care for an elderly couple who both had cancer. My first task was to prepare their breakfast of half a grapefruit each, porridge, and toast and marmalade. I then did the washing, vacuumed and dusted the house, and then cooked their midday dinner. After washing up, I would do the ironing, get the clothes off the line, and then make it home in time for the bus. My hours were from 8.30am until 3.30pm, and I was paid $3.00 an hour. It wasn't a princely sum, but it helped, and Fred and Marie were lovely people.

After a year with this service, I was approached by Mrs. Enid Pratt, who had begun the service years before originally to help new mothers after having a baby or a Caesarean operation, to train for

153

Family Support. So my job became less physical, and was more in the line of counselling, advocacy and advising with ongoing training.

When Libby and Philippa both had their first babies in 1981, I decided I needed to be free to give them a hand occasionally, so I gave it up, but a few years later, when Family Support advertised for workers, I said nothing to the family and surprised them when, after an interview, I became part of the team of four workers and a coordinator, of the newly formed Family Support Service of NSW. The pay was much better, and I did a Welfare Course at TAFE and had to attend many workshops during the ten years I was with the service. The money I earned was handy when old household items like a vacuum cleaner, washing machine or TV set needed to be replaced, and besides, the work was challenging and rewarding.

This was when I became known as Mardie, as there were four of us, and three of us were named Margaret, so I said airily, 'Oh well, my grandchildren call me Mardie, so I might as well be called that,' so Mardie I am to this day to a lot of people. I remained in the job until my 70th year when the driving became too much for me as I was in the car every day, and feared I might doze off coming home, so I retired. After I retired, I wondered how I ever had time to go to work each day, because if the Devil didn't find work for idle hands, farming husbands certainly did.

Michael, during these years had finished his training and was now teaching in Cobar, and loving being a teacher. He played Rugby and was in the cricket team, and I remember him being very distressed when a carload of fellow cricketers returning from a match against Nyngan had an accident, and a couple were killed.

Mike was 6'4' tall and loved his football, but towards the end of his time in Cobar, he suffered an injury to his back which had long-reaching affects on his involvement in all the sports he loved, which included tennis, squash, football, and long distance bike riding. He still played cricket with his former Teachers' College, Oak Hill, but down the track he had a fall while running and slid along injuring his forearm and this necessitated an operation which wasn't entirely successful, so the only sport he enjoys today is swimming, and the inter-family cricket match each January in Sydney.

During the year and after being 'sashed' as Miss Parkes Show Girl, Mary-Ann flew to Dubbo for the regional judging where the winner would be in the Sydney Showgirl Competition, along with all the other regional winners. The entire Parkes Committee drove to Dubbo where the announcement was to be made at a Dinner at the Civic Centre that night.

Mezzie was at Gwen's dressing for the dinner when we arrived, having flown from Sydney, and I noticed band-aids all over her legs. When I asked what had happened, she said her legs were covered in sores, and she hadn't felt well all day during the judging.

Nevertheless, we all went to the dinner during which a committee member kindly went out and bought some Panadol for Mezzie, and then she and her partner had to dance with the other contestants. The only way I can describe it is to say she shuffled, not danced, and then they all had to walk up to the stage, and once again our girl just shuffled up beside her partner and had to stand on the stage for speeches and the presentation of the award, which went to the local Dubbo girl.

We left as soon as we could, and Frank carried Mary-Ann over his shoulder to the car and she lay in the back for the trip home. The next morning we took her to the doctor in Parkes and she was put in hospital where they ran numerous tests, the result being she was taken to Prince of Wales Hospital by ambulance the next morning where she remained for at least a week. It was all about her liver of course. I smile when I think of the conversation we had when I was helping her pack for hospital. I noticed she was putting the mother of pearl rosary beads the nuns had given her in her bag, and I said 'Oh Mez, do you think you should take those, they might get lost,' and her reply was, 'Yes Mum, I think I'm going to have a short life and a merry one, so I intend to use all my good things!'

About this time, Mary-Ann's voice became very husky, and when she answered the phone at work, which was part of her job as receptionist, people whom she knew would remark on her 'sexy' voice. In the end it became a bit of an embarrassment to her, so she would reply, 'Oh, my voice is always like this now.'

There was to be a healing ceremony in Forbes in the Anglican Church, and coincidentally, Mary-Ann was flying home for the weekend, so I put it to her that we might go over as the minister coming to conduct the service was well-known and respected in the field of healing. When you have a loved child with a debilitating chronic illness, you will try anything that might help that child, and I was in

155

that situation. She wasn't really keen and was nauseous when she got off the plane, but she agreed, for my sake I think.

We had a light tea with Jean McLean, a friend of mine, and Mary-Ann, Jean and I drove over to Forbes. We were kneeling together, and when the local minister introduced the visiting one, he said, 'Father so and so has had a very busy tour, and will be here tomorrow night as well, so I urge you only to come up for healing tonight if you are unable to come another night.' This was a bit off-putting, so I wasn't sure Mezzie would go up, but when the time came, she rose and walked up to the altar rails, followed by Jean and me.

The celebrant came along and laid his hands on our heads in turn, praying for our healing as he did so, having first asked us what our problem was. Mary-Ann told him she had a damaged liver, Jean said she had arthritis and I asked for healing for my touchy back. On the way home, Mez said airily, 'I don't expect much Mum, but it will be a miracle enough for me if my voice comes right!' (This had been a worry to her for over a year.) That night at home, she vomited and in the night I heard her moaning, and when I checked on her she was asleep, but holding her liver, which you could see was enlarged.

Come Sunday morning she wasn't well enough to go to Mass, and we put her on the plane that night carrying a vomit bowl. She usually made quick calls every day, but we didn't hear from her until Friday night and her voice was jubilant. 'Hi Mum, I didn't go to work Monday, but I did every other day, and guess what? My voice has come good and I sang all the way to work!' So Mezzie thought she had her miracle, and she did really, but it was a small one compared to what we were asking.

Frank's brother, Pat, who was four years younger, had developed diabetes when he was twenty-eight, and this was an ongoing trial to him. His doctor said to him, 'I think I'll send you down to Dr. Shannon, he practices in Orange.' Pat's reply was typical of the Dwyer/ Donnelly men, 'I don't want any bugger practicing on me.'

Pat had episodes when they were working together, when Frank would bring him in for a cup of tea and something to eat to stave off a hyper attack, and of course he was hospitalized at times. Frank tried to make life easier for him, and once, during a dry time, he suggested to Pat that he might take the dogs and tie them up at one end of the lane, take a newspaper to read, and let the sheep eat out the lane. Pat went off but was back after an hour. This inaction didn't suit his active temperament at all, whereas Frank would have been quite comfortable with doing it, knowing it to be a useful exercise.

By this time Pat had a family of his own, and boys to help him, so the partnership was dissolved by mutual consent, and the property divided equally, also the sheep and machinery. There was a feeling of freedom in no longer being in a partnership, and I learned from it why my father never really liked partnerships, especially within a family.

Frank was fairly healthy, and for forty-five years he bagged the outside toilet straight after breakfast for the main job of the day! With so many children to get off to school, it was fortunate we had built a shower and another toilet on the veranda. However, this regularity came to a sudden stop, and at first it was only puzzling, until really severe pain set in. I won't give a blow-by-blow description, but we had many trips to doctors, then a specialist who diagnosed diverticulitis, and each time there was an attack, prescribed Bactrim tablets which caused the inflammation to subside. His condition caused extreme pain, especially when he was prescribed Argarol, which is a laxative, but the abscess wouldn't let anything past it, so it was pain, pain and more pain.

Finally, after a year of this distress, Dr. Garry Scarf from Cowra told Frank he would operate, as each time an abscess formed, there was a real danger of it rupturing the bowel, and he added, 'Then you would be in real trouble.' Frank had the operation in Cowra Hospital, and Dr. Scarf removed twelve inches of his bowel, and after recovering, he had no further trouble. In the hospital, the staff asked Frank for his full name and without hesitation, he told them, 'Francis William Michael Patrick Patterson Donnelly Dwyer.' They accepted that, but asked him again the next day. He repeated it verbatim and added, 'I was born the same day as the Queen, and she was given half a dozen names, so my mother wasn't going to be outdone!' He also told them, and this WAS true, that the bells rang in London the day he was born!

While Frank was in Cowra Hospital, one of our heifers began to calve. Michael was the midwife, and after a given time, sought the help of a more experienced man, our neighbour, Jack Wild. They delivered the calf, and to their surprise, there was a second one. Both calves were huge for twins, and shortly after giving birth to them, the cow died. They were both heifers so we named them Ada and Elsie, and then we had to rear them by hand, and I think we bottle fed them.

Marguerite was happy at home, playing with her dolls and bears and her imaginary friends, Sally, Bonita and Fred Crowley. She followed me wherever I went at Fana, and one day when I was taking grain in a big bucket to a sow with a litter, she stopped me and said, 'Wait for Fred.' I waited patiently for imaginary Fred to catch up, and in the car, she would become agitated and ask me to wait as 'Fred wasn't in yet' so I'd wait that extra second for him to climb aboard. Her 'imaginatory friends,' as she called them, were very real to her until she started school, and then they disappeared, and real friends took their place. Margie says to this day that she could actually see them, one had blonde hair and one black, and she was the 'naughty' one.

After she started school, aged five, Margie would line up all her dolls and bears, and the ones she had inherited from her older sisters, in a semi-circle and she would sit at a table in front of her class. She was Miss O'Neill, and I would hear her admonishing her class of Big Ted, Little Ted, Andy Pandy, etc., with a touch of severity in her tone. Then she would watch TV and cry over Lassie the dog when he was in trouble. Her feelings were very transparent, as the following story shows.

She was watching Young Talent Time, hosted by Johnny Young, whom she absolutely adored, and someone congratulated him on the arrival of a baby girl. She swung around to me with a woeful face, and huge eyes, and cried out, 'Mummy, I'm jealous!' I wondered what I would have done without my little Margie-Moo. Her bedroom was a long way from our living areal, and a bit scary for a little girl, so sometimes I allowed her to go to sleep in front of the TV on a bean bag, and then someone would carry her up to her bed. Grandma Dwyer would have defended this action of ours by saying, 'Well she's not in an orphanage, is she?'

She was only just five, having been born in December, when she had to catch the bus to school, and she often went to sleep coming home as the bus driver took a roundabout route. David was eleven and had jobs to do after school as well as his homework. He showed early his love of farming, and became indispensible to Frank. Both young people made life-long friends at school, David's being Stephen Cusack, and Margie's Fiona Donnelly, or Foof, as she became known to us all.

There was a bit of the larrikin in Stephen and David, and one incident shows this streak in them. At Holy Family, they were fortunate in sixth class, to have as their teacher a lovely man, Mr. Keith Cheney.

During the lunch hour one day, they put a whoopee cushion on his chair and when back in class, waited in gleeful anticipation for the moment when he sat down and activated it. To their horror, it wasn't Mr. Cheney who entered the classroom after lunch, but Sister Brigid, the former having gone home not feeling well. Every time Sister Brigid walked past the chair, the two boys slunk down in their seats, and started to breathe again when she didn't sit down. What happened when she did, I leave to your imagination!

Fiona and Marguerite actually met at pre-school when they were both three, and were in the same class right through to the Higher School Certificate, and when each girl married, the other was a bridesmaid. David also had Stephen in his bridal party as a groomsman, and though they don't live close enough for regular contact, when they do meet it is like it always was between them. Their youthful enthusiasm for pranks disappeared at the appropriate time, and Mother Bertram, who told me once about the two boys, 'Oh Mrs. Dwyer, I don't know what I'm going to do with them!' would not believe the responsible and high-achieving men they became . . . no more whoopee cushions!

CHAPTER 17

SONS AND DAUGHTERS AND PARENTS

We had our first twenty-first birthday about this time, as Mary-Ann celebrated hers in Easter 1974 with a party at Fana for a large crowd of family and friends. We provided hot and cold dishes, the Dwyer girls from Dubbo helping out with salads, and Miss McLeod, who was Father John Kelly's housekeeper and a chef of a high standard, cooking some of the hot dishes. Frank presented our first-born with the key on the lawn and Dick and Maree brought my Dad over for it, but sadly, he died in August that year from a cerebral haemorrhage.

He was nearly eighty-five, having lived six years after he had an accident in his car following a stroke. Once again, Frank showed his devotion to my father by sitting with him that last night in Wontana Nursing Home in Orange and giving him sips of water until morning, when we all joined him for Dad's last moments. It is such a feeling of loss when one is told that a parent 'is gone.'

June said to me once, 'Dad died for me when he had the stroke', but I couldn't agree with her as we had many happy times with Dad after his partial recovery, and even once at Fana. He came when Marguerite was very young, and I would put her in her stroller near Dad's chair on the sunny back veranda. After a while her stroller would roll away a bit, and Dad would hook his walking stick around it and bring it back, saying something like 'Come back, my little pet.' He was always such a busy man at Mt. Pleasant, but after his hospitalisation, we visited him in Wellington where he was in Allanville Private Hospital, took him to the park where he used a walker, and thoroughly enjoyed his company. As I've said before, I loved and admired him so much.

About this time, I read in a *Land* newspaper an article about the-then fledgling Farm Holidays scheme. I was immediately interested as I had been trying to think of some way to make extra money. I made enquiries and then had a brochure printed with a cover with Philippa on Coppertop's back, and inside advertising Fana as a holiday place for teenagers.

My first intake was a group of twelve young people from a Catholic Youth Organisation from Sydney, ages ranging from seventeen to twenty-four. We hired a car from Bert Leary in Peak Hill, an old Holden, but in good running order, and met them at the station in two vehicles. It was before seat belts were introduced, so we used the 'back—back' (as the Dwyer kids called it) in our station wagon and we had no trouble fitting them in for our various excursions.

We had cleaned the cottage thoroughly and done some painting, and that provided accommodation for the seven boys, while the five girls slept in the house. They were all good kids and took turns riding the three horses, joined in farm work when it was suitable, and fronted at the table five or six times a day for meals or scones, jam, and cream. One girl, whose name was actually Marguerite, was twenty-four and had a license so that was helpful too and freed Frank for his farm work.

One night the girls, and my own girls, borrowed some old sheets from me and some torches, and walked around the cottage in the night with the torches held under their chins, in an endeavour to scare the boys, pretending to be sepulchral beings. They set up a high wail and did a lot of moaning. I don't know if the boys were really scared, but the girls had a lot of fun doing it.

One excursion we took was to Burrendong Dam, near Wellington, where they water-skied and picnicked, and for that we hired a small bus. They found plenty to do at Fana, and as for me, if I could have hired a cook for the week it would have been easier, as their healthy appetites as well as that of my own six who were at home for the holidays, kept me busy in the kitchen.

The day before they left to go back, some of them slipped into Parkes, and when they returned, they presented me with a large bouquet of flowers, saying as they did so, 'We noticed you didn't have a garden, so thought you might appreciate these!' I was touched, and stunned as well, as I thought I did have a garden of sorts, but it was a nice gesture and I appreciated it. The garden came later when I knocked off work and had time for such things.

My Farm Holidays venture expanded into families in the cottage, and guests in the house as well. One time we had so many guests in the house that we needed the children's' bedrooms, so we put a huge tarpaulin around the front veranda and that is where the Dwyer kids slept. Both Michael and Philippa were at Teacher's College, and they each said when they arrived for the holidays, 'Mum, I need a room with a desk!' They had to be satisfied with a desk each in our bedroom, which luckily was quite large.

There were two families from England staying once, one in the cottage and one in the house. They were having a lesson on mounting and dismounting from the horses, and Frank introduced them at the yards. It was amazing when Frank introduced them and they discovered that they lived in the same street in Liverpool, in England, and they met at Fana!

Marguerite was a little trick, for when the guests arrived, we would go out to the car to welcome them, and she would be peering anxiously into the car to see if there was a little girl her age, and you know, there always was. Then when she set eyes on the other child each day, she would disappear for a while, and reappear dressed in exactly similar clothes herself. I have photos of two little girls, aged about four, in sleeveless vests, fluffy hats, jumpers and pants, and I remember one time she came to me with big sad eyes because the particular friend was in a blue cotton dress with a halter neck, and she couldn't find anything remotely like it. I must have been mad, as I was no sewer, but I cut out a dress from some blue cotton material I found, and in a matter of ten minutes there were 'two little girls in blue', both with halter necks!

I received a booking from a Lionel Long and his two children, and we joked about it and thought it couldn't possibly be 'the' Lionel Long who was a well-known folk singer. I prepared the cottage and went to work in Peak Hill, returned about 4.00pm to find the children excited as Mr. Long had arrived and he 'carried a great big guitar into the cottage', they told me. We decided to give him his privacy and the chance to get away from performing, so didn't mention his guitar to him.

One day, Amberly, his little daughter asked us, 'Why don't you ask Daddy to play for you? He plays for us every night.' So then we invited them over, and we had a musical treat every night. Mary-Ann was home and with Mez around, there was always plenty of laughter, and I think Lionel enjoyed our young, unsophisticated family. He must have, because he came again without the children, went with the men occasionally, and set up his easel and painted, and he told me he enjoyed the peace and quiet of the cottage, and the open fire. He even came to the Christmas Tree night at the Alectown pool, and entertained the locals by singing with his guitar.

We had people from all walks of life, from bus drivers to Bank Managers, and they always wrote in the guest book in the cottage their thoughts about their Farm Holiday. We had a Major and Mrs. Porteus and their daughter, son-in-law and grandchildren, and Mrs. Porteus told me their son, Julian, was studying for the priesthood. Years later he became a bishop and now he is in charge of the Cathedral Parish in Sydney and is attached to St. Mary's Cathedral, and I read about him from time to time.

Another lovely couple was Mr. and Mrs. Bilby. Mr. Bilby was high up in the education field, and worked with the Director of Education on the Wyndham Scheme when it was introduced about the time Mary-Ann started at Rose Bay. Enid was interested in fossicking for gold, so we tried our luck in the creek at Alectown, and she actually took back a few little pieces in a small bottle. I also took her somewhere near Johnny Morrison's place where there were old shafts, and she had a little hammer and smashed open white quartz. No luck there though. When she left she wrote in the book, and I thought it was rather lovely, 'Don't seek gold anywhere else, Margaret, you have all you need right here.'

When Professor Davis recalled Mary-Ann to Sydney so he could keep an eye on her, and Michael left to begin his teaching career, Philippa was left in the lurch a bit as regards accommodation, as she was in fifth form at the local high school, and had been sharing Balmoral House with them. We obtained board for her, firstly with Miss Noble, and later with Letty Howell. In both houses she received only kindness, and on completing her exams, started at Mitchell College in Bathurst, now called Charles Sturt University.

When aged sixteen, she made her debut at the Catholic Ball in Parkes and was partnered by Peter O'Donnell, one of the five sons of Jim and Pat O'Donnell. They became good friends, and when she started at Mitchell College, he 'burnt the rubber', as the kids say, most weekends and visited her. Frank was concerned, and told Philippa that 'study and romance don't mix', and my motherly advice was that, although we liked Peter, she should give herself a chance to meet other boys at College and not tie herself down too young. But Peter courted her assiduously and he became the only one for her.

The result was she proved her father to be wrong by obtaining her Diploma of Education, and also announcing her engagement to Peter. Somewhere in between all this, we had a twenty-first birthday party for her at Fana, and once again my sisters-in law helped me with the catering, though this time we stuck to cold food only for such a large gathering.

Their wedding was our first in the family, and it was truly beautiful. As Philippa had been School Captain at Our Lady of Mercy, and then boarded with the nuns until the boarding school closed, the nuns sang at the Nuptial Mass and the singing was ethereal. She had five bridesmaids, her three sisters, Mary-Ann, Libby and Gemma, her friend from childhood, Narelle Wild, and a friend from Mitchell College, Margaret Grange, who came from Gundagai where 'the dog sits on the tucker box.'

Marguerite and Ann-Marie O'Donnell, aged eight and five, were flower girls, and Peter's attendants were two of his brothers, Paul and Michael, our Michael, our nephew, Ross Freeth, and Peter's friend, David Carey. Phips was a beautiful young bride in white, carrying red rosebuds, the girls were dressed in five shades of blue, from pale blue through to navy blue, and the little girls wore long red dresses with frills.

David Dwyer and Bernard O'Donnell, who were fourteen and fifteen years old, were ushers and wore red jackets with dark pants. The bridegroom and his groomsmen chose navy suits, so it was all colour coordinated very well. I sang 'The Song of Ruth' at the Signing of the Register, and our dear friend, Father John Kelly, said the Mass and performed the wedding ceremony. It was, I thought, a marriage made in Heaven.

Philippa was married in September and had to go back to Mitchell College until she graduated in May, and Frank and I attended the Graduation with Peter. After this, the young couple moved into their first home in Parkes and Philippa began a teaching career which has spanned thirty-five years, with a break now and then to give birth to five fine boys. We have always admired her dedication to teaching, which she loves even more today than she did then. She taught for three years before her first son, Damien Grafton, was born on 23rd March 1981, and resumed teaching as soon as he was weaned. Simon Francis followed three years later in 1984, then Nikolas Peter in 1986, Benson Paul in 1988, and finally James Thomas in 1990.

Libby had done the School Certificate at Our Lady of Mercy School, and after doing voluntary work with Mrs. Ros Bruncher in the Occupational Therapy Room at the local hospital, was employed as a Teacher's Aide at St. Joseph's Infant School where Mrs. June Baker was Principal. Libby enjoyed this involvement with the teaching staff and June Baker still speaks of her ability as a competent Teacher's Aide. She remained there until her marriage in November 1980, to Arnold Kealley. In 1981, her first child, Katrina Maree was born, followed 16 months later by another daughter, Anita Louise.

Mary-Ann met Mark Boan in Sydney, and was instantly attracted to him, so much so that she went home and told her flatmate, Pam Andrews, that she had met the man she hoped to marry! This, in spite of the fact that he had ended a very early marriage and was divorced, and also he was Jewish! Well, Mark wasn't very Jewish as he never made his Bar mitzvah, but his father was Jewish. In true Mary-Ann style, she wrote all of this to her very Catholic aunts in Dubbo, adding that she hoped it could be worked out.

Mary-Ann was hospitalised again about this time, and before proceeding with her relationship with Mark, insisted that he have a talk with Professor Davis, who had treated Mary-Ann since the hepatitis struck when she was seventeen, and she was now twenty-seven. Mark asked Prof, as Mezzie called him, 'Life expectancy, Professor?' Alan Davis was quite frank, but he said, 'She may make forty-five,' and Mark, being the optimistic man he was, thought, 'Fifteen years, that's not too bad', so they continued bravely with their plans to marry.

In due course, Mark asked Frank for Mary-Ann's hand in marriage, and there was great rejoicing in many homes, all around Parkes, Dubbo, and Mt. Pleasant and district. The marriage could not be fast-tracked as they had to go through the Tribunal, an office which deals with the re-marriage of divorced people within the Church, and Mark was the one who was interviewed and had to furnish the details of his earlier marriage. The information and application form for the marriage was sent to Rome and I worried for them, remembering how many *years* Princess Caroline of Monaco had to wait for the dispensation of her first marriage. In fact, the dispensation only arrived a few weeks before the wedding date, and Mary-Ann joked that they might have to get married in Cooke Park!

In the meantime, Gemma, at twenty, had caught the eye of one of her bosses, Brian Churchill, in the insurance firm in which she worked, and I'll bet he never had a chance! So he came up and did the right thing and approached Frank. The night all this happened, there was a huge crowd sleeping at Fana, and Gemma opted for sleeping on a mattress with the other young ones on the lounge floor. I went in to say goodnight, and whispered to Gem, 'We really like Brian, Gem.' She cocked one sleepy eye up at me, and said, 'Oh Church! Yes, he'll do!' and thirty years later, it looks as if he has 'done' very well.

So we had two engagements, and then the girls got together and decided to have a double wedding. What excitement there was, and one of the reasons put forward by both girls was typical of them: 'It will save Dad the cost of two weddings!' Their frugality, though I think it was more their consciousness of tradition within the family, prompted them to decide on Mary-Ann wearing my 1952 gown of cream satin, and on Gemma asking Mollie and Kath for permission to wear the other ivory satin gown, worn first by Molly, in 1951, and then by Kath in 1953. This permission was readily given, but both girls were sworn to secrecy, as we wanted the full impact of the bridal party to be seen and felt.

And seen and felt it was, when on March 6th 1981, Mary-Ann, on her father's arm, preceded by eleven-year-old Marguerite, and her bridesmaid, Pam Andrews, then Gemma's bridesmaid, Morna McColl, and finally Gemma, partnered by eighteen-year-old David, walked up the long aisle of the beautiful Church in Parkes, their long satin trains spread out behind them to the triumphant sound of Sister Michael on the organ playing the Wedding March and Ray Payne playing the trumpet!

As it registered with each row of guests, especially family members on both sides, that these heirloom gowns were actually those worn by three of us in the early fifties, nostalgia was rife, and there were a few tears! It was especially felt by my sisters, Gwen and June, who had such a soft spot for this much-loved niece who had such a fragile grip on life, and for 'Saucers', which was what Stella called Gemma as a child, and I'm sure Molly, Kath and their husbands were transported back a few years too to their own wedding days.

As Michael was in the bridal party, David was chosen to bring one bride up to the altar. Unselfishly, and predictably, Mary-Ann announced, 'Dad can bring Gem up, and I'll walk with David,' but Gemma said, 'No, you're the eldest, you should go with Dad,' so it was decided that, when David and Gemma arrived at the altar, David should hand her to her Dad, and he was to place her hand in Brian's. Both Philippa and Libby were heavily pregnant, so being fresh out of eligible sisters, the girls chose their best friends and flatmate as attendants, and Pam and Morna wore lovely maroon gowns made by my good friend, Kitty Harper, of Parkes. Their dream to have Marguerite as a flower-girl when she was first born, materialised that day and she was dressed in cream to match the two brides, but we classed her in more dignified terms, seeing she was eleven, and called her a junior bridesmaid.

Mary-Ann had always dreamed of an overseas trip, so that is where they went for their honeymoon, beginning in England and after the British Isles, continuing to Europe, and she enjoyed every moment of it. If she was sometimes too tired to continue on into the night, she was happy for 'her boy' to carry on with the others, and they were in Assissi when Peter rang to tell them that Damien Grafton O'Donnell had arrived safely. A fortnight later, another 'phone call informed them of the safe arrival of Katrina Maree Kealley, Libby's daughter, so they had two babies to meet on their return.

They moved into a nice unit at Waverley and Mary-Ann resumed the job she had at Prince of Wales Hospital, working down in the basement in the archives. She was handy there for her fortnightly appointments with Professor Davis, and I think he recommended her for the position. One day, after her visit, she said to him, 'You know Prof, my mother prays for you every day.' Professor Davis was startled. 'That's very nice of her, Mary-Ann,' he said. 'Oh yes,' Mez said breezily, 'because she knows that when you go, I go!' Mary-Ann said he laughed all the way down the corridor. What a joy that girl was to so many people.

When Philippa's son, Damien, and Libby's daughter, Katrina, were four-months-old, Mary-Ann and Mark came to Fana for a weekend visit. They arrived, as always, at midnight, as they travelled from Sydney after work, and it is a five or six hour trip to Parkes. Over a cup of tea, Mezzie-Ann entertained her father, as she always did, with stories of the characters at work, the one she called 'Uncle', what this one said and what that one did, and the house literally rang with her laughter from the minute she arrived. In bed by about 1.00am, she was always up early to have breakfast, then she would cook Mark an egg when he got up, and after her shower, she would carry the clothes they had worn the day before out to the laundry, and busy herself washing 'my boy's' clothes, as she would say to me.

The rest of the family from Parkes—Peter, Philippa and Damien, and Libby, Arnold and Katrina—would visit, and Mezzie had a lovely time getting to know her niece and nephew. We took photos and there is one of her with the two babies in her arms, and it is the only one we have of her with any of her nieces or nephews so it is very precious, if not quite as clear as we would like. This was in August 1981, and after a lovely weekend and meeting their first niece and nephew, Mary-Ann and Mark returned to Sydney and their work.

CHAPTER 18

WE SAY GOODBYE TO MARY-ANN

In early October, we attended the wedding of Molly Sheridan's daughter, Valerie, to Neil Hindmarsh, at Coolah. Mary-Ann and Mark were there, but she was most unwell at the wedding reception which was held at their home, and showed me how swollen her stomach was, saying, 'I look seven months pregnant, don't I?' They returned to Sydney in Mark's small MG sports car, and they had an extra passenger so it was a miserable trip for her as she was far from well.

However, she returned to work when she felt a bit better, and we hoped to hear of an improvement within a few days, but knowing how ill she'd been at the wedding, we thought she might be hospitalised. Someone said once: 'when Mez is in hospital, just go and see her and you'll find out all the news and what everyone in the family is doing.'

She always kept busy in hospital too, making lovely macramé hangers of knotted white rope, and she would present us with one when we went to see her. You are meant to hang potted plants in them and I've always had a couple around. There was always fun and laughter around her bed, and she was a favourite in Parkes Ward on the fourth floor at Prince of Wales Hospital at Randwick.

This time was different. Mary-Ann visited Professor Davis and he sent her straight up to Parkes Ward, telling her to get Mark to collect her clothes and bring them to the hospital after work. The first shock came when we had a phone call from Mark, saying Mary-Ann wasn't well at all, and Professor Davis thought we should come down. This was a departure from the usual procedure of her hospitalisation, so we were a bit alarmed; but oh no, God had always been so good to me and this could not be happening to my beloved daughter. If we went down and saw her, and prayed hard, she would be OK again. Optimism was the creed I lived by, and it didn't desert me now.

We rang Professor Davis, who told us she was very ill indeed, so we packed hurriedly and left with David and Marguerite. Philippa and baby Damien left from Parkes, Peter followed next morning, and Michael caught the first plane he could from Mildura, which was the next day, Saturday. We gave Libby the opportunity to come, and I'm sure Arnold would have driven her, but because of her anxiety phobia, she was unable to face the ordeal.

Gemma's boss gave her the day off and she was able to sit with Mezzie until we arrived, and to be with Mark. Though quite ill, her face lit up when we walked in, and she said, 'Oh Mum, Dad, it's lovely to see you.' Then as I kissed her, 'I'm quite unwell this time, Mum.' And she added, 'Mark got really upset when I couldn't sign my name.'

Gemma and Mark had been ministering to her all day, attending to her every need, and they told us she had been a bit disorientated in the morning, that Roma Condon and her daughter Cathy had visited and she knew Roma, but not Cathy, and this disturbed me as Cathy was a close friend of hers from earlier days. At this point they decided 'family only.'

Frank and I stayed with her all night and she was very restless, and would sit up and ask, 'May I please go to sleep now, Mummy?' or 'May I please have a sleep in tomorrow, Daddy?' We lay her back gently and told her of course she could, but it wouldn't be long before she would repeat the procedure again. About 2.00am, she started a high loud moaning, all on the one note, and Sister came in and asked us to leave, as they wanted to put a catheter in. We waited about an hour, as every time we tried to return, we heard the same high wailing. Finally, all was quiet so we tentatively made our way back to her room with our hearts in our mouths, only to hear her talking quite lucidly to the doctor, and when we crept in, Mary-Ann was beaming, and exclaimed, 'Oh Mum, Dad, isn't it wonderful to feel well again!'

The next morning she was again coherent, and able to speak to us all. Philippa and Peter had arrived, and took turns with Gemma and Mark to attend to Mezzie, with pans and sponging her, and the love flowing from them to her, and her calm acceptance of it was beautiful to see. They were so gentle with her, and Gemma was having her little jokes, and Mezzie would smile and say 'Oh Gem Gem, you're so funny, you always make me laugh!' Mary-Ann asked Gemma, 'Am I still lucid?' and Gem said, 'What does lucid mean?' and that amused Mezzie too as Gem wasn't famous at that stage for her language skills.

Eighteen-year-old David felt like a fish out of water, and went in and sat beside her, put his chin on his hands and said 'I dunno Mez, I haven't done a bloody thing,' and his big sister smiled and said 'Well you're here, aren't you, Davy?'

Michael was shocked to see her so ill, and he said 'I want to apologise to you Mez. In all these years, I've never realised the seriousness of your illness.' She said, 'Oh that's all right Mike, it was my attitude to it that stopped you from realising that.' And that was true as she never dwelt on it, and kept a positive attitude all through. Mike told her he was sorry all the same, and she told him, 'No guilt, Mike.'

The next day was Sunday and Father Shallvey, the hospital chaplain, arranged a special Mass in her room, which we all attended. Our dear girl was so pleased, and so peaceful after receiving Communion. Earlier, she had spent a quiet time with Father and received the Sacrament of Reconciliation, or Confession as we used to call it. Father Shallvey came out of her room and said, 'You have a very, very special daughter there, Mrs. Dwyer.' He himself was a beautiful man, and has relatives in Parkes: Graham, Bill and Evelyn Shallvey, and Bill's mother, Doreen, and cousin, Marlene Freeman, to name a few.

Michael kissed his sister goodbye very tenderly and left for the airport, as he was due back at school next morning, as did Peter who also had to go. Peter, like his mother, Pat, and brother, Paul, was very fond of Mary-Ann, and I have an enduring memory of Peter looking down at her and saying very tenderly, before kissing her, 'Goodbye, Mez!' and she replied softly: 'Goodbye, Pete.'

I can only imagine Michael's feelings as he travelled back to Wentworth where he was teaching, knowing he would never again see the beautiful sister who had shared the responsibility with him of being the two eldest of seven. They were more than our children, those two, they were two adults who shored us up, you might say, in our endeavours, the same way a stay props up a strainer post when one is building a fence, and we relied on them. So Michael's relationship to

Mary-Ann was unique, as indeed was that of all her siblings, unique to them, each in a different way. That was the magic of Mary-Ann.

Frank and David left for home the next day, Monday, as Professor Davis had told Frank it may be a couple of weeks before anything happened, and he intended to start David off on the hay baling, and then come back. On Tuesday morning, eleven-year-old Marguerite was dropped at the hospital very early and gave Mary-Ann her breakfast, then cared for her until after lunch. She was very mature for her age, and handled all phone calls, one being from Mez's good friend, Father Paul O'Donnell, who was stationed at Broken Hill, but unfortunately she was asleep so didn't speak to him. However, she was able to speak briefly to Aunty June when she rang from Brisbane, and that was her last phone call.

Philippa, who left seven-month old Damien with her cousin, Cathy Dwyer, with whom she was staying, took over then and continued the loving care until 4.00pm when I arrived, and she went back to feed her baby. Earlier on that last day of her life, Mary-Ann said to Mark, 'I think I'd better see your Mum and Dad today.' So he arranged for Norman and Jocelyn Boan to come in. This was so typical of Mezzie, as she found her mother-in-law abrasive, but if I could have felt any more proud of her, it was this single act that made me even more so. I think it meant a lot to Mark's dad to have the opportunity to say goodbye to this fine girl his son had married.

When I arrived, Mary-Ann said, 'Mum, I was saying to Phips and Gem that, if the worst happens, I would like to be buried in the Lawn Cemetery at Windsor where little Mary Hogan is buried.' This was a bit too direct for me, but I said, 'Yes darling, but Mark and Dad have had a talk, and Mark is quite happy for you to come to Parkes.' Her face lit up all over, and she said, 'Oh, did he really? I wanted to come home all the time, but I thought Mark might want me down here!'

She then said, 'Put your head down and have a good cry, Mum. I'm strong!' I did just that, and she added, 'And you know Mum how I've always loved the earth—I used to eat it when I was a little girl.' Numb though I was, I couldn't believe how she was protecting me, covering the things mothers think about when a child is dying.

When she was in pain, she asked me to pray to Jesus, the Infant King, as someone had loaned her a large picture of the Infant de Prague. It was on her locker, a picture of Jesus as a child, but wearing a crown.

When I did, she would say, 'Thank you Jesus, it's gone now,' meaning the pain, and then, 'Mum, isn't it wonderful the way the Holy Spirit is looking after everything? I even enjoy my meals.' She asked me to brush her hair, but said, 'Not too hard though Mum, it makes it oily.' Then she added, 'You know, Mum, our prayers were answered in different ways. My appearance was always important to me, and despite all the cortisone tablets etc. I still looked all right!'

Mary-Ann told me she was full of peace, that she was glad she had seen Norman and Jocelyn, and I was to tell Libby that she knew why she couldn't come down, and she understood. She told me she had been reading the Jerusalem Bible a young girl in the next room had given her, and for the first time, the bible had made sense to her. She said, 'Matthew just came alive for me.'

Mark came from work, and announced in his positive way (thinking of the two tiring weeks ahead I guess), that he and I would go home and get some rest and come back early in the morning. I was quite submissive and didn't think to question this, so we kissed her and went home. Mary-Ann had given me her bible to keep, so before I put the light out and got into the bed I shared with Marguerite, I opened it at random, and it was the story of Jesus and His disciples being caught in the storm while fishing, and Jesus told Peter to walk on the water to shore, and Peter's faith wasn't strong enough, and he sank. I took this as a sign that if my faith was strong enough, Mary-Ann would recover.

How wrong I was! At 2.30am, the phone rang. It was the Sister in Mezzie's ward, telling us she was very low, so Mark and I raced to Prince of Wales. We found her, as if sleeping, with her head gently to one side and looking very beautiful. We said The Lord's Prayer together, my Jewish son-in-law and I. We both kissed her, and then she quietly and peacefully stopped breathing. My darling, pretty little first-born daughter had gone to Heaven. Mark sobbed and sobbed, but I just felt numb, and I asked myself what was wrong with me when I loved her so much, and I was as cold as a fish.

*　　*　　*

The morning after Mary-Ann's death, it was decided that I should go and find a hairdresser who could do something to my hair as we had the funeral to face on arriving back at Fana. I set out, not knowing

Waverley at all, and not even knowing where I could locate a hairdresser, in fact, not caring much about my hair at all, and feeling very desolate as I walked along. I looked in the mirror as the girl was cutting my hair, and wondered what she must be thinking of this white-headed, haggard old lady of *fifty-two*, who was answering her polite questions in monosyllables and looking like I was.

Peter brought Frank to Sydney and picked up Philippa, baby Damien and me that night, and when we arrived at Fana, I saw that my dear friends, Zilda, Vilma and Helen, and my sister-in-law, Kittie, had been there and cleaned the house, and put flowers in, even a vase of rosebuds beside our bed.

The funeral was arranged for Friday, 23rd October, but Father Paul O'Donnell, who was our first choice as celebrant, was very sick in Broken Hill with a severe gastric attack, and was unable to come. We therefore contacted Mary-Ann's special friend, Father Walsh, who was a Jesuit and a medical doctor as well, and he instantly agreed to fly up and conduct the funeral and Requiem Mass.

This was very beautiful, with Sister Michael at the organ, and the Parkes Choir singing throughout the Mass. Father Walsh spoke of the schoolgirl from the Sacred Heart Convent, Rose Bay, who, with her friend, Dorothy Walsh, who was also Father's niece, used to come over to Lavender Bay where he was Parish Priest, and spend their weekend cooking for him in the absence of his housekeeper. He told of her laughter and joyful nature which 'gladdened an old man's heart', and I knew Mary-Ann would have been so pleased that he celebrated her Mass.

I was quite numb throughout, and also at the graveside, which I realised afterwards, was God once again looking after me as He had always done. I have pictures in my mind even now, thirty years later, of all Mez's siblings and cousins, huddled in small groups at the cemetery, with their arms around each other, forming circles of love and strength for each other. It was a comfort to us to see how much everyone cared.

On returning to Fana, I sat on my bed, while the many friends and family members were being made welcome and comfortable in the rest of the house, and suddenly I smelled the perfume of roses very strongly. I glanced at the small vase of roses, which the girls had placed on my bedside table a few days before, and knew that they were drooping, and no perfume could come from them, and yet the scent was very strong. I visited the bathroom and when I returned to my room, the perfume had absolutely disappeared. I even lifted the vase and sniffed the limp roses, but there was no perfume at all. I may, in my grief, have been overly fanciful, but I simply accepted it as a very small sign that my daughter was happy where she was, and we should go on with our lives as she would want us to do.

CHAPTER 19

LIFE WITHOUT MARY-ANN

When we returned from Sydney after Mary-Ann's death, Libby told us of an event that happened early on the morning of 21ˢᵗ October. Mary-Ann had died at 2.40am in Prince of Wales Hospital, but Libby didn't have a phone, so she didn't know until Pat O'Donnell went to the flat and broke the news to her at 9.00am. Apparently, Arnold got up about 5.00am as usual to get ready for a 6.00am start at work, and Libby was awake too and told him that she had a dream that was really more like a vision, because it was real and she was awake. She said, 'Mary-Ann came and floated above the bed, and was smiling down on us, then she hovered above Katrina's baby basket still smiling, then she disappeared!' When Libby told me this, I said, 'Well Lib, you couldn't come to say goodbye to her, so she came to say goodbye to you.'

Libby was very upset at hearing this, and much later, when she was telling Gemma and Philippa about it, any skepticism we might have been feeling was swept away, when Libby added something she hadn't thought to mention to me: 'And Mezzie had a nightie on with red on it, and there was red at the neck.' Her sisters were amazed as Philippa had put her own nightie on Mary-Ann that morning, and it was white, with little red dots in the pattern, flock I think it was called, and it had a narrow red ribbon tied at the neck and that was what she had on when she died!

We didn't speak of this to anyone at first, but as the years passed, and the girls would be in a group talking with people, and the conversation might get around to events similar to this, they would recount the little story, and there was never any skepticism. Many believed it was entirely possible that her big sister, knowing the crippling panic attacks Libby was subject to which prevented her from coming to say goodbye to her, had somehow reversed the situation.

Before leaving the subject of Mary-Ann's sad death, I need to mention again the wonderful support we received from our families and friends. Our brother-in-law, Bernie Crowley, and my brother Harry, expressed their support in a special way. In the mail we received a sizable cheque from each of them and their wives, 'to help with the funeral', and with hard times on the land we were very touched.

Life went on at Fana, with the rotation of crops, shearing and general sheep work. 1982 brought the good, and the bad, the good being the arrival of Libby's second daughter, Anita Louise, dark-haired and olive-skinned and a mate for sixteen-month old Katrina, and the bad being a continuation of a terrible drought which dried up dams, creeks and water holes. Mark paid us his first visit without Mezzie-Ann, and he spent his days working with Frank, and assisted him with shifting sheep and dredging the creek to bring water to the surface for the sheep to drink. Fairly drastic measures when you think about it, but this drought had been very severe, and water was beginning to be a problem.

Rain did come eventually and we were able to buy a new car, a blue Holden Vacationer, and I was delighted as it was the first automatic car I had ever driven. We had been managing with second-hand cars for years, and repair bills were high, so our new car was a thrill. Mary-Ann had actually said to me those last few days, 'Mum, I'd love to see you and Dad with a decent car', and actually one of the nights when she was in hospital, someone had stolen our little Torana from outside Mark's unit at Waverley, and it was discovered a short time later, with a dint in it. It was not mentioned to Mezzie though, and she just spoke about a new car out of the blue.

November 1983, brought sorrow to the Derrymore folk when Pat died on 30th with all of his family, and most of his extended family, present. Pat had endured living with diabetes ever since he was diagnosed with it when he was only twenty-eight, and he was fifty-three when he died. He handed the reins to Bernard, his youngest son, who had worked with him all his young life.

A couple of months later Peter's father, Jim O'Donnell, died on 28th January, having come through a kidney transplant operation successfully, but was then diagnosed with leukemia. Before his kidney operation, Jim had dialysis treatment a couple of times a week on a kidney machine, and this greatly reduced his quality of life. He was a very fine man who did much for his town, and had served in the war. We felt sad for both Kittie and Pat on the loss of their husbands, and Damien was never to know his paternal grandfather.

I noticed my family were all affected differently by the loss of their eldest sister, who, if we were casting for Louisa M. Alcott's 'Little Women,' would have won the role of Meg, a second mother figure in the March family. Michael felt lonely away from us all at Wentworth and applied for a move a bit closer. He was sent to Condobolin, and was able to come to Fana more often, and I noticed he needed to talk about Mez. Not so Davy, who chose not to talk about her, at least not to me, but I knew how much he missed her, and I know that when he met Joanne Carney, his future wife, he did tell her all about Mary-Ann, and both he and Jo wished that Jo had known her. Gemma, who had lived with her and been so close to her, had a lot of anger, I suspect mainly with God because He had told us 'to ask and you will receive, knock and the door will be opened to you.' We had prayed so hard and so long for her recovery, so Gem's faith took a beating.

I didn't worry too much about this, as God must be used to it, but there was a change in Gemma's plans. She had said when they had the double wedding, 'Don't expect children for four years, Mum' and I thought, 'Well, she is only twenty', but this changed when Mary-Ann died, and she wanted a baby straight away. It didn't happen at once, but Samuel William Churchill arrived in 1984, a very cute little boy, and Lucy Mary-Ann in 1986. If there was ever a doll, it was Lucy.

Philippa had been quietly adding to her family too, and when Lucy arrived, she had three O'Donnell cousins, Damien, Simon and Nikolas. With them and the two Kealleys, Katrina and Anita, grandchildren became very much a part of the scene at Fana, with bunks on the lounge floor becoming commonplace at family gatherings. Gradually, we began to carry on with our lives, and grandchildren certainly helped.

Frank was never one to wear his feelings on his sleeve, so he seemed to go on much as he always had, but he confided to me once, that whilst on the tractor or header, he continually prayed Hail Marys and the Lord's Prayer after losing his daughter. Everyone's spirituality is different, and Philippa's grief was very private too, but she had her baby to care for and had resumed teaching.

Molly, Kath and their husbands, Jack and Neville, stayed a week with us after the funeral, Molly taking over in the kitchen, and one day she said, 'Margaret, we can't go home while you look like this.' It shocked me into looking at my white face in the mirror, so I put on make-up, especially lipstick . . . and they went home the next day!

This was during the period when I had stopped working in order to be a support to our new mothers, especially Libby, so with Frank and Davy away all day and Marguerite at school, I did battle loneliness and missed the daily quick phone calls which always began, 'Hi, it's me!'

One day, I was feeling especially sad, and went into a little grotto where there was a statue of Jesus, which we had inherited after the sale of the church at Alectown. There is a misconception that Catholics worship the statues and pictures of Jesus and Mary in our churches and homes, but nothing could be further from the truth. In the same way as we adorn our walls and side tables with photographs of our loved ones, Catholics, in general, like to have a picture of our heavenly Father, or His mother, Mary, around, to glance at and be reminded of our spiritual journey. Many Catholics use devotion to Mary to 'get on the soft side' of her Son, Jesus, in much the same way as teenagers will approach Mum to get around Dad with some request. Definitely we don't worship her, we ask her to intercede for us.

Anyway, this rather large statue was returned to Frank because Uncle Pat had denoted it to the church. I tried to offload it onto the priest, and then the nuns, in Peak Hill, but they didn't want it, so initially I put it in our bedroom in the corner near my bed. Gradually, it began to provide a very unspiritual service, as I started to hang things on it, as the hands were extended just asking to be utilized. After a few weeks, I was horrified to find my bra hanging from it, so I removed the hands (which were expendable) and it remained there. Marguerite asked me why Jesus had no hands, and with the idea of, 'Here is a chance for some spiritual input', I told her, 'It is because we are His Hands now, He asks us to do His work for Him.'

Eventually, I put it outside under the wisteria, and that is where I was drawn this day when I felt 'under the weather.' I really needed someone to call, but it was a remote possibility indeed. However, I asked for just that in my prayer under the wisteria, and would you believe it? A utility pulled up and a familiar figure started to walk towards the house. It was our good friend, Geoff Jelbart, who occasionally called in on his way to his farm, as he lived in Parkes.

Geoff may have been surprised at the enthusiasm of my greeting that day, but we chatted over a cup of coffee for half an hour and then 'Doctor' Jelbart went on his way, having certainly been used as the Lord's Hands that day! He spoke of Mary-Ann and told me that when his daughter, Vivienne, was in the judging of Miss Show Girl with Mezzie, he hoped that if his daughter didn't win it, Mary-Ann would.

Before leaving the subject of the statue, I will share a small anecdote about Damien O'Donnell. He was just two and was following me around in the garden when he noticed the statue, hands once more attached, in the grotto. His little face lit up with surprise, and he ran over and put his arms around it, and looking up at the face, exclaimed, 'Hello Jesus, I haven't seen you for ages!' (Though he actually said 'f'ages'.) Another gem from a toddler's mouth.

David started playing football with Trundle, which was about an hour-and-a half drive from Fana, and he always borrowed our Torana to go out there for training. We worried about him as he was tired from working all day, then the hard training, and finally the drive home. Our fears were well founded because one night about midnight, he came into our bedroom and told us he had dozed off and rolled the car on its side just before Alectown. Luckily, he was not hurt, and the car wasn't damaged much, but after that he became one of the many lads for whom Christine Harrison provided a bunk after training. She was very generous to the boys, and eventually married Lloyd Nock, one of the players.

The training paid off, as that year Trundle swept everything before them, winning both teams in the Grand Final. Incidentally, David played in both games that day as one of the boys unfortunately broke his leg just minutes into the game, and David had to go on. Rugby Union was to become a passion with Davy and he played for many years in the Boars with Parkes, and even now in his forties, has a run in the Golden Oldies. There was a large picture of him once in the local paper, the *Champion Post*, with the headlines, 'Doggie plays his hundredth First Grade game of Rugby Union,' and unfortunately from my point of view, he has passed this ability and passion on to his son, Lewie, who now plays for the Boars.

In February, 1984, Michael set off for a trip overseas which took him to the United Kingdom and Ireland, much of Europe, Turkey, Egypt and finally North America and Canada, a journey of nine months. Mark also felt the need to travel, and he and Mike met in Jerusalem and spent six weeks together working in a Kibbutz in Israel, then travelled together to the Dardanelles and to Anzac Cove, then on the Nile to the Valley of the Kings and the Valley of the Queens in Egypt.

They separated, and Mark journeyed to Moscow, while Mike pushed on through Europe, stayed for a few days to get his breath with a friend of ours, Evelyn Fritch, in Switzerland, then spent a further few days in Sweden with a friend he'd made in the Kibbutz. After Portugal, he took a ferry to Ireland, bought a bike, and with his tent and swag on his back, rode thirteen hundred kilometres around the green isle. He stayed in County Tipperary with Frank's second cousin, Joan Kehelly, and her husband, Jerry, and met most of the O'Dwyers who were part of Grandfather Dwyer's family.

He went into a pub in Ireland, and asked a local, 'How do I get to Thurles?' The Irishman put down his glass, scratched his head, and said, 'Waal, I wouldn't start from here!' When he was in Northern Ireland, he asked a farmer if he could pitch his tent inside his fence, and the farmer agreed, saying, 'I can do better than that, come up to the house and you can sleep in the caravan.' Mike was very grateful, but even more so next morning when the farmer arrived over with a huge egg which, when Mike cooked it in his jam tin over his primus, turned out to be a double yolker.

It's funny how what goes around, comes around. Twenty years later, I was driving home from work one freezing winter's night, and I had chosen to come the back way, past the Telescope, or the Big Dish as some people call it. Just as I was about to turn in off the black lane, I noticed a small car, a dull light glowing near it, a tiny tent pitched beside the car, and when I pulled up, there were two apologetic young girls there.

I said hello to them, and cut short their apologies with, 'Of course it's all right, but it's too cold here. I've got empty bedrooms over at my place so pack up and come over.'

'Oh no, they were all right', they said, 'but thank you all the same.'

I drove the couple of miles home, and raced in to Frank, told him about the girls, and suggested we load the trailer with logs and firewood, and go over and light a fire for them. This we did, and I took a rug as well, and when we got to the girls, they were cooking something on their primus in a very bad light. Our fire soon fixed that and they had plenty of light, as well as warmth. They offered us a cup of white wine, which Frank declined, not being a wine drinker, but not so Margaret, and I enjoyed a small plastic cup of wine with them.

The girls told us that they were studying at a Canberra University and were on their way to the Macquarie Marshes. One was from Amsterdam, and the other South Africa. When we said goodnight to them, I said, 'You can bring the rug back when you come over for breakfast in the morning.' They did just that, and enjoyed a wash and the use of the toilet, before setting off. When they thanked us, I said, 'I've been waiting twenty years to return the hospitality afforded my son when he was travelling', and I told them the story.

In 1988, David and his football mates went to Ulladulla on the South Coast for a holiday. He met some young nurses there, and Joanne Carney was one of them. He was on his way home in Michael's old brown Holden which he had inherited when Mike bought a better car, and Jo and her friends followed as far as Canberra in Jo's car. In Canberra, Jo had an accident in her car, so David drove them back to Ulladulla, and then rang me and asked if he could bring a girl with him to Fana, as he really liked her.

They arrived, and Jo stayed a week. Then a pattern seemed to form as the little red car crossed the mountains fairly often. Sixteen-year-old Marguerite was making her debut in May and Jo arrived a day before to go to the ball. I came home from work about 6.00pm to find the red car in the driveway, and when I asked where Jo was, Frank told me that she and Davy had gone over to Wancurra on the motorbike so Davy could bring the tractor home.

A bit worried, I asked how the motorbike was getting home, and Frank said carelessly, 'Oh, Jo's riding it.' Now I was alarmed, as Jo had only the smallest amount of experience of riding the bike, and it was already dark. I was cooking dinner, and I watched the two lights coming from the kitchen window, not feeling at ease. The bike was turning into the driveway and I heard a scream and the bike had stopped. So I ran out and Jo and the bike were on the ground, and she was in pain. Apparently she was heading for a big gum tree and she pressed the accelerator instead of the brake, so instead of driving into the tree, she threw herself off the bike.

David arrived five minutes later to find we had covered Jo with a blanket and were on the phone with the hospital. The boys made a splint with a broom handle and Mike drove while David supported Jo in the back. The result was that she certainly didn't make it to the ball, as she was still in hospital, and Marguerite went there and showed herself to Jo in all her girlish splendour.

Jo had done serious damage to her knee, and stayed with us for a month, and then her mother, stepfather and Nanna arrived to take her home. I think the relationship developed during that month and it wasn't long before Jo came to Parkes to live, got a job at the hospital, and shared a house with Debbie Simpson, later Debbie Hewett. She and David announced their engagement eventually, and were married in 1989 in her home city of Wollongong. They chose to buy a house in Parkes, as Jo was nursing at the hospital and we all thought the trip out to Fana after a late night shift might not be a good idea.

In April 1989, three months after David and Jo were married, I celebrated my 60th birthday. It was the first real birthday party I ever had as Dad didn't really go in for twenty-firsts, and none of us had one. I was very excited about the luncheon, and invited friends from Mt. Pleasant days, cousins from Orange who had never seen where I lived, the sixty-year-old nuns who had been my best friends at Perthville, including of course, Sister Marie Therese.

When the car from Perthville arrived, I went out to meet them, and Carmel said to the others, 'I think we'll tell her straight away and get it over with.' I was a bit startled, but they went on to tell me that Phillo Gearon had died the night before from the tumour, which she had been battling for fourteen months. I had sat beside Philomena for all of 4th and 5th form, and had visited her in St. Vincent's Hospital in Bathurst while she was ill. We all had a hug, and Marie Therese said in her commonsense voice, 'Phillo would want us to just get on now and have a great day.' So we did!

An event occurred that day which made the day memorable. I had 150 guests on the lawn or arriving, and Philippa came up with eyes as big as saucers, and exclaimed, 'Mum, Wancurra's been blown up!' I brushed her off with 'Don't be silly,' but she persisted, 'Mum, it's true. Peter and David have been over and seen it.'

Frank contacted the police who came and interviewed us, also asking if any guests arriving had seen any cars. The guests from Wellington had come past Wancurra and reported seeing a green car, so subsequent police investigations revealed that a stolen car had overturned near Bogan Gate and there were explosives in the boot, stolen from the mine. Four arrests were made and the young men aged between seventeen and twenty-four later appeared in court in Forbes and each was ordered to pay Frank a sum of money. When asked why they did it, their reply was that they were bored! Incidentally, only one of them ever paid the money, but the others either absconded, or were put in jail for other offence. Frank happened to meet the local sheriff one day, and he told him to hang off charging the others 'until they pay me my money.' That money would have been very handy at that time.

I had never thought I would travel, but my cousin Claire Garty, and her husband, Denis, came to Fana for one of their visits, and were planning a trip overseas. Suddenly it occurred to me that I might be able to go to Bavaria for the Oberamagau Passion Play, which is enacted from May to September every ten years. Frank had no wish to go, but Denis told me how to go about booking, and so on the 2nd August 1990, I was booked to fly by Thai airlines on a Trafalgar tour taking in Italy, Switzerland, Austria, the Passion Play in Oberamagau, France, England, Scotland and Ireland.

I was working so was able to take out a loan, which incidentally took me four years to repay, but it was worth every penny. I received a phone call from Judy Thornton, our local librarian, asking me if I minded if she travelled with me, and of course I was delighted. Judy asked me if Frank snored, and I told her he did sometimes after a few beers, so she was relieved as she said she snored badly and we would be sharing a room all the time. I was later to discover what an understatement that was!

The year 1990 brought floods to our area and Frank was to drive us to Sydney, but no one could get past Bathurst because of the flooded Macquarie River, so we drove to Parkes Airport for our flight to Sydney. After a while, we received word that the pilot couldn't land at Parkes and we were taken in two taxis to Cudal where we waited for the plane. That plane couldn't land either because of the low ceiling of cloud, so we eventually took off from Orange Airport.

Never a lover of flying, as I've mentioned earlier, I was made even more nervous on the little eight-seater we were in, by the instructions coming from the pilot to leave our seatbelts buckled, and even once he said to tighten them. We ducked and wove our way to Mascot and just before landing, the pilot announced the wind was at such a high velocity that we were in for a bumpy landing. Imagine my relief and great surprise when he made a textbook landing, with hardly a bump at all. I felt like kissing him, and credited my heartfelt prayers all the way down as well as his skill for our safe arrival.

The next day we were at Mascot awaiting our take-off for Rome, which was to be the first city on our itinerary, when I suddenly thought I should make a will. I wrote out how I wanted my few possessions to be distributed and stipulated that Philippa was to have my sapphire and diamond engagement ring, as her ring didn't have a diamond, only a sapphire. I also left my white bedroom suite to Libby as she had bought it for us when she was working as a girl in Parkes, and the list went on to include all of them.

After we had taken off, Gemma rang Philippa. 'You'll never guess what Mum did! She made a will at the Airport!' Combined laughter from both of them, and Philippa said, 'I've always loved Mum's ring,' then Gem continued, 'Then you'd better be good at scuba diving, because she's got it on!' This time the laughter was even louder as they both reflected on their crazy, slightly eccentric mother, and they agreed Dad wouldn't be too pleased either to lose his bed and wardrobe!

Judy and I found ourselves seated in the Thai Airways Jet beside an elderly man with an accent. He introduced himself as Doctor Edgar Gatt from Melbourne. He was a retired anesthetist and an International judge of photography, had lost his wife after a long illness a few months before, and had had bypass surgery in May (this was 2nd August). He was from Malta originally but practiced medicine in Melbourne for many years.

You might say we befriended Edgar, as he had heavy, expensive photographic equipment, which he carried wherever we went, so we offered to help him with it. We became a threesome, as all of the others on the Trafalgar Tour were married couples, so wherever Edgar went, we trailed along too to help carry his equipment.

As we travelled over the Swiss Alps, I nearly had to pinch myself to make sure I was actually making this trip, and with the coach radio playing the songs from 'The Sound of Music,' I felt like Maria von Trapp who sang when Captain von Trapp proposed to her, 'Somewhere in my youth, or childhood, I must have done something good!'

We enjoyed our trip very much, and it ended in Dublin after we had been driven all around the south of Ireland. The others flew to London en route for Australia, but we had made plans to go to Tipperary so we caught a train and stayed with Joan Kehelly and Brigid O'Dwyer in Thurles who were first cousins of Frank's father, William Dwyer.

They made us very welcome, as did all Frank's Dwyer relatives when Joan drove us to see them. To my dismay, Joan put us in a room with one three-quarter bed in it so I developed a pattern in order to survive. After Judy was asleep, and Beethoven's Symphony in E Flat Minor had started up beside me, I grabbed one of the many eiderdowns on our bed, and crept down the stairs to a divan in a room with a heater in it just off the kitchen, and there I stayed until six o'clock when I climbed the stairs and was in bed beside her when she awoke. I have never told Judy this story, so I had better tell her before she reads this!

We visited the original Fana where Bill and Biddy Dwyer lived on a dairy farm, and I helped Bill take the Freesian cows back to the paddock after the evening milking, aided by Brandy, the dog. We made a couple of visits to Fana, where Bill had built a lovely new home to replace Grandfather Dwyer's former one which is still there, and has a thatched roof. Joan's brother, Father Laurence O'Dwyer, who had assisted at our wedding, was visiting Ireland from his parish in Australia, and he drove us to the West Coast to visit our own Father Pat Murray's grave at Milltown Malbray, on the wild west coast of Ireland.

It stands with a few other graves in the grounds of a small church, and its close proximity to the beach means one can hear waves crashing on the sand. It is marked with a large Celtic Cross, and imbedded in the centre of it is a large Australian opal, which Father Pat had given his older sister, Mary, and she knew just the spot for it when he died. I stood in front of his grave with the wind howling around me and the waves thundering in to the beach, holding on to my felt hat as it was a stormy day, and I said, 'Oh Pat, what a wild spot you've chosen to be buried in!' Silly words when we all know he is in a far better place and with the Lord he served for forty years.

After about ten days with Joan, we caught the train to Dublin and flew from there back to London and the next day home to Sydney. With apologies to Joan, who was a marvellous hostess, Judy and I both agreed that the most dangerous thing we did whilst on our trip was being driven by Joan who had never managed to get her license (or so we were told!)

While we were away, the 1990s war between Iraq and Kuwait was raging, and Frank wrote and said, 'I know how you like to help people, but don't go anywhere near Kuwait!' Funnily enough, Thai Airways avoided bringing us home via the Middle East because of this conflict, and we flew over Moscow, landing at Delhi to refuel. Just before we landed there, some sari-clad older women beckoned to me to come over, and when I did, they asked me, in sign language more than anything, to fill in landing forms for them. I did this for two of them and when I returned to my seat, I asked Judy: 'Have I got Family Support written on my forehead?' because helping with forms was part of my job at home. And then I remembered Stella saying to me once when something similar happened to her, 'I must have a kind face like a cow!'

The floods were well over and Frank was at Mascot to meet us, and he couldn't believe it when it said on the Landing Board that my flight, naming it, was due to land at one minute past eight, and sure enough, at one minute past eight the sign declared that Flight such and such from London, had just landed! He really couldn't get over it, and was so pleased to see me that I wondered should I have gone in the first place.

I'm glad I did though as the Passion Play was an unforgettable experience on its own, and ever since watching the Passion being re-enacted on the huge open-air stage in Oberamagau, the Mass has held so much more meaning for me. When Father lifts the Host for all to see, and says, 'This is My Body', and then a little later while lifting the Chalice, 'This is My Blood', I see in my mind's eye, the long table at the Last Supper, with all the Apostles seated, and Jesus in the middle, saying just those words, and I see poor Judas sitting at one end, seated a bit sideways as if already distancing himself from the others, and I always feel sorry for him. Is it right that he was pre-destined to play that role in the death of Jesus in order for the words of Scripture to come true?

And would he necessarily have gone to Hell, because we know he was sorry by what he did in his despair? I often wonder.

I was away six weeks and came home in time for a twenty-first birthday, and a new grandson. Marguerite's birthday was close to Christmas, so she chose to have it on 23rd November at the Parkes Bowling Club as I was just back from overseas. James Thomas O'Donnell made his appearance on 20th November, so with a three-day-old baby, Philippa got gate leave for the party, which was catered for, and the main meal was a pig on the spit, with the usual salads. Marguerite had asked every one to come dressed in black and white and everyone obliged, the most amusing being Peter and Brian in baggy, black and white check trousers. Life was getting back to normal for the Dwyer family.

CHAPTER 20

CHALLENGES TO OUR FAMILY LIFE

While rearing her girls, Libby became a Day Care Mother, and while the girls were at school, was kept busy looking after pre-school children. Mostly, she cared for children whose mothers were nurses, which meant that she would get them before the mother started the 6am shift in the morning, until 3.00pm, then with those children gone, another nurse would drop her children off before her 3.00pm shift, and those would be with Libby until 11.00pm at night. This meant bottle-feeding, and changing nappies, and with two schoolgirls of her own, and a husband who was a shift worker, it made for a tiring and busy life, as she wasn't allowed to go to bed until the children were picked up.

Sadly, we suffered the first marital break-up in our happy family, when Arnold worked in Dubbo for six weeks with his job on the railway. Katrina was ten, and Anita eight, and they, and their mother, were looking forward to his return when he rang to say he wanted 'out' of their marriage and wasn't coming back to Parkes. Libby was devastated, but managed to ask him if there was a third party involved and of course at this stage he said there was not. This later proved to be untrue. On this particular morning, Libby had five day-care children, all under the age of five, as another carer had to go to Orange, and asked Libby to take hers as well.

I received a phone call from her and I could tell that she was striving to keep control of herself when she told me about the call from Arnold, and then she added, 'I can't be left alone today, Mum.' I felt incredibly sad for her and I told her I would be in as soon as I could. This would take me three quarters of an hour as I was having a day off work because I wasn't very well, so I had to shower and change, and then drive 30 kilometres in. So I rang my coordinator and asked her to send someone down to Libby.

When I arrived, my colleagues had everything under control, having rung the Day Care office to place the five children with other carers, so it was an improvement not to have all those little tots roaming around, and their carer in a shocked condition. A neighbour made Libby a cup of tea, and after that she stopped pacing around the house, had a good cry on her neighbour's shoulder, and seemed to settle down. Our coordinator, Ivy Rooke, had herself gone to Libby and I think Marg Troy, too.

I tell you these details because to be told something so final, with no warning, can be likened to hearing of the death of a loved one, and to have to go on without the support of a husband, and cope with everything, as well as rearing two little girls on her own, must have seemed to her a monumental task. I vowed then and there that if I could help her in any way, I would do so, and though living a distance away, I tried to do just that whenever I could. In my work with Family Support, I was aware of the powerlessness of single mothers whose husbands had walked out on their families, and of the many tears shed into their pillows at night.

The first thing I did was to buy her another microwave as she needed it to heat up bottles and food for the children in her care, and Arnold took that, and many other things when he came back a few days later with a trailer. Katrina, at the age of six, used to whip an egg with a fork, pour in a little milk, put that in the microwave and when she made a piece of toast, she had scrambled eggs on toast for a snack. As the two little girls loved music, they laughingly told me recently that they think they mourned the loss of the stereo which Arnold took, more than they did their absent father! They are now aged thirty and twenty-eight, so perhaps, like me, they blocked out the pain. They also assured me recently they wanted me to tell it like it was.

Libby had only driven a car on the farm, and didn't have the confidence to get a license and had no car, so when Arnold left, she and the girls had to walk everywhere they went. Katrina and Anita told me they remember the three of them walking home from Woollies, each carrying her share of the groceries, and how the bags got 'a bit heavy' before they made it home.

Arnold was well paid in his job and he was a good provider, so Libby missed that security, but after a few months she began to manage as well as anyone in that situation could, and of course the Family Support Service made her aware of whatever help was available to her. The children attended Holy Family School, and Libby did tuck shop duty all through their primary school days, as well as assisting with Library and cleaning the Chapel, so I am not the only one who has admired her for all that marathon walking she did over so many years, rain, hail or shine, literally.

Four years later she became friendly with an older man, Brian, and to our very great surprise, presented us with another granddaughter, Bethany Ann. Though the relationship didn't continue, having the baby was good for her because she had to focus on rearing her little girl, and through her involvement with the Family Support Service with whom I worked, came to parenting classes and group sessions and brought Bethany. Here she made a couple of good friends, who were also single parents again, and these friends she has retained for the past twenty years, and they have supported each other.

Katrina and Anita progressed to Red Bend Catholic College at Forbes for their secondary education, and both achieved their Year 12 Certificate and benefitted from all that such a good college offered. Libby received sympathetic concessions from time to time as regards school fees, but always contributed what she could, and was of a frugal nature, only buying what the girls needed, and not much for herself.

Bethany started school at Holy Family in Parkes and my involvement was mainly running the girls about when they had appointments out of town. Katrina did some TAFE courses in Orange, and there was the occasional missed bus, so I would get a phone call and off we'd go. She also had knee trouble for a while and needed to see a specialist in Orange and I would take her to these appointments.

After her final exams, Marguerite spent a year in a traineeship in the Public Trust Office in Sydney, dealing with wills and so on, but didn't find it very exciting so she went to Concord Hospital and gained her Certificate as an Enrolled Nurse. She returned to Fana and was accepted into Charles Sturt University in Bathurst to further her nursing career, but Cupid intervened when she met Scott Burns, her first ever boyfriend, and fell in love.

They were married in Parkes on 7th February 1993 and Marguerite chose an all-white wedding with the bride and her attendants, Fiona Donnelly, her best friend since preschool days, Kristie Shambrook and Maryanne MacGregor, friends from high school days, all in white with beautiful flowers for colour. Her flower girls were Kimberly Jackson, Scott's niece, and Lucy Churchill, Gemma's daughter, and the groomsmen included Scott's brother, Brady, and friends, Brad Jayet and David Parker. It was a pretty wedding, I sang throughout the Nuptial Mass, and then was joined by Frank Donnelly, or Kamaal, as Frank calls him, in singing 'All I ask of you' from Phantom of the Opera at the signing of the register.

After her marriage, Marguerite worked at the Southern Cross Village in Parkes as a nurse carer for a few years and then gave us the joyous new that she was pregnant. Like Ruth in the Old Testament, she followed Scott to Sydney not long before Grace Estelle Burns was born on 7th November 1996 and we were thrilled not only because she was healthy and beautiful, but she also had the titian hair Stella had always wanted my children to have, mainly because Frank's hair was such a nice shade of auburn, and curly.

Gemma had many good friends in Sydney and started bringing them to Fana for long weekends and sometimes longer. One of these was Joanne Ford who, with her husband Neal, had five beautiful children: Mitchell, Lauren, Paula, and the twins, Jessica and Natalie. Joanne and Gemma would arrive in two cars, with or without their husbands, and Gemma, by this time, had four children, Sam, Lucy, Edward and Jack, so there would be kids everywhere, some learning to drive the paddock bashers on the flat lanes through Fana, the younger ones feeding chooks and collecting eggs, or going with David or Frank to feed sheep, and all coming home hungry and dirty.

If we were marking lambs, there would be lots of child labour involved in bringing the sheep in to the yards and catching the lambs, while Joanne and Gemma assisted with the more sophisticated work of giving them needles to guard against fluke, and scratching them to prevent scabby mouth. David and Frank would cut their tails off or use rings, and castrate the wether portion. All would arrive at the house for lunch, splattered with blood and needing a good wash before eating, but, as Frank was fond of saying, 'Happy as a pig in muck!'

Jo Ford was great at helping with the cooking, and Gemma was generally off somewhere with David. Philippa would arrive out with her five boys, Damien, Simon, Nikolas, Benson and James, and if Gemma was home, Marguerite would bring Grace, and Jo Dwyer would arrive with Sally, as Lewie would have come earlier with David, as he considered himself chief lamb-catcher! This scenario was repeated when Franny Power and her four children, Leanne, Daniel, Chris and Erin, came, and also when Gail Gloag and her two little girls, Erin and Bridie, visited Fana. Sometimes, all four families came together and what wonderful times we had then, with the older ones learning to drive, or off somewhere with the men, and the younger girls inside playing charades or dress-ups inside the house.

It was sometimes wet, and they would all take off their sneakers at the kitchen door, and there would be a long row of wet, muddy sneakers stretching halfway along the back veranda. One time it rained every day and I was distressed by these wet shoes, fearing that if they put them on wet next morning they would get colds, so I got lots of newspaper, and stuffed each and every shoe with this. I then spread them out on more newspaper in front of the open fire in the lounge, as well as the closed combustion heater in the family room, and they were dry by morning.

It's amazing how good I felt when an adult Mitchell Ford was here a couple of weeks ago, and he told me how his sneakers got wet recently and he remembered what I did at Fana with the newspaper, so he gave them that treatment and it worked!

I need to stress here that our visitors did not come empty-handed, as the girls would do a big grocery shop in Parkes on their way to us, or the next day, and I would also have bought up big, so there was always plenty of food.

Dinner time meant all the children were fed first, and they would make themselves comfortable in front of the television watching a video, some on the lounge or chairs, the rest sprawled on big cushions on the floor, while the adults ate their meal in the dining room. Then, with the young fry settled for the night, the Mums and Dads would move to the front veranda and bring out the chardonnay for the ladies and well-earned beers for the boys, and eventually Frank and I would go to bed and listen to the hilarity coming from the veranda.

Finally, about midnight, there would be silence and I would creep out and make sure the children were covered in their make-shift mattresses on the floor in the lounge, and that all lights were off. They were good times, and those children are grown up now and successful in their chosen fields. Two are married and have children of their own, and when I had my eightieth birthday a couple of years ago, every one of them came from Sydney to Fana for it, absolutely making my day.

Scott had two children before he and Marguerite got married, but they lived with their mother in Narromine, and though Scott didn't get to see them, he supported them financially. Jeremy was thirteen and Elizabeth eight when their mother, Jennifer Barry, had a car accident on her way to Tullamore, and sadly died a few weeks later as a result. Jeremy had left home, but Elizabeth was living in Narromine with her stepfather and three younger siblings, above a hotel owned by her uncle. She knew about her father, but had never met him.

While visiting her maternal grandmother in Parkes, she was brought to meet Marguerite and baby Grace, but didn't meet her father as he was working in Sydney at the time, and came home at weekends. She expressed the wish to come and live with Scott and Marguerite, so it was arranged, and she was dropped off, and later in the week I went with Marguerite and Elizabeth to Narromine to pick up her belongings. Scott met her for the first time when he returned at the weekend. She was a comely little girl, very like her Dad really, and showed that she was capable beyond her years, probably being the eldest and having to help with her mother's three young children. Grace took to her straight away and she seemed to like her baby half-sister.

Grace was two when Scott was transferred to Jabiru in the Northern Territory with his job with Telecom, so they left, taking Grace and Elizabeth with them. Scott loved the Territory with its wonderful fishing, but Marguerite found it extremely hot and too far from all her family. She started Elizabeth at school, made friends and joined in the social life at Jabiru of mainly barbeques, but she wasn't totally happy, and neither was Grace.

She, Grace, caught a dreadful infection from the local swimming pool, and it was concentrated in her mouth causing huge ulcers and cold sores. The poor little pet couldn't suck her dummy (of which she was very fond), found it hard to eat, and was really miserable. She, like Marguerite, missed us all, and when they went to a barbeque she expected to see Aunty Jo and David, her little cousin Sally, Grandfather and Mardie, and everyone was a total stranger to her.

I rang Margie, and she put Grace on, and the little girl said, 'I've got a sore mouth, Mardie', and then she nearly broke my heart when she said tearfully, 'Mardie, can I come to your house? I'll be good!' I sobbed when I got off the phone and Frank was his usual comforting self, telling me gruffly that there was no use crying as I couldn't do anything about it. I still regard this as one of my saddest moments.

The next thing we heard was that Marguerite had chicken pox, and I knew that she always developed giant hives whenever she had a temperature, and these only subsided when she took phenergan, which calmed the hives but totally zonked her out for twenty-four hours. It would be well-nigh impossible to take this prescribed drug with Scott off working somewhere on Groote Island, and two children to care for, so despite Frank telling me I couldn't do anything about it, the little girl who prayed behind doors as a child knew she could do something, and that was pray! So I did, and miracle of miracles, we received word they were coming home, as Scott had applied for a transfer to NSW and was coming to Winston Hills in Sydney.

We were thrilled, because Sydney was manageable for me when any of them were sick, but Jabiru! They might as well have been on the moon! There was further exciting news that Margie was pregnant again, and I knew how much she wanted another baby as Grace was going on for three. They travelled in their four wheel drive, their furniture etc coming by removalists, and during the trip home heard from us that Michael and Virginia were getting married.

That is a story in itself, as both of them were forty-four, and at that age each finally found their soul mate. Virginia told us later that Michael was the one for whom she had been searching all her life while Michael said Virginia was exactly the girl whom he had been seeking all his life.

This is how it all played out. Virginia's family from the Philippines were visiting and were due to return at a certain date, flights booked etc. When they drove to Canberra for an overnight stay, Michael decided not to go with them, but to give them time alone as a family. However, he was looking at a dreary, wet weekend, so on an impulse, travelled to Canberra to visit one of his College friends, Tim Boynton. Over a nice drop, or two, of red, Tim convinced him to go and see the family at their hotel, so next morning he invaded the family, abducted Virginia and took her to the Canberra International for breakfast. Over bacon and eggs, he popped the question: 'Will you marry me?' Virginia teased him by saying, 'Oh Michael, I'll have to think about it', bowed her head for three seconds, and then looked up radiantly, and said, 'YES!'

The next step was to approach Virginia's parents, and when they agreed, it was a case of 'Why wait? Why not have the wedding before the family return to the Philippines?' There was great enthusiasm for this idea, but of course there were formalities according to the law, in both Church and State. They had no trouble with the priest, but in NSW, a month's notice must be given for a marriage to take place. The travellers had to sign an affidavit, and produce their tickets, and Virginia's father, Rudolpho Calub, wrote a letter in perfect English and in beautiful handwriting, supporting the application. That may have clinched it, because after Mike had travelled a few times between Penrith and the offices of Births, Deaths, and Marriages in the city, permission was given. They had just two weeks to plan the wedding.

Our family received the news with great jubilation, especially as Virginia announced that any little girl, who could find a cream dress and blue flowers for her hair, could be a flower girl. She ended up with eight beautiful young girls, Grace, at 2 years 10 months, being the youngest, and the others from the Dwyer clan were Lucy Churchill, Elizabeth Burns and Sally Dwyer, who was four. Virginia's nieces, Mayna, Jenny-May, Mimsi and Geraldine, were the others and they all fulfilled their role perfectly.

Every member of the two families was given a role as reader, hostess, altar boy, etc, and I was honoured to be asked to sing, especially as I knew I was past my use-by date! Lewie had just started school, and his job was to read out one of the Prayers of Intercession. He was given the hand-printed lines before we left Gemma's house, but when his big moment came, he couldn't find it in his pocket, so someone handed him the wedding booklet. This was unfamiliar to Lewie, so he made a stab at remembering it, and said, and I quote, 'Dear Lord, bless Michael and Virginia, and send them lots and lots of babies!' This caused some amusement, as most people there knew the bridal couple was getting close to their 'use-by date'!

It was amazing that such a wonderful wedding, with every detail attended to, was arranged in just two weeks, Virginia dressed in a lovely bridal gown with a little veil, Michael a handsome groom in black dinner suit and white shirt and a bevy of gorgeous little girls. Some brides take twelve months to plan a wedding, and after this, I wondered why.

Marguerite was eight months pregnant at Michael's wedding, and they had moved into a house at Winston Hills where they booked Elizabeth into school. I came down to care for Lizzie and Grace when the baby came, and, though he kept us waiting a while, William Francis Burns was born on 20th November. In actual fact, he was 'William' for probably half an hour, because Scott had always wanted a son called Billy, so that is what he was when I met him the morning he was born, a bonny boy and the image of his Dad.

Marguerite was as happy as a lark, as her house was only a few blocks from Gemma's, Foof was not far away, and Gemma's friends were her friends too, so there were plenty of 'sisters' to make a fuss of her little family. They were there for a year, but were eventually to return to Parkes where Scott opened his own business, End to End Communications, and they rented while their new home was being built. Marguerite resumed her job at Southern Cross Village, Elizabeth caught the bus to Red Bend College, and I was delighted to have them so accessible.

If the year 1998 brought great joy with the Burns' return from the Northern Territory, Michael and Virginia's marriage, and the birth of Billy Burns, 1999 was a different story. In about July, Peter and Philippa's marriage sadly ended.

It affected us all, as Peter had been part of our lives for twenty-six years, and this decision changed our relationship with him forever. We missed him at family gatherings, though we still retained and cherished the five beautiful O'Donnell boys. Philippa gradually adjusted to single life becoming stronger in the process, made arrangements for sharing the boys, and found salvation in them, her teaching, and her family.

Life moves on, no matter what has happened, and Christmas is always Christmas, with all the family heading for home, the pool cleaned and ready, the roster sorted so everyone knows which family member he, or she, has to buy for, and each one knowing what food each particular person has to bring. These times are healing times when one is in the bosom of the family with no post-mortems being held, only healthy interchange of ideas and acceptance of things as they are, and plenty of merriment.

About this time, with me approaching pension age, we transferred the family farm, Fana, to David who had been working on it virtually all his life. We still lived there for another ten years and started calling ourselves 'the manager and housekeeper', and when nuisance calls came, this was a polite way to turn away repeated calls for monetary assistance. I'd say, 'I'm only the housekeeper', which in actual fact was true. We already had our pet charities like Guide Dogs, Careflight and Childflight (and we had three occasions when we needed those, so we always support them), Rural Fire Service, Mission Australia and of course, our contribution to the maintenance of Holy Family Church.

Before New Year 2000, I rang all of our Alectown friends, and a couple of special ones from Parkes, and invited them to a New Year's Dinner, suggesting that we all dress up in our best and make a gala night of it. They were all enthusiastic and it was decided what 'plate' each one would bring to contribute to the meal, and, as the younger members were all celebrating in true Parkes style at one, or a few, of the venues, we had the place to ourselves.

I used the good crystal wine glasses I had bought in Waterford in Ireland, and my best crockery, and spared no effort to have the table set to rival the glossy magazines, and my guests arrived looking fantastic, the women in their lovely dresses complete with bling, and the men dressed in sartorial elegance. You couldn't spot a farmer among any of them.

There was Zilda and husband Norman, Vilma, Ronda and Dennis, Helen and Jack, Beverly and John, Margaret and Jim, and of course Frank and me. We had a fun night with music playing, old stories being retold and lots of lovely food. And that was the night I had my first and only ever smoke! And it was a cheroot!

It happened like this. Beverly, being a thoughtful and creative girl, thought she was adding to the fun of the night by bringing out a tin of cheroots for the men. I thought it was a great idea, and I was expectant when Bev produced the 'surprise' on the veranda. To our amazement, it went down like a dead balloon, as each man in turn refused to take one, being I guess a reformed smoker and not wanting to kick-start the habit. I thought Frank at least could have had a go at one, as he hadn't ever been a smoker, so no danger of restarting a habit. But no, the males stuck together, and I couldn't stand Bev's crestfallen face, so I said brightly, 'I'd like one Bev', and you could have heard a pin drop.

She gave me one, someone produced a match, and I smoked that cheroot right to the end. I was thinking, 'I must not do the drawback, whatever that is', and, do you know I didn't, I just smoked it nice and smoothly like a veteran. My friends from the time of my marriage, Zilda and Vilma, were laughing hysterically in the dining room, but worrying as well as to whether their eccentric friend might choke on the smoke.

David came out towards the end of October, just before harvest, and told us his marriage was 'pretty ordinary at the moment.' It was the euphemism to end all euphemisms, as in actual fact, his marriage was over. The shock Frank and I got was enormous, Frank because one would have to hit him with news like this right between the eyes before he would notice anything amiss, and like me, he was fond of Jo, who for some reason, he always called 'Joseph.' And me, well I had suspected nothing either as Jo had only recently been extolling David's virtues to Zilda and me whilst driving us to Sydney.

We had been running down our poor old husbands, as women who have been married a long time are inclined to do, knowing that the three of us knew we didn't really mean it, and were just sounding off, when Jo put us in our place by saying blithely, 'Well, I can't complain about my husband, he's this and that, and does this and that and he's a wonderful man and a fantastic father!' Well! Zilda and I looked at each other and said no more. And now here was Davy with this bombshell.

David said they hadn't told the children yet, and that upset me to think what a shock was in store for them as Lewie was eight and Sally six, and they loved their Mum and Dad equally. Children are resilient though, and they came through it all with no obvious ill effects, but David lost two stone during that harvest and though he could afford to lose weight, we didn't want it to be that way. The local farmers were fond of David, and the general opinion among them was expressed by one older farmer at the wheat terminal one day, when he said to Frank, 'I feel very sorry for Doggie.'

The first time I saw Jo after hearing the sad news from David, she repeated the complimentary things she had said on the way to Sydney about him, only she added, 'But I don't love him anymore.' Those six words were hard for a mother to hear, I guess because, despite his faults, I always thought David was lovable. I was, you see, still naive at seventy-one.

Jo stayed in Parkes for some time after this, and David could go after work and bowl a few balls to Lewie in the back garden, and wrestle with Sally, his little princess, on the lawn, but then Jo moved back to Wollongong, taking the children with her. I said to David, 'Look at it as if they are at boarding school, and will be home every three months', and they were home fairly often for school holidays as Jo was working, and school holidays are hard for mothers who work. When they came to Parkes, they had so many families with whom to stay when their Dad was busy, and cousins with whom to share fun times, and Grandfather and I were always there at Fana. David would slip to Wollongong to see them in between holidays, or for long weekends, and flew them home to Parkes occasionally.

Gradually, David and Jo developed a friendly relationship, a bit like a brother and sister who disagree occasionally, and I guess we all moved on and accepted the situation, especially as Jo was generous in encouraging our involvement with Lewie and Sally and we saw a lot of them.

Shortly into the New Year, Margie and Scott had some exciting news for us, which we certainly needed after David's bombshell! They were adding to their family in late September and Grace, Billy and Lizzie were excited to be having a little brother or sister. Lizzie was such a help at this time as Marguerite was still working at Southern Cross Village, and she would do the daily washing early and Lizzie would hang it before she caught the bus at 8.00am, which wasn't a bad effort. She was competent for her age, and would sometimes make a cake when she came home from school, loved Billy and Grace and adored the new baby when she came.

Daisy Mary-Ann Burns arrived on 1st October 2002, with the same lovely dark hair, which her mother had when, she was born, and nice and chubby at 9lbs 6ozs. She was a picture, everyone was thrilled to bits and she grew into a fetching little girl with quite a sense of humour. She resembles her mother, Marguerite, so much that I am constantly reminded of her as a child, and I state categorically here, that despite the assumption that the youngest of a big family is sure to be spoiled, Marguerite certainly was not, and furthermore, we have not had one moment's worry with her in her 41 years of life. Daisy is also the youngest and I see no sign of her being spoiled, though she has however got plenty of spirit, and I say she is like Scarlett O'Hara from 'Gone with the Wind', with attitude!

So we moved into the twenty-first century with these challenges behind us, and I guess there will be more, though hopefully not the same, for life is made up of challenges of all sorts. In the years following these sad events, Frank was inclined to tell people that the Queen rang him for his birthday, which he shares with her, and during the conversation, Frank told her we had three broken marriages in the family. According to Frank, Her Majesty said, 'Well, we have had the same problem with our children', so I think Frank thought he was in good company.

CHAPTER 21

RETIREMENT AND OUR GOLDEN WEDDING

The year 1999 had brought more than another marriage break-up. It was the year I turned seventy, and I noticed I wasn't handling the daily travelling within the shire, which my work entailed, very well. I had to stop once or twice when returning from Manildra, or Trundle, as I was feeling sleepy, and I realised my stamina in driving wasn't equal to the stamina I showed in my daily life. Reluctantly, I tendered my resignation to Family Support and they gave me a nice morning tea, and suddenly I was free to do all the things I had been unable to do for the thirteen years of my working life.

The first thing I thought was, 'How did I ever have time to go to work?' I was back to being available so that meant I could run the men here and there, slip into town for a part for a tractor, move vehicles when an extra driver was needed and generally make myself useful. My first aim though was to try and create a lovely garden, and this became a priority with me. I wanted it to be a typical country garden, but all my efforts over the next few years resulted in a garden that was rather like me, homespun. It did however have green lawns, shrubs, walkways, archways, garden seats and hardy flowering plants with the odd piece of statuary, and on family occasions, also provided an excellent cricket pitch!

I did create an area in memory of my lovely daughter, with flowering shrubs, a clock, a few angels, water plants, a path through it, and a table and chairs, and it was circled by trees that were part of the driveway. It was rather charming, and lovely Joanne Ford, my 'sixth' daughter, excelled at art and painted a beautiful sign, 'Mary-Ann's Garden', which hung on a tree. I loved it when we called everybody from the shed and elsewhere, for a cup of tea, and someone would say, 'Are we having it in Mary-Ann's garden?'

For Christmas one year, the family gave us tickets to Phantom of the Opera in Melbourne, so we took the coach to Flinders Street Station and were met by Edgar Gatt, who had invited us to stay with him in his magnificent home in East Keilor. He cooked nice Mediterranean dishes for us, and looked after us very well, taking us to the Botanical Gardens, and for a visit to the city, where riding in the trams evoked memories of doing this in Sydney as a young girl. I caught up with my cousin Ailsa (the one whose hair I had put through the wringer!), and her husband John, and they invited us to a lovely Australian roast dinner in their spacious family home where we met some of their family.

Of course we returned the compliment, and Edgar came to visit us at Fana. He was anxious to spend time on a farm, and to see where we lived, as I had talked non-stop to him while we were overseas about Fana, Frank and my family. He arrived at shearing time, and next day, after visiting the shed, asked me what I was going to do next.

I told him I was going to water the garden and he said he would help me, so I told him to go outside the fence and I would throw the hose over the high wisteria, and he could water the vegies I had planted there. He was walking along to catch the hose, and suddenly I heard an exclamation, then a thud, and when I raced around to him, I found that Edgar had fallen in the second chamber of the *sewerage pit*! He had stepped on the cement covering the pit, which had a crack in it, and it had given away taking poor Edgar with it!

I said, 'Oh Edgar, you poor man, can you get out?' and he said, 'You will have to help me a little bit, I think', so I heaved and he did too and he climbed out. He went straight into the shower on the veranda, and I brought him some fresh clothes.

In the kitchen we inspected the damage to his shin which was bleeding, and I put some antiseptic on it, and declared, 'We are going straight in to casualty', but Edgar demurred and said reasonably, 'In a little while, after you have given all those men their lunch.' So the shearers came down, we had our lunch and then fronted up at casualty at the hospital. Jo Burke was on duty, and the conversation went something like this.

Jo: 'Are your tetanus injections up to date, Doctor?'

Edgar: 'No, Sister.' So the phone call to the surgery resulted in the necessary permission, and Edgar had his tetanus injection. Jo began cleaning and dressing the leg, and asked, 'How far did you fall in, Doctor?'

Anyone but Edgar would have said, 'Up to my armpits', but Edgar was nothing, if not specific, and he told her, 'Up to my nipples, I think!' I felt a bubble of mirth rising in me, but suppressed it, as Edgar was very serious and it was no joke.

Jo: 'You were nearly floating, Doctor!' At this I nearly choked, but managed, 'Don't mention floating, Jo.'

On the drive home, I said to Edgar, 'You were lucky, Edgar, in the chamber you fell in', meaning the water was fairly clear there, but he looked at me balefully, and said with his Maltese accent, 'Lucky! You think I'm lucky!' so we talked of other things for the rest of the trip. Edgar was happy with the competence shown by Jo Burke, but said his son-in-law was a microbiologist, and he would check with him on his return to Melbourne. Everything must have been all right as we heard no more about it, and I made sure the sewerage pit had a new cover as soon as possible. Incidentally, Edgar remarked to me that 'Farms are very dangerous places.'

My brother, Harry, and his wife, Olive, had two daughters, Lesley and Pam, and these girls were very bright and especially good at languages. Both became language teachers, and taught Indonesian and Japanese in Sydney High Schools, and Pam, at an early age, was made coordinator of Asian Studies at the University of Technology in Sydney. As a schoolgirl, she had spent a year in Japan as an exchange student, won a competition in Japanese public speaking the following year and returned for another year as her prize, and she and her husband Ken Carpenter, have made many trips to Japan over the years, sometimes so Pam could choose teachers of Japanese in Australian schools.

Lesley taught Indonesian and she made her mark also in that field, introducing that language into many schools along the South Coast. In 1981, she and her husband, Bob McLean, became the proud parents of identical twin girls, Christina and Xanthe, and they were also very academic, later gaining passes in the Higher School Certificate in the first 5 per cent of the state.

When the twins were four, Lesley and Bob had taken sabbatical leave, and travelled to the centre of Australia and then north to Cairns. While they were there, they noticed that Xanthe wasn't responding to requests, and thought she was being naughty, until Christina told her mother, 'She can't hear you Mummy!'

Investigation proved she was indeed deaf, and, on their return to Sydney, specialists could find no cause for it so put it down to an infection. Everything that could be done was done, and she was fitted with hearing aids in both ears, but her hearing was very much below par. Despite this affliction, Xanthe obtained a TER result in her final exams of 95.7 and studied physiotherapy at University.

In her third year she struggled a bit, so decided to have a Cochlear Implant, which made a huge difference and she graduated and worked for two years at hospitals in the Hunter region. After a nine-month trip overseas, which included Japan, she began working in a practice in Sydney.

Christina received a TER result of 97.6 in her final school exams, and became a chartered accountant while working for PriceWaterhouseCoopers. Harry was very proud of his only grandchildren, and indeed his daughters, and though a very modest man, said of them once, 'Not bad for a couple of little girls from Stuart Town!' Christina has been living overseas for a couple of years, and while in France, learned the French language. She is thinking of returning to Sydney in September 2011.

Dick and Maree's three children have all been equally successful in their chosen careers. Both Warren and Stewart received their secondary education at St Joseph's College, Hunter's Hill, and after graduation, Warren became a fully qualified electrical tradesman, and obtained his electrician and electrical contractor licenses later that year.

While working as Technical Officer with Ophir County Council's head office, he undertook design, planning and implementation of the electrical distribution network, specialising in substation design and telemetry.

Like his father, Dick, he also played Rugby Union for the Orange City Club, and through that met and married Donna Matthews. His work at Ophir Council expanded into micro computing and in 1989 he moved to Parkes where he joined the RTA and got to use his electrical, electronic and computer skills across a region that covers 60 per cent of the State. Consequently, he travels extensively by plane and car and gets to see much of Western NSW regularly.

Warren's rise was consistent and he now holds the position of IT Telecommunications Services Manager with the RTA, a statewide role that causes him to travel extensively and spend considerable time in Sydney. Along the way, he and Donna have produced three fine sons, Mitchell, Ryan and Alec who are also pursuing careers, except Alec who is in Year 11 at Red Bend College, Forbes.

Dick's only daughter, Margot, qualified as a P.E. teacher at Wollongong University, and later married Murray Read, an accountant, and had four children, Samantha, Danielle, Penelope, and Jason. Murray became the subject of a Sydney newspaper and magazine article when he developed breast cancer, from which he totally recovered, but the story generated watchfulness among the male population for that condition. They live in Wollongong and visit Mt. Pleasant in school holidays.

Stewart married a Sydney girl, Anne Littrich, and he is a 'man of the land', working his own property near Wellington, and cooperating with Dick on Mt. Pleasant and a couple of other places they own. They have five children, Jack, Max, Charlie, Hugh and Lucy, and all have a love of horses, competing in polo, and horse events. Dick's children return to Mt. Pleasant, where they were reared, for holidays and family events and I must admit, I envy them these visits, and have been included in some of them.

In our own family, the youngest grandchildren are treasures, and Grace amused me one day when she was a tiny tot. The family called Scott's mother, Nan, and because Nan's mother lived down the hill from her, the children called the older woman Bottom Nan! When Bottom Nan's sister died, I drove two-year-old Grace to see her great—grandmother. On the way, I suggested she be very kind to Bottom Nan as she would be very sad about her sister, and might even cry. Grace reassured me, 'It's all right Mardie, I'll just say, 'They're only crocodile tears!' It was obviously a phrase Grace had heard but didn't realise its meaning. I said hastily, 'Oh no, don't say that, just give her a big hug.' Thankfully, she had forgotten about it by the time we got there.

When Bottom Nan, or Mona as was her name, died at 92, I had the privilege of singing 'Gentle Woman' at the graveside ceremony, and it was a fitting song for a lovely, gentle lady: 'Gentle woman, quiet light, morning star, so strong and bright, gentle mother, peaceful dove, teach us wisdom, teach us love.'

Elizabeth still lived with Marguerite and her dad, but became dissatisfied and rebelled against their basic rules, and with urgings from her maternal grandmother, moved in with her. She didn't stay there very long, found a partner and left to live her own life. Now at twenty-three, she is a single mum and has a part-time job and a gorgeous two-year-old boy, Hunter. She knows her dad and Marguerite are there when she needs them, as they have always been, sending her to Red Bend College, having her and the baby live with them during a rocky period in her relationship with Hunter's father, and building a self-contained flat for her in their back garden, which she eventually chose not to live in.

It is currently occupied by a very dear friend of Marguerite's, Lisa Kelly, or Poss as we call her, who is having a battle with her health at the moment, and it cuts both ways as she is a godsend to Marguerite, always being there to keep an eye on the children if she is delayed coming home from her work in Forbes, and everyone knows how handy it is to have someone bring clothes in off the line if it suddenly rains! I have to monitor her attempts to help me out by driving me to Orange or Dubbo for appointments, and her health is not good enough to do this at the moment.

Grace and Daisy learned dancing from an early age, but Billy was a natural athlete, playing football in under 8's, under 10's, under 12's and now at only twelve years of age, plays a good game in under 14's. He was also selected in the Polding Team, which is a state representative team, and in 2010, this team actually won the State Finals. He also plays hockey and touch footy, and he is training for some sport every night of the week. Grace and Daisy still learn dancing and both play soccer, and Grace is interested in the Musical and Dramatic Society, and goes in shows when she can. She is now fifteen and attends Red Bend College at Forbes where she is in Year 10, while Billy is there also in Year 7, and Daisy, who is eight, is still at Holy Family Parkes in 3rd Grade.

Meanwhile, in Sydney, Gemma's family is pursuing their careers. Sam trained initially as a landscape gardener, but abandoned that in favour of the police force, and trained at the Academy in Goulburn. Frank and I attended his graduation, and watched nearly 800 young police cadets throw their caps in the air at the conclusion of a gruelling parade, which included a couple of hours in the blazing sun. Gemma and Brian were very proud of their first born in his spanking new uniform and even more so when he applied for, and was accepted, into the Riot Squad. He has currently been nominated for a bravery award.

Lucy worked for a year in a Nursing Home where she was much loved, then did an Enrolled Nurses Course before going to University to gain her degree in Nursing. She followed this with another year in Obstetrics and graduated in that in 2011. Lucy really loves delivering babies, and plans to specialize in midwifery eventually. She is currently working at Westmead Hospital, in Sydney. She met her soul-mate at the Gold Coast, when they were both there for Schoolies Week, of all things, and the romance blossomed for four years before she and Matt Johnstone were married in St. Stanislaus College Chapel in Bathurst in 2010. They were attended by all eighteen grandchildren; the youngest, Daisy, being the flowergirl.

Edward Churchill excelled at football, and played in the 1st 15's at Oak Hill College while at school, travelling to New Zealand and Argentina to play. He wanted to be a Jackeroo and applied to the Clyde Agricultural College for entrance to the course and, after a successful interview, was accepted. His first position was at a large property near Walcha called 'Wirribilla' where they muster on four-wheel motorbikes and Edward is in seventh heaven and just loves the outdoor life. He plays Rugby for Northern Central Districts and also in a local Walcha team, and unfortunately has taken to riding bulls in rodeos, which I'm not too happy about. 'You can't wrap them in cotton wool', I'm told . . . well I'm here to tell you that riding bulls is vastly different from wrapping them in cotton wool!

Jack is the youngest of Gem's family, and he was christened Jack Boundy, after W.B. (Wilfred Boundy). Jack also played a good game of football, but it's not a passion with him as it is with Edward, though he also travelled to Argentina to play at the end of school. He obtained employment with Bunnings on leaving school, which tickled Frank, and he would refer to Jack as 'the Manager' of Bunnings, just as he has called Sam 'Sergeant' ever since he graduated.

Jack is studying business management at University but still working at Bunnings, and Gemma proudly tells me how well he is doing at Uni lately, getting distinctions. Jack is as meticulous and tidy as Edward is carefree and a bit of a larrikin, but they always got on well. When Ed was at the harum-scarum stage, Jack would pack for him when they travelled to Parkes, otherwise Ed might live in what he wore up for the whole weekend! True! It is amazing to me that Edward is now the responsible head stockman of Wirribilla, and is turning twenty-two shortly and has been given a cottage of his own of which he is very proud.

The interaction between Gemma and her friends never ceases to amaze me. When her children were at school, they would often be playing at a different oval, sometimes in different suburbs, and Gem's army of friends would transport the one who was playing with their child, and vice versa. It was an amazing support network that Gemma was part of, and what I witnessed many, many times at Gem's was an exercise in real Christianity, mostly every day and every week.

Gem and her friends all worked, and each knew their children were safely at Gemma's house after school and being nurtured exactly the same as her own. No child ever felt unwanted, or a nuisance, and were totally at home there, frequently staying overnight after a late night out. By the same token, she had no compunction about calling on her friends either when she needed help. This has gone on until this very day, and I've always admired this interaction between them all.

I felt the same closeness to Frank's sisters because every time we had a large function, I had no hesitation in asking for their help in the shape of a salad or a slice, and it was always forthcoming. Before the 'Farewell to Fana' luncheon, I extended this request to most of my friends as we had decided the dessert was going to be an ice cream each and slices, and the idea of providing this for 210 people was daunting. So my family and friends arrived with a delectable array of slices.

Each of her friends has the same loving attitude to their friends' children as Gemma has, and so call on each other when necessary. Seeing them all together reminds me of the New Testament when St Paul said, 'See how these Christians love one another!' If only we all did, life would be sweeter. When Gemma and Brian were selling their house a couple of years ago, and they had all the furniture moved into other rooms so new carpets could be laid, Gem just said to one of her friends who is also her cousin, 'Oh Jeanette, you'll have Lucy and Matt staying with you tonight', and to Margaret, 'Marg, Brian and I will sleep at your place tonight', and so on. Maybe she knew she had enough Brownie points in hand to be able to say it, or more likely, the relationships were so strong that it just seemed natural. Of course, she also knew that if it didn't suit, they would just say so.

After my retirement, the visits from my cousins, Claire and Ailsa, and their husbands, were a special joy to me. It was great when the two couples came together, and we had lazy breakfasts, full days, and then at a respectable hour, Frank would get a beer for the boys and Denis and John would do the honours for we three ladies, and mix us a brandy, lime and soda which we would sip as we prepared dinner.

There would be much laughter among us as we recalled old times, and Denis was always able to come up with a joke or two, mostly Irish. My sisters, Gwen and June, were advanced in age by this time and too unwell to travel the long distance which separated us, so we three cousins have become more like sisters, and their friendship means a lot to me. Of course as we get older the tyranny of distance makes it harder for some of us to travel, but we do manage it, if not as often as we would like.

In fact, in October, 2011, they are hoping to visit us, as the Radio Telescope is the venue for 'Opera at the Dish,' a night with four young opera singers performing 'From Bellini to Broadway' and featuring the Macquarie Philharmonia Orchestra under the baton of Mark Shiell. Two of the young singers have strong Parkes connections, Dallas Watts having been reared here and Helen Barnett is married to a former Parkes resident, whose grandmother, my friend Kitty Harper, still lives here. It has been billed as an enchanting evening of music under the stars, with the Dish lit up as the spectacular backdrop, and Ailsa and John, Claire and Denis and I have been eagerly looking forward to it.

The year 2002 was a special year as our Golden Wedding Anniversary fell in May, and our children planned a luncheon at Fana for close friends and family. It was a long way for Gwen and my cousins of similar age to travel, so Gemma arranged another luncheon for fifty at her home at Cherrybrook to be held a week before the one at Fana. She actually seated us all in her very spacious rumpus room, and in true Gemma style, engaged the help of her friends with the catering, and her own, and her friends' children, to wait on us at the tables. It was a memorable day, and, as it happened, the last day I would ever see Gwen walking about, and, despite encroaching Parkinson's Disease, being her usual bright self.

During the week between the two luncheon parties, Gwen sustained a fall during the night and fractured her hip, more or less shattering it. The result of the operation was that, despite the pin, screws and a bolt that the surgeon inserted, Gwen was unable to walk again, and for the next eight years was in a wheelchair in an aged care facility on the Central Coast. Her fortitude was an inspiration to us all, especially as she had always been a very active participant in all that life offered. I wrote to her often and told her many times, 'Dad would be so proud of you!' and I reminded her that he said that God hadn't given us these chins for nothing!

Despite the fact that her only daughter, Jayne Wilson's husband Paul was battling renal cancer, Jayne lavished as much care on her as she could, though Gwen would say to her, 'I'm all right, you look after Paul.' And Jayne did look after him, her nursing experience proving invaluable, giving interferon injections on alternate days, and finally nursing him at home until he lost his four year battle against cancer, and sadly, died. She had the support of her three fine sons and their wives, and the comfort of five little grandchildren, but it was a sad loss for all of them.

The 50th wedding anniversary at Fana was a grand affair, as the family generously hired a large marquee and Marie Maguire to cater, and we could gaze out over the Fana acres through the plastic windows as we enjoyed our lunch. As we cut our cake, made by Gemma's wonderful mother-in-law, Edna Churchill, and decorated by Brian's sister Kerrie, the music that echoed through the marquee was 'Love conquers Everything' from Andrew Lloyd Webber's musical, 'Aspects of Love.'

As I listened to it, I thought how true it was, for Malcolm Fraser was right when he said, 'Life wasn't meant to be easy', and we had survived many worrying times over those fifty years, battling the vicissitudes of life on the land which caused financial worries, watching Mary-Ann's struggle with her health, and finally seeing the heartache caused by three marriage break-ups.

There were more anxious moments to come though, and we had no inkling of it on that happy day. In 2004, David was reaping a wonderful harvest after many drought years, and told us buoyantly that the crops in Wancurra paddocks were registering 25 bags to the acre. We were so pleased for him, and then he had to knock off stripping to fight a fire which had started the other side of the Newell Highway in towards Parkes and which, with the wind velocity very high, was potentially very dangerous indeed.

The firefighters battled all day, but the fire jumped the Newell Highway and was heading for the Radio Telescope, which is not far from us. They stopped it near Coobang Creek, and all of us thought the drama was over. I had invited our friends, Mary and Brian Carroll, and Coral and Jim Maunsell, for dinner the next night, and after the fire was declared out, I proceeded with my preparations. I was happily setting the dinner table when David was called out to the fire again as it had started up at the spot where it had started the day before and the wind velocity was again frightening.

I heard David say to one of the truck drivers, 'Make sure they leave early enough', but I didn't think it likely we would have to leave as we had lived there fifty-two years and never had a fire. I did however, find someone who could drive David's new header and asked him to park it on bare ground. I was busy with my thoughts and my preparations, and Fana was surrounded on the western side by so much high shrubbery that when I looked out I couldn't see any fire. Suddenly, Frank rushed in and said urgently, 'Margaret, we have to go.' I said stupidly, 'Go where?' and Frank told me the fire was almost on us, and Mick (the truck driver) had told him to get me.

I was so shocked, and I remembered the children telling me that if we had to leave, to make sure I took Mary-Ann's large portrait, so I ran in to get it, realised it was too high and heavy, and Frank was yelling at me to come, so I ran into my bedroom, grabbed a dress I had bought the day before, and two pairs of panties, and raced into the car. It's funny the choices one makes sometimes.

I drove to the garden gate and we could see at once that the fire had cut us off from the driveway, the back road out was burning too, so I thought at first about the dam, but then decided to park the car on the bare ground between the house and the cottage, which was about the size of a tennis court, where earlier I had organised for the header to be put 'just in case.' That seemed a good spot for us too so I parked beside it. As we sat there, with Mick terrified in the back, we could see the fire as it attacked the house, and the dust and smoke was horrendous and the noise terrifying. We saw the tree outside the kitchen window burning, and then the dust and smoke was so intense that we could barely see the bonnet of the car.

At this point, I *knew* my house was going to burn down, and that we might die, but strangely, a feeling of peace crept over me, a very strong feeling of peace, and I knew instantly that my house was *not* going to burn, and we weren't going to die! It was a conviction without anything to substantiate it, and I may be presumptuous, but it was as if God was reassuring me. Frank told someone later, 'I know how you feel when you are going to die . . . you just go numb!' Venus and Mars? Who knows?

After the fire had passed, Tim O'Brien and Terry Job, the captain and vice—captain of the Parkes Rural Fire Service, pulled up beside us and asked if we were all right, and they told us that they had ridden it out under a fire blanket under their truck, and had radioed the plane and told them, 'Get down here to Fana, they're still inside!' meaning us. So they water-bombed the house and saved it, and that was the deafening noise we had heard, the plane zooming so low over us. If I had known that, I might have been more frightened of the low-flying plane than I was of the fire!

The boys said they were going around to the front of the house to put the garden and fences out, so I got the buckets I had filled from the swimming pool earlier 'just in case' and put out the dog kennels, and the sleepers around my tomatoes. We learned later that the fire had once again jumped the highway, as the wind was as strong as the day before, missing Bernard Dwyer's house and crops, and heading straight for us, taking David's bumper crop with it, as well as many of Bernard's sheep which had got caught in the tree-line.

We learned later that David and his mates had a lucky escape that day, as they were on the back of a truck in a paddock unfamiliar to them, with smoke and dust making it impossible to see, when their driver had an asthma attack and passed out. They stopped and replaced the driver, and thank God, made it out safely, though David told me 'It was a bit hairy!' I believe the Unger team had a similar experience, so we were all lucky to come through without loss of life, and only one house burnt down, and that was an unlived-in former dwelling.

Meanwhile, my poor visitors were heading out to my dinner party, and were stopped by the police and had to return to Parkes. They could see the smoke and I think they were worried about us, not knowing if we were safe. The fire continued for another eight miles past Fana, burning lots of stubble but also destroying many crops.

Bishop Harry Westcott came to see us as soon as traffic was allowed along our lane, gave me a hug, and told us this little anecdote about his experience of the fire.

Apparently, he and Doreen were on their knees praying that the fire would miss them, then realised it was going to miss them, so were rejoicing and thanking God, when they noticed the wind had changed and it was heading straight for their daughter, Rebecca's, house. It went something like this, 'Oh, thank You God, and bless You, thank You Lord', then seeing the wind change and the fire heading for Rebecca's house . . . 'Oh, God, No!'

There was an inquiry and the result was that electric wires on the way to the Northparkes Mines were slack, and in the high wind and intense heat of the day, had apparently rubbed together in a dry gum tree, ignited a flame and burning leaves had fallen into a dry crop of wheat, thus starting the fire which instantly had a mind of it's own. Country Energy bore the brunt of it and had to recompense farmers who put in a claim.

After the excitement had died down, we were back in the house and still worried about the boys fighting the fire further on, when the phone rang and it was Lewie and Sally ringing from Wollongong to find out how their father was. Sally was ten at the time, and the little voice sounded pathetic: 'Mardie, is my Dad all right?' All I could think was that we hoped so, but I told her that he was still out at the fire but he would be fine. She told me that she was praying for him and I could tell both she and Lewie were worried. In fifty-eight years it was the only time we had suffered a fire.

Gemma and Brian had been looking for a small place of about 100 acres with a house on it in the Parkes district for their retirement, and came and inspected a few, but they were not suitable. While discussing it with David, the idea emerged, 'What about Fana homestead and some acres?' This pleased Gemma very much as she loved our old home and could see possibilities in it for refurbishment, and as she said to me, 'We will still be able to have family gatherings like Christmas there, Mum.' So the Churchills bought Fana and eighty acres from David, and Frank and I were very happy about it. The legal aspects were all taken care of, a surveyor was brought in, and the deal was settled in 2005, so I realised I would be moving to Parkes in the next few years.

On 6th October 2005, I heard some grim news on the ABC morning program. There was a helicopter crash in the northwest and the pilot, an older man, was killed and his forty-two-year-old passenger injured. I thought; 'How sad', and didn't find out until later that it was our nephew, John Dwyer, who had been flown by the Flying Doctor Service to Royal Adelaide Hospital. His father-in-law was killed and John had a leg amputated and spent many months in hospital. It was a terrible time for John, his wife Alison, and children Mitchell and Jayne, not to mention his mother, Kittie, and his siblings, and John is still battling with the pain of his 'good' leg.

In 2008, Brian and Gemma began to prepare their home in Cherrybrook for sale, painting and laying new carpets, and I started to haunt the estate agencies and could be seen peering at the houses for sale posted in their windows. There was no hurry as Brian was not retiring until he was sixty, and he was still only fifty-eight, but I felt we had to start looking, and also begin to get us both used to the idea.

Finally, on 13th March 2010, we moved from Fana to Elizabeth Street, Parkes, and just in time too, because Frank's health took a downward curve in the ensuing winter months and I had to ring the ambulance a number of times, and he always ended up in hospital. I would have found the constant doctor's appointments and hospitalisation very hard to manage had we still lived at Fana.

Frank is in hospital as I write this, and yesterday I was sitting beside him while he ate his lunch, and out of the blue, he said, 'Thanks for looking after me.' Surprised, I replied, 'It's my pleasure Frank. Anyway, that is what I promised to do nearly sixty years ago.'

CHAPTER 22

GRANDCHILDREN AND THEIR ACCOMPLISHMENTS

After the break-up of his marriage, David was very lonely so he started to have the odd romance with a nice girl, but it always petered out. One Easter he invited a young woman and her two teenage daughters to Fana and before they arrived, we were eating at the kitchen table and I knocked a full mug of scalding tea all down the front of myself. David jumped up, grabbed a jug of iced water off the table and threw it right at the sight of the injury, which was from my waist down! It was certainly quick thinking, and saved me from a more serious consequence, but we had a good laugh about it. There was nothing wrong with his reflexes, and his action saved me from a painful burn.

Later, when David's friend had arrived, we were sitting on the front veranda having a glass of wine and someone started to tell her about me knocking the hot tea over myself. I finished the story off and in my impulsive way, picked up a glass, which I thought was empty, threw it straight at the lass, saying: 'David threw a jug of water over me, like this', and literally showered her with Chardonnay! Everyone was thunderstruck as she had only been there half an hour and I had thrown a glass of wine over her crisp, white blouse!

She was a good sport and joined in the hysterical laughter, which was no doubt fuelled by the Chardonnay, and slipped inside to change her blouse. I was mortified, but it was a milky kind of wine glass, and I honestly thought it was empty. Gemma quipped, 'No wonder David can't find a partner with Mum chucking glasses of wine over them!' and I was just thankful it wasn't red wine.

As a family, we had not suffered any serious accidents, but that changed about this time. Marguerite and her family and a few other friends were invited to a property to have a picnic on Anzac Day. David couldn't go, so Marguerite and Scott took Lewie and Sally with them as they were home for the weekend from Wollongong. After they had eaten, one of the teenage boys needed to go the toilet, so one of the older boys offered to drive him to the shearing shed where there was a toilet and washbasin. He was a careful driver, so several young people, including David's son, Lewie, climbed on the back of the old utility and sat down. Lewie remarked that he had better not lose his mobile as it was his mother's and had cost a fair bit, so someone said 'Show it to us, Lewie.'

He stood up (and at not quite fourteen, he was 6'4' tall), and took the mobile out of his jeans. It slipped out of his hands and in his efforts to grab it, he could see he was going over the side of the ute, so decided to jump out as the ute was slowing down. Unfortunately, his big size 13 boot caught on the side of the ute, and he slammed his head on the rocks when he landed, rendering him unconscious. Someone drove to the campsite for Marguerite and Scott, and Marguerite took charge while Scott rang the ambulance.

She wound a towel around his neck to keep it rigid, and when Lewie drifted in and out of consciousness, kept speaking to him quietly telling him that she needed him to keep quite still for her. The Parkes Ambulance people arranged for the Careflight Helicopter to come from Orange, so Marguerite called for a blanket to cover Lewie and herself as the huge chopper stirs up a lot of dust when it lands in a paddock. The crew put our boy in an induced coma and they flew to Orange, then later that night on to Westmead Hospital in Sydney, where Gemma, and his mum Jo, and her sister Samantha, were waiting for him at 2.00am.

David was tracked down in Parkes and was there when the chopper landed, feeling very distressed and apprehensive of course. He was unable to get a flight to Sydney until early next morning, so he rang us at 9.00pm from Orange to tell us the worrying news and that Lewie was being sent on to Sydney. When I told him his dad was in bed asleep and perhaps I should leave it until morning to tell him, David insisted,

'No Mum, I think you should tell him now as we don't know what's going to happen and it would be too big a shock for him.'

I saw the wisdom of this, so I poured us both a small brandy before bringing Frank down to the family room, and telling him. Lewie has always been 'the apple of Frank's eye' but he took it better than I thought he would, so I suggested we say a few prayers for Lewie, which we did, and then we went to bed. This was about ten o'clock and I finally dozed off just before 2.00am, when I was alarmed to hear the phone ringing, and when I answered it with a fast beating heart, it was David saying Gemma had rung to say the helicopter had just landed safely at the hospital.

A friend of ours drove Marguerite, Sally, Grace as company for Sal, and me to Sydney the next day and we spent all our time at the hospital where Lewie was in the children's ward with his feet stuck out a full 12 inches past the bed. There were some worrying days, and a lot of prayers were offered for him, but a fortnight later, he was discharged and Jo took him back to Wollongong where the brain injury team kept an eye on his head injury. Thank God, he made an amazing recovery, though he has never regained his sense of smell.

He turned fourteen in hospital so we made a little fuss of that, and I was touched when I was sitting with him and he said, 'Thanks for coming down, Mardie.' I ask you, what do you say to a beloved child who says that to you?

This was a freak accident and it was no one's fault, and, considering the number of grandchildren and the contact sports they play, plus the travelling they all do daily, not to mention their globe-trotting, motorbike riding and now Edward's bull riding, I feel very blessed indeed that they are as I write this, all in one piece.

While his younger brother was searching for a soul mate, Michael was moving from strength to strength in his job in Sydney. After he had been teaching for twelve years in Cobar, Wentworth on the Murray River, Condobolin, Peak Hill, and Forbes, he had become disenchanted with certain aspects of the administrative side and the lack of support from one principal in particular.

This led him to give up a vocation he genuinely loved and to which he had given his all, and to seek another career that would be less stressful. Nothing was available in Parkes to suit his qualifications, so he joined the Commonwealth Employment Service in Sydney, and rose rapidly through the grades to become a Senior Case Manager. When the CES became Centrelink in 1998, they offered him the same position, but he decided to try for the private sector. I rang him late one night to see how his job search was going, and he said: 'I had an interview today with the Salvation Army Employment Plus because they won twelve contracts around Sydney, and the interview went well, but I haven't heard from Ivan yet and he was going to ring me tonight.'

I said: 'Ivan! Was that Ivan Kelly?'

Michael was surprised. 'Yes,' he answered.

I asked: 'Has he got a red beard and is fairly stocky?'

Again Michael answered 'yes,' and I said: 'Michael, Ivan Kelly from the Salvation Army and his wife and family stayed in the cottage a couple of times for Farm Holidays years ago!'

Michael sounded like Mr. Chips, from the movie 'Goodbye Mr. Chips', when he said wonderingly, 'Is that so?' Then he added, 'I must have missed out on the job though, and I'm flying to Jabiru tomorrow morning to stay with Marguerite and Scott for a fortnight and have a look at Kakadu, but I gave them my phone number there.'

That was the end of that conversation, but a few nights later, he rang from Jabiru to say he had got the job as manager of the Hurstville Branch. On his return he met Ivan Kelly at the first Regional meeting, and told him who he was, a Dwyer from Fana. Ivan was amazed and said, 'The last time we went there to stay, Marguerite was only a little girl, and she met us at the gate with the news that 'Mum and Dad are at a funeral, and Dad said for you to feed the pigs, and water the dogs!' After a couple of years at Hurstville, Mike progressed to Blacktown, then Penrith and is currently at Mt. Druitt, but lives at Penrith. As would be expected of Michael, he is very dedicated to his job, and as manager, is able to utilise his people skills and also those he learned during his training and years of experience in the field of teaching.

That career started twelve years ago, and shortly after, he married Virginia, and they help each other, as she works as a Senior Case Manager in the same field, but for another company at Parramatta, so you might say there is friendly rivalry. Michael has high praise for the many skills Virginia brings to her job, at which he claims, 'she is outstanding.' She has a Bachelor in Psychology, and a Masters in Education, and in the Philippines, was administrator of a school for 3,000 girls. Michael also told me, when I started writing my story, that Virginia was Literary Editor of the University Paper in the most prestigious university in the Philippines. I thought Michael might have been a bit one-eyed about this, so I checked with Virginia, who rather reluctantly, told me it was right.

While I am discussing educational achievements, it is gratifying to see so many young Australians attending University as mature age students. This has happened to some of my grandchildren, who, though they have jobs, with maturity, have recognised the value of further study and qualifications.

Philippa's boys are a case in point. Damien and Simon, the two eldest, at thirty and twenty-seven years of age, have started at university for the first time, while retaining their jobs to finance their courses. This means all five boys are currently studying for their degrees. Damien lives in Wagga Wagga where he manages his father's G.W.S. office there, and Simon recently started up his new job, which leads to travelling to all the IGA stores in a large area of NSW, and it fits in well with his Uni studies.

Her third son, Nikolas, did very well at university, winning the Chancellor's medal and gaining eight Distinctions in his last two semesters, one of these at another university. He then spent twelve months overseas, and while over there received word that he had been awarded a scholarship to do his Honours at Charles Sturt University, Bathurst, where he was given an office, and also the opportunity to tutor, lecture and mark papers for the Uni. He has since moved on and is contemplating a trip to Spain, then Cambodia, after which he plans to do his Masters.

Benson, at twenty-one, despite being dyslexic, is also at Charles Sturt in his last year studying Advertising and succeeding beyond our wildest dreams. He achieves distinctions and credits, even two high distinctions recently, and even today did a presentation at the University. Benson has always read prolifically, which surprises me considering his dyslexia, and he is a lateral thinker, an attribute I would consider an advantage in advertising.

James, the youngest O'Donnell boy, is now twenty, and studying civil engineering at Sydney University, though he has done the external part of it in Parkes this year while working for the Parkes Shire Council, members of which have spoken to Peter and Philippa very favourably about James. He is a very caring lad who spends time with both his mother and father, and has been very generous in helping me out on numerous occasions with my computer problems. I will miss him when he has to resume his studies in Sydney, and I guess his Rugby Union team will too.

If the boys get their sense of adventure and the love of speed of car and bike racing from their father, there is no doubt in my mind that they inherit their interest in education and learning from their mother. I have seldom seen Philippa give anything except a book as a gift to her nieces and nephews and young friends, and most surfaces on her dining table and breakfast bar are covered nearly every night with school-related work. By morning though they are loaded in her boot ready for school, and the kitchen and dining area are once more clear and uncluttered.

Libby's daughter, Katrina, the little girl of ten whose dad moved away, has amazed us all with her achievements. She always wanted to be a Primary School Teacher, but a severe bout of Glandular Fever during the HSC examinations plus the break-up of her first romance which meant a lot to her, resulted in poor results, albeit glowing reports from her teachers. Previously, aged fourteen, she had written a poem and, when I read it, I asked her to allow me to enter it in the under 16 section of an Australia-wide Banjo Patterson Competition. She agreed, so I entered the poem called 'Questions' in which a young girl asks her father endless questions, 'Do you still love me? Do you still care? Do you remember how close we were? We were as close as God and priest', and it continues in that vein.

To Katrina's great surprise, but not mine, she came second, and the prize-giving dinner was at the Canobolas Hotel in Orange. Libby was unable to go because of her phobia about travel, so David drove Katrina and her proud grandparents to Orange and we attended the function in the ballroom with the huge chandelier hanging down, the same room where Frank and I had our wedding reception many years before.

Katrina had now turned fifteen and though she was dressed to suit her age, Mr. Laurie Neville, the manager of the ABC radio station, was surprised to find this tall, attractive girl was so young. He told us that the judges were very moved by her entry and it was a beautiful, poignant piece of writing. She has written many poems since, but I've not read all of them yet.

Her career as Branch Manager of National Australia Bank in Parkes and Condobolin for nine-and-a-half years was the culmination of several enterprises, beginning with a Business Certificate 111 course at Orange TAFE, which unfortunately she was unable to finish, as she was only 18, had no car, and accommodation was a problem. Then she had a series of casual jobs which included Teacher's Aide at a Forbes School, receptionist and general all-rounder at the Parkes International Motel, waitressing at the Twisted Fig restaurant at the Cambridge Hotel and also the Henry Parkes Motor Inn, serving behind the bar at the Parkes Hotel, clerical work helping out at Golden West Services, working at the Pizza Hut, and Fosseys etc. All of this kept the wolf from the door until she ended up where she was meant to be, at the NAB as branch manager.

She bought three houses along the way, the first when only nineteen, and later sold them, won the best dressed female at the Parkes Picnic Races, and met her future husband, Glen Johnston, who seemed to be a confirmed bachelor, in 2003. She gave birth to Angus in 2005 and Frankie in 2008. She and Glen were married later that year, Estella was born in 2009 and finally Boundy (called after W.B. and his great, great grandfather) arrived in February 2011. Space only allows for half of her story but you can see she is a busy girl, and is now a very happy wife and mother.

Libby's second daughter, Anita, met her partner when extremely young and naive, but gained her AIN (Assistant in Nursing), and cared for the elderly in Niola Nursing Home in Parkes and also in Cherrybrook in Sydney when she and her partner moved there. She was highly thought of in both these facilities, as she was an efficient and compassionate nurse. Her daughter, Hope, was born in 2005, and Lillian in 2007. She separated from their father in that year, and he died tragically in 2009. She manages her life and her two little girls very well, and was coping well enough to get a job this year at one of the motels and is currently working at three jobs. She is very generous with her time where Frank and I are concerned, and often calls in to shave her grandfather, something that is a great help to me.

Bethany, Libby's youngest daughter, is in Year 11 at Red Bend College, and after an up and down year last year, has now knuckled down to study and her teachers are pleased with her efforts. She made her debut at the Catholic Ball this year and was partnered by my nephew Warren's son, Alec Edwards, so the Dwyers and Edwards are sticking together. They made a delightful couple, he in a dark suit and Bethany in a white gown cut on simple lines, but with two flying panels hanging from the shoulders at the back. I only made one request of her: 'Don't get a dress that is too old for you, leave the more sophisticated styles for the brides.' And she looked perfect for her age.

Before discussing what David's children are doing, I should bring my readers up to date with his life. When I last spoke of him, I had just thrown a glass of wine over one of his female friends, but quite a lot of time has elapsed since then, and he has certainly moved on with his life.

In late April 2010, David sustained an injury to his leg, which required 22 stitches. It became infected, and he was unable to work for three weeks, and this right at the height of sowing time. When Lewie had his eighteenth birthday party on 1ˢᵗ May, David made it to Wollongong, thanks to Katrina and Glen, who drove him, but because he was sowing, arrived very late.

Katrina introduced him to a very nice blonde lady named Lisa Eastment, and according to Katrina, the attraction was mutual, and they talked all night. Things moved very fast between them, and it wasn't long before David was flying up to the Gold Coast where Lisa lived with her thirteen-year-old daughter, Brittany, and her twelve-year-old son, Tyson, and she was reversing the journey and coming to Parkes. The children came down fairly soon and loved Parkes, and before we knew it, Lisa had bought a house here, and it was all in a matter of months.

She had some renovations done to the house which opened it up more, and Brittany and Lewie have a room each, and there is one for Sally and Tyson whenever they come to Parkes, as Sally lives with Jo in Wollongong, and Tyson at the moment is with his father in Cairns. Brittany goes to Red Bend College with Grace, Billy and Bethany, and her good friends Ruby Byrnes and Illy Hewett, and is in touch footy and basketball teams.

Now we come to the tricky bit. It is all legal of course, but David's ex-wife Jo is now married to Lisa's brother, Craig, but all parties seem to have adjusted to the situation, and Jo will always have a spot in our memories. I say a special thanks to God for bringing them together for we all love Lisa, and haven't seen David so happy for years. He has a partner and helpmate who goes with him wherever he is working and helps him, then goes home and cooks them all a wonderful dinner. David told me 'It's a bit like "Packed to the Rafters" here', as David's worker, Adrian, lives downstairs for the time being in a flat, and Lisa is providing for him too, and of course he, David and Lewie have hearty appetites, Brittany is a busy school-girl and Tyson comes for school holidays. Sal comes when her training schedule allows, but she is doing the Higher School certificate next year so won't have much time to spare.

David's son, Lewie, has come from Wollongong to live with David and Lisa, and is employed by Parkes Pumps, working with a couple of older men and enjoying every minute of it. He is taking on a couple of night courses when TAFE resumes next year, and will begin footy training next football season. I'm not happy about him playing football because of his former head injury, but he loves it and plays a good game. However, no one listens to an 82-year-old born worrier, so it's overtime on the prayers for me.

Sally is in Year 11 at St Mary's in Wollongong and I'm told is a good student. She is also very athletic and has been playing in the Illawarra Mixed Touch Footy team since she was fifteen, and she is now seventeen. She is conscientious about her training and has her sights set on the Australian team, but only time will tell about that. Just recently she was selected in the NSW Catholic Schools' Team and I guess it is good to have a dream. Meanwhile, she is very fit and runs kilometres with little effort, and that is remarkable when one considers she was the baby who had a huge heart operation when only a week old. Like Oprah Winfrey, I have always felt God's grace in my life, and can see how He looks after me, and mine.

I sound as if I think my children and grandchildren are perfect, but indeed they are not, and who wants them to be? I am however, aware of their struggles and achievements, and I've always said 'If any of them were pulled up for DUI or some other offence, it would be in the newspapers for all to see', so if their efforts in life have been successful, be it in bull-riding, teaching, policing, parenting, sport, or just being a good-living normal person, in a journal like this, I am recording it. And thank you for your indulgence in reading it.

The Edwards family at Mt. Pleasant shortly after Margaret announced her engagement. Margaret, W.B., Harry, Stella, June, Jack, Gwen and Dick in front

Dick, Margaret, Harry, June and Gwen at Harry's home at Lake Macquarie. Absent is Jack, who was deceased

Margaret and Frank Dwyer share a moment
at her 80th birthday celebrations

Margaret and her grandchildren, Lewis Dwyer, holding
Billy Burns, Sally Dwyer and Grace Burns, visit Aunty May
Donnelly, on her 102nd birthday. She lived to be 107

Margaret and co-travellers on the coach party in Edinburgh

The bride, Libby Dwyer, with her family, Mary-Ann,
Philippa, Marguerite, Michael, Frank, David and Gemma.
This is the only photograph with all the family together

Margaret and her co-workers, Margaret Troy and Robyn
McDonald, with coordinator, Ivy Rooke

Some of the Dwyer family at the wedding of granddaughter,
Katrina Kealley, to Glen Johnston

Some of Margaret Dwyer's school friends at a reunion.
Sister Margaret Baker (Bake), Clair O'Regan, Sister Marie Therese,
Kath Freeth and Sister Christina (Joan Morrissey)

Michael Dwyer and his wife, Virginia, at Fana

Philippa O'Donnell at the Parkes picnic races

Libby Kealley at her 50th birthday

Marguerite Burns (centre) with Joanne Ford and her sister, Gemma Churchill, at her 40th birthday

David Dwyer and Frank Donnelly at Marguerite's birthday celebrations

Philippa's boys, Simon, James, Nikolas, Damien,
and Benson O'Donnell

Libby and her girls, Anita, Bethany, Katrina, and
her new husband, Glen Johnston

Gemma and Brian Churchill and their family
at Lucy's wedding to Matthew Johnson, Sam, Brian, Lucy
and Matt, Gemma, Jack and Edward

David's children, Lewis and Sally, with their mother, Jo Toban

Marguerite's family, Daisy, Marguerite, Scott, Billy, and Grace

CHAPTER 23

FAREWELL TO FANA

It was March 2008 and we were at the sad funeral of Craig Whittaker, the husband of one of Marguerite's friends, Mandy, relaxing at the wake at the Railway Hotel in Parkes. I turned away from Frank to get him a cup of tea, and hearing exclamations of consternation, turned to see Frank slowly falling backwards to the floor. My immediate reaction was to start shaking as he had never had any sort of turn before, but the amazing thing was that the men lifted him up and he had his tea as if nothing had happened.

I was to witness this episode many times in the coming months, sometimes three or four times a week. The blackout only lasted a very short time, and he always fell backwards. The doctors treated him with Warfarin tablets, or 'rat poison' as he would tell people, but nothing changed, and I was fearful he would hit his head on the coffee table or something as he landed. And with Frank on Warfarin, I was nervous of a serious bleed.

Luckily, he was in Sydney with Gemma when it happened once, and she took him straight to Casualty at Hornsby Hospital. After a number of tests, he was admitted, and a few days later he was transported to Royal North Shore Hospital where they put a pacemaker and defibrillator under the skin on his chest. I went to Sydney and after his discharge, and the team from Royal North Shore came twice daily to Gemma's and taught me how to look after him and how to handle his medication.

On our return to Parkes, the doctors from the Clarinda Street Medical Centre took over and he has been closely watched and monitored ever since. I have been told he has a 'tired and floppy' old heart and he gave us a serious fright on Fathers' Day 2010, when he was in hospital in the high dependency unit and unable to breathe. The locum and nursing staff were talking about calling the Careflight helicopter to move him to Westmead Hospital in Sydney and Doctor Harwood was called in.

Frank wasn't altogether with us, and was making a lot of noise trying to breathe. Dr. Harwood told us he knew Frank wouldn't want to go to Sydney away from us all, and he mightn't make it anyway. He ended by saying, 'But it's up to you Mardie, I know it's hard, but you have to make a decision now because we have to order the chopper.' I asked Marguerite what she thought, and she said she couldn't disagree with David Harwood, so I asked Davey, and he said to the doctor, 'Well what's the alternative, David?'

David said, 'We keep him here and make him as comfortable as possible for as long as possible.'

At that moment, Frank opened his eyes, spoke to Davey and Lewie, then looked up and saw the doctor, and said, 'Oh you're here, David.' David welcomed him back and told him we were just about to send for the chopper. Frank's reaction was purely Frank: 'No way in the bloody world!' And I was relieved of the responsibility of making the decision and he is being kept comfortable and enjoys his quieter life.

We are frequently in the waiting room at the surgery for his regular blood tests and he is like a child let out of school, talking to everyone: 'What's your name? Are you from here?' and so on. One day the waiting room was full, and he told a gentleman he was speaking with, 'The Viagra tablets they give me aren't working!' The room was full of elderly ladies, and the odd young Mum with a child, and the room just exploded with mirth . . . I've never seen such a shake-up in a waiting room before.

Everyone was laughing but I think I was 'laughing on the outside' and 'grinning and bearing it' on the inside, if not actually crying as in the words of the old song.

I have added another title to my name . . . I am now Frank's carer. He tells everyone I am the best carer in the world, but he forgets that sometimes, and I go from being Mother Theresa to Mary Magdalene very quickly. He used to sit on the front veranda when the weather was mild, with a rug across his knees, and his men friends often called in to sit and yarn with him there, but it's winter now and the sun is warm at the back of the house so he sits there in what I call 'my garden room', because of the palms and hanging plants that fill it, and if too cold, he sits inside with the gas heater on.

Frank Donnelly, Bob Collins, John Davey, Cliff Westcott, Neil and Ian Unger, Don Littlewood and Lyndsay Watt are very generous with their time, and the other day, Len Unger, who is 94, rode his gopher up and spent an hour-and-a-half with him. Frank really enjoyed Len's visit and he said he'd come again. I like seeing him enjoying his friends' company and I love making them tea or coffee, that's one of the joys of being in town, having people pop in.

I didn't want to disrupt the house too much before the 80th birthday and 'Farewell to Fana' luncheon, so I didn't start packing all the boxes until after it was over. It was a huge job, packing and sorting 58 years of possessions, some precious, others just clutter, and though my girls helped a bit, they are busy people and work fulltime and most of it, especially the sorting of photographs, needed me on the job.

Marguerite and Scott were the ones who found a house for us. As soon as Margie saw 10 Elizabeth Street, she knew I would love it, and rang me to meet them there at 3o'clock. I knew instantly I would be happy there as it was a Federation house with high, patterned ceilings and beautiful stained glass windows and doors throughout. Our requirement had been three bedrooms and two bathrooms but it only had a second toilet on the back veranda, and no second shower, but we all said confidently, 'We can soon put an outside shower near the toilet.' This has been harder to achieve than we thought, but moves are in hand to fix the problems we have in that area.

Everyone who sees it for the first time is struck by how it reminds them of Fana, and when someone walks in, he or she will say, 'Oh, this is Fana!' so we are calling it 'Little Fana' and I plan to replace the name 'Kelso' which is on the front wall with that. Gemma and Brian are renaming our former home too, and it is now Fana Beug, which is Gaelic for Little Fana. Many people say when they walk into 10 Elizabeth Street, 'Mardie, this is sooooooo you!'

It is in a pretty street lined with jacaranda trees, and in a great position with close proximity to the hospital, the supermarket, the doctors' surgery and Woolworths, and the Church is only a few minutes away. So we were thrilled when the sale went ahead without much delay.

We were to move in on March 13, 2010, so every time I came to Parkes, I loaded the car and the boot with whatever I could carry and would put them in place and also measure spots to see where my furniture would fit. I was still packing boxes, and it was decisions, decisions, decisions! I didn't realise that I was physically and emotionally exhausted, and I was driving in on March 3, three days before Lucy and Matt's wedding in Bathurst, and I prayed that nothing would spoil the wedding. I prayed that I would not have an accident, in fact, that no one would have an accident, or do anything to disrupt Gemma's first wedding, as they were all looking forward to it so much.

When I finished the shopping, paying the bills and leaving things at our new house, I felt fine so I left for Fana. I waved to Liz Dwyer and Karen Pearce as I turned off the highway into Dwyer's Lane, was listening to music on the radio and everything was normal . . . until I was approaching the first left-hand turn on the lane. I was driving the usual pace (about 80 kilometres) that we all travel on the lane, when suddenly I was in loose gravel on the wrong side of the road.

I knew not to apply the brake, but I did try to steer the car gently over to the correct side. To my dismay, it started to rock, and it seemed to have picked up speed, so I knew I was in trouble. I just grasped the steering wheel firmly, pressed my back into the seat, and my neck firmly into the head rest, and the next few minutes were chaotic, but I dimly realised the car was turning over.

Suddenly it was all over, and I was sitting behind the wheel of a car which was facing back the way I had been coming from, parked half on Unger's fence and with a badly shattered windscreen. My first thought was, 'I'm alive!' and my second was a fervent thank-you to God. I could not open the front doors, but I managed to open one of the back ones, so crawled out and down to the road. I had picked my mobile phone off the floor in the back as I crawled out, so I rang my friend Ronda Hewes, and she and Denis came. They retrieved my glasses, unbroken, from under the driver's seat, and everything else out of the car, and wonder of wonders, a case of Frank's Toohey's Old beer from the boot. There was only one bottle ruined, and that had blown!

Marguerite came in answer to Ronda's phone call, and instructed me to pack an overnight bag for Dad, as she had arranged for him to go to Philippa's for the night and she was meeting us at the hospital, and one for myself as I would probably be in hospital overnight. They met us at the doors to Casualty with a wheelchair and neck brace and told me I should have rung the ambulance instead of Ronda, as neck injuries sometimes don't show at first. I was X-rayed, and everyone was amazed that I didn't have at least some sign of whiplash, but put it down to my reflex action of pushing my head against the head rest.

I was discharged the next day, and Lucy's wedding in Bathurst was in three days' time. I was to sing at the wedding, so my main concern was to get the old voice in shape and sing as pleasingly as I could. There were a lot of prayers said, and pineapple juice sipped, because as I said, I was past my 'use-by' date for singing and I honestly didn't feel confident. I didn't want to let my beautiful granddaughter down.

My prayers were answered, and I asked myself, 'Is there no limit to God's indulgence when He saved the father of the bride at the wedding feast at Cana from the embarrassment of running out of wine, by changing water into wine, and now, centuries later, caused an 81-year-old lady with a perpetually husky voice, "to sing like a bird", to quote those present?' As I gazed down the chapel, I saw my family's tears, my big, brawny sons and grandsons as affected as the girls in our family who are sometimes emotional wrecks, and I realised they were thinking of what might have been because of my accident.

My friend Joan (Sister Christina) accompanied me on the organ in St Stannies Chapel, and managed this unfamiliar organ very well, and it was so reassuring to look up to the choir loft and see her playing so confidently. At school, her chosen musical instrument was the violin, but as choir mistress for many years at Perthville, she is very familiar with the organ.

The wedding was beautiful, Lucy a petite and delightful bride, Matt a very handsome groom, and six of Lucy's girlfriends, Paula, Leanne, Kate, Jo, another Gemma, and Jess, were a bevy of beauty in coral, a lovely shade of pink, and Lucy asked each girl to choose her own style. Seven-year-old Daisy Mary-Ann shone as the sole flower girl, and Matt's attendants were Lucy's three brothers Sam, Ed and Jack, Lucy's cousin, Simon O'Donnell, and two of Matt's friends.

Father James Sutcliffe celebrated the marriage in a very personal way, and mentioned how much thought the young couple had put into choosing their readings. They followed tradition, as Matt's father and mother, Mick and Liz Johnstone, had also been married in that Chapel, and both Matt and his father had gone to school at the College.

The young couple went to Thailand for their honeymoon, and five of the groomsmen very kindly gave them a week there on their own, and then *joined them*! I mean, how thoughtful, how kind, how very like them! They are great friends, always ready to help out!

CHAPTER 24

WE LEAVE FANA

In 2009 I was to celebrate my 80th birthday, and a house in Parkes had been found for us, so as I said in the last chapter, I began sorting my possessions in preparation for the big move towards the end of the year.

Suddenly I realised the enormity of what was happening. Fifty-eight years of living on our lovely farm and rearing our seven children there; fifty-eight years of friendly contact with our neighbours whom we now called friends; fifty-eight years of solitude and privacy; fifty-eight years of gazing out of every window to an ever-changing vista, sometimes chocolate-brown ploughed fields, then the emerging pale green of newly-sown crops followed by the burgeoning deeper green as they matured, and finally the gradual ripening of the heads when the weather warmed, and they turned brown. And the canola . . . from green and verdant to a vibrant sea of yellow as far as the eye could see until it also ripened and turned brown.

I felt a strong urge to celebrate those years and to share the event with as many friends and neighbours as we could, so we planned a 'Farewell to Fana' day to coincide with my birthday. I wanted to thank God publicly for all He had done for us during those years, for His constant care of each of us and for the many blessings he had bestowed on our family, so I incorporated a short Thanksgiving Service in to the celebrations.

He didn't make us rich in monetary terms, far from it, but we felt rich in our family, the affection we had for each other, and in the friends we had gathered over the years.

Our Parish priest was unable to come, so I asked Sister Joan Keogh, who is in charge of pastoral care in the Peak Hill Parish, to conduct the twenty minute service, and in her generous way, she not only did that, but printed the booklets we used. We held it in, and around, Mary-Ann's Garden and I added a photograph of her to the sign that hung on a tree trunk in her garden.

Michael acted as MC, and a grandchild from each family read a short verse specially chosen from scripture, Virginia representing Michael and herself, as they have no children, and Bernard's son, Patrick Dwyer, read one too as he is a special friend of Frank's. At the end of the readings, Sister Joan read a special blessing, with her hand on our shoulders, for Frank and me, and we ended with everyone singing The Galilee Song:

> 'As I gaze into the night. Down the future of my
> years . . . I'm not sure I want to walk,
> Past horizons that I know! But I feel my spirit called.
> Like a stirring deep within,
> Restless, till I live again, beyond the fears that close
> me in!
> So I leave my boats behind, leave them on familiar
> shores,
> Set my heart upon the deep, follow you again my
> Lord!'

This hymn typifies how I felt, apprehensive and vulnerable, as I had never lived in a town, and only in three places in my life, Mt. Pleasant, Perthville and Fana, all of them in the country, and all so very safe and familiar. And I knew Frank had similar feelings. But the hymn says 'beyond the fears that close me in,' and I felt a bit like when I embraced playing bridge, very apprehensive. I had to step outside my comfort zone, grit my teeth and start a new life, leaving my former life behind.

After the service, everyone moved into a huge new shed, with a cement floor and several windows, which Gem and Brian had built just outside the garden gate. We found the family had set long tables and chairs to seat at least 150 (the younger people were eating at tables outside) and two smaller tables were laden with identical food platters, to save everyone crowding around one table. There was a large leg of ham, lamb from Derrymore and Mt. Pleasant, beef and chicken platters, and 'three-only' special and delicious salads, and of course, tossed salads.

The shed was decorated in the colours I had chosen for my eightieth birthday, green and orange, and my invitations had been couched in words to proclaim my ecumenical upbringing, with the theme 'Oh me father, he was orange, and me mother, she was green!'

Michael continued as MC inside, and the main meal was followed by a novel dessert, which, with over two hundred guests to serve, was a very practical idea. Daisy Burns and Jackie Dwyer took Magnum ice creams around on trays and we ate those while we listened to Philippa, Marguerite and David extol our virtues, while Joanne Ford spoke of how her family loved Fana, and had been coming there for twenty-two years, and our brother-in-law, Ritchie McKay, remembered the many happy occasions when he and many present had enjoyed the hospitality of Fana.

Our niece, Jacinta Weekes, told of growing up beside us and sharing so much with our children over the years, and she especially remembered car trips when we all sang as we drove along. John Davey and Linda McGlynn, friends for many years, were also generous in their comments, and my brother Dick told me he wanted to speak, but he knew he would be too emotional. Harry would have been the same if he had been there, and as we all get older and start remembering things, we all get a bit emotional.

It was a very special day for me with all my children and grandchildren there, my sole surviving brother, Dick, and his wife, Maree, their son Warren and his wife Donna, Gwen's daughter, Jayne, and her brother Gerard, and his wife Dagmar, who all travelled long distances. My special cousins, Claire and Denis, Ailsa and John, had been invaluable in taking charge of the morning tea when everyone had first arrived and also served tea, coffee and slices after we left the shed. My sisters-in-law from Dubbo, Parkes and Trundle and many of my local and Parkes friends came bearing slices, which were part of the dessert, and

Margaret, one of the 'little ones' when I first came to Derrymore, made and decorated a beautiful birthday cake.

Michael had prepared a wonderful PowerPoint presentation, but there was too much light in the shed to do it justice, though some of us enjoyed it later inside. And Michael chose my favourite music with the presentation, 'Nessun Dorma', sung by Pavarotti, 'Lookin' forward, Lookin' back', sung by John Williamson, and the one we all love in our family, You Raise Me Up.

A special joy was that my very first and only boyfriend, Kevin Peters, brought by his daughter Judy, and her husband, Joe, came from Orange and he was on the cusp of turning ninety. When I saw him in his walker, the years rolled back and I was that young, naive girl at Mt. Pleasant again, and I remembered how good he had been to me and it was wonderful to see him. So I had old friends and new friends surrounding me and making it all so special.

Our children combined their efforts to make it a memorable occasion, and I was pleased that so many of their friends came to share the day with us. I was especially touched that all those children who had been coming to Fana for years with their parents, made the effort as adults to be present at my 80th birthday and the Farewell to Fana. They are all very dear to me, as are their parents.

The year 2009 however held sadness for a lot of Parkes people, including me, when Sister Michael who was loved throughout Parkes and districts, suffered a stroke and died just before her 90th birthday. A couple of weeks later, Sister Marie Therese also died in Bathurst and though she was 96, I felt her loss. She was my teacher, my basketball coach, my mentor, my most constant correspondent and my friend, and it was Marie Therese who urged me many times to write my story. Marguerite drove me to Perthville for her funeral and I sat with Joan, Sister Christina, and she and I placed items on the coffin of our former, beloved teacher.

The next year brought a deterioration in Gwen's condition, and Jayne rang to warn me that she was slipping. I had a sick husband at this time and I was his carer, and thought I couldn't get to see her. She confounded the medical staff by hanging on for a month and no one knew when that strong heart would stop beating. Knowing her as I did, I knew it would take some time.

One day Marguerite said, 'Mum, if you want to go and see Aunty Gwen you could put Dad in The Southern Cross Village for respite care', and suddenly I decided I would. I rang the Village, they agreed, so I rang our chemist to get a Webster Pack ready for the Village, drove swiftly to the Railway Station and got a return ticket to Penrith, and then I rang Michael to see if he could pick me up that night and take me to see Gwen the next day. Michael assured me he could arrange for someone to fill in for him at work and he would take me.

I packed Frank's overnight bag and medications and a suitcase for myself, phoned Philippa at her school and asked her to pick Dad and his belongings up after school and take him to the Village. I made one more phone call to my granddaughter, Anita, to come and take me to the station as I didn't want to leave my car there. I made Frank a sandwich for lunch and Anita arrived with Hope and Lillian in their car seats. I kissed Frank goodbye and left him serenely watching the ABC on television, and Anita delivered me to the station ten minutes before the coach left. It was 12.30pm when I made the decision to go, and 2.10 pm when I boarded the coach. So the saying, 'Wishes have wings' must be true as I am not usually a fast mover nowadays!

Michael was called on his mobile (which luckily is not handheld) so many times by the acting manager on our way up to The Entrance, and back, that I felt slightly guilty for taking him away from work. The guilt disappeared when I approached Gwen's bed and saw how lovely she looked, and how frail, and I knew I could have done nothing else but come. She couldn't speak, but Jayne said, 'Margaret's here, Mum,' and I know she knew I was there by the awareness in her eyes. I simply sat there holding her hand and talking to her about how she had been a second mother to me, and how much I loved her.

At one stage I reminded her about the time she was singing 'Shine little glow—worm, shine oh glimmer' at the piano, and Harry was passing through, and he sang 'Shine little glow-worm, shine you bugger!' She turned her head slightly and looked at me with the tiniest little smile, and I knew she remembered. I suggested that perhaps we were making her tired, and maybe we should go, and Jayne told her and asked, 'If you want them to stay, press my hand', and she did just that, so we stayed a bit longer.

Memories flooded over me as I sat there, of a small girl standing impatiently while this older sister tied my hair with a red ribbon to keep it out of my eyes at school, of the same small girl standing even more impatiently while she cut my nails. I remembered how she tried to explain to me the changes happening to my teenage body, and how 'squirmy' I felt, but most of all I remembered how honest and fine she was, and how talented.

A week or so later we made the trip again, but this time it was to lay her to rest beside Bill in the Palmdale Cemetery. She was five months away from her 90th birthday, and left a string of achievements behind her, but I always remember her as a loving sister, scrupulously honest in all she said, always cheerful, and as I've said earlier, very quick at whatever she did.

At Gwen's funeral, I caught up with Gwen's three children. With Jayne, who had had lost Paul, and their three sons, Matthew and his wife, Jay, Nathan and his wife Michelle, and Luke, who is single, and met Jayne's five lovely grandchildren. Her sons are fine boys and successful in their line of business, and Jayne has finally come through the tunnel of her great grief at losing Paul, and is presently holidaying with a female friend in Italy, and planning more trips.

Robert, who is actually my godson, lives near Tweed Heads and has two sons, Justin and Joshua, who came with him to the funeral. No longer 'Wobs' as we called him when he was little and used to love all that went on at Mt. Pleasant, he has progressed through a banking career, bookmaking, owning a Pet Food shop in Dubbo, to now doing what he loves best, working with polo horses on his small acreage, and playing polo as well. He owns a couple of horses, but the others are thoroughbred polo horses which he has on agistment on his property, which his brother Gerard told me is of a very high standard.

Gerard is the youngest of Gwen's children, and he lives at West Pennant Hills in Sydney with his second wife, Dagmar. He and Debbie had four children, Cameron, Jennelle, Tammara, and Brennan, but sadly, Debbie died from cancer when Brennan was just five, and later he married Dagmar who is wonderful to them all. Gerard followed his father, Bill, into the teaching arena, his first school being one at Mt. Druitt, where he taught for nine years. He then moved to Braddock High School in Cranebrook in North Ryde for three years, after which he was appointed Head of Science at Prairiewood High in Fairfield.

I remember my former teacher, Bill, being very proud of Gerard when he became Senior Curriculum Advisor, travelling around NSW to all the high schools, and it was at this point that he lost Debbie. With young children to rear, he gave up the travelling, and became School Development Officer in Western Sydney for five years. Currently in his early fifties, he works as Assistant Director of Education Measurement, and School Accountability, in Sydney, and his children have branched out in their own careers, except for Brennan who is in his last year at school.

My brother Jack's daughter, Robyn, is married to Bill Keech, and they live in Bundaberg. They have four daughters, Devarni, Amber, Jenaya, and Ebony, and also five grandchildren, one of them called Jack. They have run their business, Bundaberg House Relocations, for many years and now own a house in Vanuatu where they discovered the need for storage sheds. Before they moved to Bundaberg, they lived in Cairns where Robyn had a boutique for young girls, so Robyn seems to have inherited her father's 'get up and go'.

I remember when Jack lost the sight of one eye after he collected a big black bull on his windscreen and consequently had a car accident while returning home from Orange one night. While in hospital he defied the orders of the nursing staff 'to rest and be quiet,' and through phone calls, sold a couple of mobs of sheep and a property or two. Jack had followed W.B. into the Stock and Station Agency and had lots of energy until struck down by cancer in his mid-fifties.

Jack's boy, Stephen, has led a wandering life, working here, there and everywhere. He married Barbara, a nurse from Orange, and they had a son, Adam, but the marriage broke up, and since then he has lived a couple of times in Darwin, worked for Waterman's Drillers in the Central West, and, according to Robyn, is currently living and working down near Bateman's Bay on the South Coast. I remember him as a beautiful little curly-headed boy, but I haven't seen him for years, so I intend to catch up with him soon.

June and Lester had two children, Lindy and Philip, but moved to Brisbane when Lindy was just a baby. Lindy was a vivacious girl, like Mary-Ann, and she was married to Noel L'Estrange and had two small boys when she found the dreaded lump in her breast, which turned out to be malignant. She was thirty-two at the time, and breast-feeding six months old Edward, and her other son Patrick, was two. It was very sad for the family when she died aged thirty-four, leaving Noel with a four year old and a two year old to rear.

Lindy's career had been in advertising, like her father Lester, and she met her husband through that as he was also in advertising. Noel eventually married Jan, a friend of Lindy's, whose husband had also died, and they have a daughter, Anna, and of course Lindy's two sons, Patrick and Edward.

June's son Philip's career started in hotel management, and then he leased a gourmet delicatessen which was named 'Oodles,' at The Valley in Brisbane for many years, only giving it up when his rare arthritic condition made it too hard to continue. He married Christine, who worked there with him, and they had a son, Harry, who is now nineteen, but unfortunately the marriage ended. Oodles supplied take-away meals for many places, including Government House in Brisbane, and Philip was an excellent chef. Nowadays, he is a manager of a local Landcare group, and engaged to Kimberly and they plan to marry later this year.

June is in a nursing home on Bribie Island, having lost Lester from a heart attack in April, 2009, and Philip says she is happy there, but like dementia patients everywhere, asks to go home as night approaches. Michael and I flew up to see her a few years ago, and I could hardly believe it! June's hair is as snowy white as mine has been for years, but hers still has the curly look that I was denied, and it looks different with her brown eyes.

We bought her a couple of bottles of rum and also a few bottles of Coke, as rum and Coke has been her favourite nightcap for many years. I said, 'Perhaps we'd better give them to the staff for safe keeping', and the brown eyes flashed, and she said, 'No way, they'll only drink them!' So we knew the young feisty June was still in there, somewhere.

As for Frank and me, we live happily in Little Fana in Elizabeth Street where I care for him, and he cares about me. Our friends drop in, or I invite them on occasion, and our home, including our front veranda and garden room at the back, cause the house to expand so we are mostly not confined to the rooms within the house. My piano is now in my lounge and I play it often, and Frank enjoys listening to the old melodies, which were so popular in his youth; 'evergreens' I think they are called. The neighbours have been remarking lately that they also love to hear it, so I am still doing what I love, using my gift of music to give pleasure to people.

I have a pleasant social life of playing bridge one day a week, attending Mass at weekends and whenever I can on weekdays, my once-a-month View Club Luncheon meeting, a garden club meeting occasionally, an odd lunch with friends when Libby kindly comes to spend time with her Dad, and of course the odd visit to Fana Beug when Gemma and Brian are in residence.

We have also enjoyed regular visits from Frank's cousins, Michael Byrnes and his wife Anne, from Kiama, and Norma Manning and her husband, Peter, from the Central Coast. Frank's cousins, Michael and Norma, have always enjoyed a very close relationship with the Dwyer family, and Frank really enjoys their visits and reliving the past with them.

We also enjoy family celebrations which are fairly constant in our family, as we had a 50th birthday for Gemma in December 2010, the birth and christening of Boundy Edward Campbell Johnston and a 30th birthday party for his Mum, Katrina, this year. Philippa's youngest son, James, is turning twenty-one in November, so I've no doubt we will be celebrating that occasion.

On 1st October this year, 2011, we, the Dwyer Family, celebrated 100 years since Grandfather Michael Dwyer, and his wife, Mary Josephine, settled in the Alectown area. The Centenary celebrations were held at Derrymore, and we were very involved as Grandfather, Frank's dad, and Uncle Pat added to their holding by purchasing adjoining properties, one of which was Fana, where we lived for fifty-eight years.

There was a committee formed, and Gemma, as the new resident of Fana, was on that. There was also a Mass, celebrated by Father Hooley, an Irish priest from Canowindra, in which all families played a role. The Offertory Procession consisted of five of our great-grandchildren, all under five, and another tiny tot who was Jacinta's grandchild, and as they say in today's vernacular, 'They were all as cute as!'

Relatives from Ireland, Mary and Michael Parsons, came out especially and attended with their son, Shane, who lives in Sydney, and it was a great opportunity for us to get to know them.

After Mass we enjoyed a lovely meal of cold meat and salads, and the formal part of the day began. Frank had declined to speak because his health had been uncertain, so his sisters spoke of their grandfather and grandmother, their mother and father, and recalled events from their growing up years at Derrymore. Frank, as patriarch of the family, cut the ribbon to unveil a plaque on a huge granite rock which stated, 'The descendants of Michael and Mary Dwyer gathered here on 1st October, 2011, to celebrate 100 years of Derrymore.'

Our Michael put together a wonderful PowerPoint presentation of all the family groups from the photographs, which he had asked them to send him, and this was accompanied by stirring and truly great music. The rain pelted down, but many of those present were reared in the mud when it rained, and we were under shelter in a great shed, so we just thanked God for the rain for which the farmers were grateful.

Rose-Marie wrote to Frank the week after, telling him he had been a real father figure to her all her life, and saying how much she appreciated his phone calls when they had fire, floods and droughts, and he would ring to see how they were. Frank had forgotten this, but he was pleased to be reminded of it, and when she said that he had taken his truck to Warren after they had a fire twenty years ago to help collect the hay which Haddon Rig Stud had given them for the stock, he remembered that too.

There are doctor's appointments to keep us occupied and sometimes hospitalization for Frank, and he has recently had surgery in the new Orange Hospital to remove a 13 millimetre stone which was lodged in a tube to his kidney, causing obstruction, but strangely no pain. Since then he has been remarkably well, no wheezing from the build up of fluid which plagued him all last year, and his doctor recently pronounced his chest the best it's been for ages. So we are grateful for that, and Frank continues, as I'm fond of telling friends, 'to live the life of Reilly!'

In writing this short autobiography, I have only made passing reference to my Alectown friends, Vilma, Zilda, Helen, Beverly and Ronda, but anyone who lives in the country knows how invaluable friends are, and I know I would have been bereft without them. Friends are necessary for one's mental wellbeing and I value them greatly, as I do my friends in Parkes, especially Helmi, who has been a faithful friend for over thirty years, my friends among the Sister of Mercy, Kitty Harper, Venie, Shirley and all the new friends I have made since coming to Parkes to live.

There is one young friend we call Poss, who somehow sneaked into my heart like an extra daughter as Jo Ford did, and when she is with me, the song in my heart reaches crescendo. Nothing is any trouble to her, and I am continually indebted to her. And joy of joys, David got Lisa's children, Brittany and Tyson, out of bed one morning recently and told them to come to the kitchen where Lisa and Lewie were organising breakfast, as he wanted to ask their mother to marry him! And he did just that, producing the ring as well, so now they are organising a wedding for early in 2012 and we are just delighted.

I have been writing about W.B.'s and Stella's children and grandchildren, in this journey of a soul, and somehow I feel they would be 'as proud as punch' if they happened to meet up with any of us today. All they asked of us was to have integrity, to be totally honest, 'to mind our P's and Q's' (good one, Dad!), to show compassion for our fellow human beings and to quote W.B., 'to look after the pennies and the pounds would look after themselves!' That would be cents and dollars now, but somehow I feel we have failed that test, as frugality is not very common now, and we live in a consumer society, totally different to the frugal times of my youth.

Thoughtfulness and compassion I do see in my children and grandchildren, not religiosity and bums on seats in the church all the time, but hidden acts of a charitable nature, and a caring attitude to friends in need of a little bit of TLC. Frank and I are showered with kindness and generosity from them, from Michael down to Marguerite, and all this while they are working fulltime and leading very busy lives.

Our grandchildren are also generous to us with their time, and in the consideration they unfailingly show us, and during the last five years we have welcomed seven great-grandchildren, Angus and Hope who are five, Lillian who is three-and-a-half, Frankie, who has just turned three and his sister, Stella, who is two. And of course, Lizzie's little two-year-old, Hunter. Then, as a reminder of where it all began with Wilfred Boundy Edwards, the arrival of his namesake, Boundy Edward Campbell Johnson, during the year, a gorgeous chubby baby boy.

I couldn't end this narrative in a better way than by saying thank you to all of them. We love them all dearly, and in some way, each has contributed to keeping The Song in my Heart alive forever.

EPILOGUE

Sadly, Frank passed away on November 25, 2011, four months before the book was published. He read each chapter as it was finished.

His legacy lives on in his family and in the pages of this story.